The Making
of a
Journalist

WILLIAM S. WHITE

The Making of a Journalist

THE UNIVERSITY PRESS OF KENTUCKY

Frontispiece: The author in his office in Washington, about 1965.

Copyright © 1986 by William Smith White.

87-3207
The University Press of Kentucky
Scholarly publisher for the Commonwealth,
serving Bellarmine College, Berea College, Centre
College of Kentucky, Eastern Kentucky University,
The Filson Club, Georgetown College, Kentucky
Historical Society, Kentucky State University,
Morehead State University, Murray State University,
Northern Kentucky University, Transylvania University,
University of Kentucky, University of Louisville,
and Western Kentucky University.

Editorial and Sales Offices: Lexington, Kentucky 40506-0024

Library of Congress Cataloging-in-Publication Data
White, William S., 1906-
  The making of a journalist.

  Includes index.
  1. White, William S., 1906- . 2. Journalists—
United States—Biography. I. Title.
PN4874.W53A36 1986   070′.92′4 [B]   86-5628
ISBN 0-8131-1603-1

To my wife June,
to my sister Doris White Rowe,
and to my daughters Victoria June White Holland
and Cia S. White McClanahan,

with much gratitude to Cia,
who edited this book for me

CHAPTER ONE

I GREW UP in rural Texas at a time and in a milieu wherein a dour Calvinism—anti-whiskey, anti-gaming, anti-horse racing, and even anti-overt-happiness—lay like a chill and scowling fog over the small landscape of my boyhood. But there was in my case a relieving break in the enveloping clouds in the persons of my father and mother, especially of my father. Like my mother, he had come to Texas from the far different aura of plantation life in the Mississippi Delta, where having a good time had been as important as getting in the cotton. Moreover, impoverished though he was for most of his life, his descent was from Cavalier and Royalist England, though he himself never rode to the hounds in his life and he was distinctly and unalterably a non-Evangelical type, passionately attached to all the uniquely *private* rights of the Anglo-American heritage, from Magna Carta down through the American Bill of Rights. His was a complicated philosophy, beginning perhaps with judge-not-that-ye-be-not-judged, genially detouring into the notion that good taste was about as important as good conduct and that gentlemen need not and did not point fingers at others, and then reaching a crescendo of conviction that no person should be deprived of life or reputation without what amounted, literally or morally, to a just trial by jury.

From my father, I got a heavy dose of this life view. It was a dose that later caused me, as an Associated Press reporter in New York, to tell the city editor to send another boy when he

1

asked me to go to a celebrated acquaintance and inquire whether he was really being divorced. It was a dose, speaking of my professional life, that caused me as a commentator to leap almost automatically to the defense of nearly any accused politician—or of any other person—provided the hue and cry against him was truly strident and provided I smelt a lust for blood in the accusers. It was a dose that caused me to have a deplorable fondness for the old Tammany Hall politicians in New York, even right up to the time when Thomas E. Dewey, a small man draped in a big cloak of righteousness, was smashing Tammany by sending its boss of the Thirties, Jimmy Hines, to prison.

This kind of attitude may have done me no good as a journalist, journalists being supposed to beam upon Bad People what Woodrow Wilson called the pitiless white light of publicity. As a matter of fact, I think on reflection that at times I carried such an attitude too far, career quite aside. But there it was, and there it is now. The Lord—and a lifelong sense of vague self-guilt somehow thrust into me by the community of my boyhood, not withstanding the stout immunity of both parents to such nonsense—made me a defense juror at heart, and I have never really got over it.

All the same, even if I have been too slow, as reporter, correspondent, or columnist, to seek to search out and destroy the Tammanys I have known, my instinctive revulsion from stentorian reformers has not always been too far off. There is, for illustration, the case of Thomas E. Dewey. I knew Dewey well when he was a special prosecutor in New York, riding a chariot of glory while the local press almost unanimously raised hosannas to him. I knew him him when, in 1938, he ran for governor against Herbert Lehman, one of the most enlightened and decent men ever to hold public office. I saw Dewey arrogantly threaten the judges of New York City in the Hines-Tammany affair—and put some of them into his pocket. I saw him coddle the prostitutes and informers whom he needed as state's witnesses. In the campaign against Lehman, I saw him snap his fingers, a Little Napoleon indeed, to so gentlemanly an associate as Paul Lockwood, with a snarled command: "Bring *me* a drink, Paul!"

2

And so when Thomas E. Dewey ran for president in 1948 against the beleaguered and brave and lonely Harry Truman, my defense juror's, my pro-underdog syndrome was useful after all. The pollsters, the politicians, and experts of all sorts were unanimous in the certainty that Truman (whose party's left and right wings were alike in venomous revolt against him) could not possibly survive. Because of the way I happen, for good or ill, to be made up, because of what I knew first-hand about Dewey the man, because as a journalist I have always sought some way to part from the crowd without making a thing of it, some instinct made me skeptical from the first of Everybody's conviction that Truman could not possibly make it.

Then, as it turned out, the *New York Times* dispatched me from the Washington bureau for an ear-to-the-ground trip through six states. Traveling by myself and taking no polls but mostly only listening, I began more and more to doubt Everybody. Some sort of pattern seemed to me to be loosely forming. Well-to-do Middlewestern farmers of old Republican habit seemed angry at the "Do Nothing" and "Worst Ever" Republican-controlled Eightieth Congress for not having provided enough corn storage bins for the fall crop of 1948. At opposite poles in cultural as well as racial distance from these agrarian types, the urban blacks appeared to me to be marshaling massively behind Mr. Truman. I spent a good part of one Sunday with an Irish Democratic ward boss in St. Louis and he convinced me that this was indeed the case. He showed me hundreds of pencil-written and mostly barely literate letters in which again and again there occurred these or equivalent words: "Mr. Truman sure stuck out his neck for us." The reference was to the steamy Democratic National Convention held not long before, in Philadelphia. From this the enraged Dixiecrats had marched out into the rain after the Convention's adoption of a civil-rights plank that Truman himself had not actually been all that keen about, although he could scarcely oppose it strongly once it had been offered by Hubert Horatio Humphrey of Minnesota. (Here entered H.H.H. into the national arena.)

At the end of my itinerary, I went from St. Louis down to

3

Oklahoma City and there encountered the large and in every way formidable figure of Governor Robert Kerr, later a most muscular senator from Oklahoma. Kerr asked me where I had been and what I had seen. I gave him about the account I have given here and he struck me an affectionate blow on the back and roared: "The kinds of movements you've found don't stop at state lines! Truman is going to win this election. When you get back to Washington go get some of that long-odds betting money we're always reading about."

Obeying his own injunction, Kerr then accosted a similarly rich friend in the street and boomingly and quite openly bet him ten thousand dollars on Harry Truman, the odds being one of Kerr's dollars against two of his betting adversary's. (Kerr was a strict-constructionist Baptist, to a violent degree. He neither touched alcohol nor tolerated it in others, and he was in this regard as fiercely intolerant as any Puritan Father who ever lit a faggot under a New England witch. But his theology most certainly never proscribed gambling.)

I did go back to Washington, not to get some of those long odds, but rather to sweat out a roundup piece for the *Times*. On my desk were various polls showing Dewey vastly ahead of Truman; the very air vibrated with the drums of doom for him. I held an inner debate. Should I follow my strong instinct and predict, outright, a Truman victory, against the undeniable fact that I had, after all, been in only six of our then forty-eight states? I found I could not quite do this, for I was a child of an Old Journalism in which Objectivity was beaten into us with an almost religious force. One felt it literally an act of dishonor not to lean over backward to reject sternly what one *hoped* would happen, lest it influence the aseptic and personless duty to report without even a chemical trace of private feeling.

So, finally, I wrote not that Truman *would* win but rather that Truman was gaining rapidly and widely and *might well* win, polls or no polls—quaking inside as I did so. The piece appeared so far back in the paper that many people never saw it at all. But Harry Truman and Truman's people did; and in the following years when I knew Mr. Truman very well, he never forgot that I had, as he put it with too little qualification, "been right."

He remembered me favorably, too, for reasons having nothing to do with what kind of journalist I was or was not, or indeed whether I was a journalist at all. For I had met him in the most unforgettable circumstances for us both. Late on an April day in 1945 I walked across the Capitol from the Senate, which I was covering for the *Times*, to the little hideaway office on the House side that Speaker Sam Rayburn, something of a mentor of mine, called the Board of Education. This was a watering hole for the Speaker's closest friends. I had not long beforehand returned from three years overseas in the war— World War II—and I knew almost nothing of Mr. Truman except that Franklin D. Roosevelt had picked him to be vice president in 1944.

As I neared the recessed and discreet little door of the Board of Education, a compact man in a white hat of modified Western style emerged from it and walked off down the corridor. I went in and saw Rayburn sitting at a window with tears on his cheeks. The man in the white hat was on his way downtown to become president of the United States. Roosevelt had just died in Warm Springs, Georgia. For years after, on the anniversary of that day, Rayburn was kind enough to invite me back to the Board of Education, where Harry Truman was always the deferential guest and Sam Rayburn always a host who made it plain that here it was he who sat at the head of the table.

Here were to be found such elevated Rayburn cronies as Chief Justice Fred Vinson. Here Rayburn alone gave the signal as to when the drinking was to start and again when it was to stop. Here there was no rank or protocol to exclude the only non-ranker present, myself, from saying anything that came to mind. Here, Rayburn called Mr. Truman simply "Harry"; that is, until the Board of Education was adjourned and Truman rose to leave. At that point, Rayburn always stood and said the same thing in the same way: "Good night, *Mister President.*"

I have been accused of being, as a journalist, pro-politician. But why should a political writer have an automatic distaste for his subject matter? Why should the captain hate the sea? (This is not to say that the captain may forget the reefs or forget that his ultimate responsibility is not to the sea but to his ship.) And if I have been pro-politician, how could it be otherwise?

There is an inexplicable chemistry at work between those who run public affairs and those who write about them. Sometimes the mix is genial; one journalist likes the genus politician and the genus politician likes the genus journalist. The relationship may obtain, moreover, even if the journalist is happily hitting the politician over the head in print; it has nothing to do, except in the most puerile relationships, with who approves of the politics—or the writings—of whom.

Barry Goldwater and I maintained an affectionate association all during the time that, as a syndicated columnist, I was belaboring him in his 1964 presidential campaign against a friend of my youth, Lyndon Johnson. Again, I turned such journalistic guns as I had against Eugene McCarthy in his 1968 presidential effort, in the belief that he was threatening a political party that now, as a columnist, I could support without the constraints of the God of Objectivity of my earlier career. After it was all over—specifically, early on New Year's Day of 1969—I went from a party at the house of Gilbert Harrison, then of the *New Republic*, to the house of Senator McCarthy. Accompanied by my wife, Sidney Hyman and his wife, and Simcha Dinitz, a future Israeli ambassador to the United States, and his wife, I more or less stormed McCarthy's door. I repeated the reproaches I had heaped upon him in my column, added a few more and then observed: "All the same, you're a good fellow, old Gene; now read us some of your poetry." I suppose I need not say that the wine was red that night; but at all events McCarthy was warmly welcoming and did in fact read a good deal of his poetry to us all. Not bad, either.

It always puzzled me, and to be honest it also hurt me, that some eminently qualified national journalists in Washington seemed truly to believe that a political writer who *liked* politicians must somehow be in their thrall or lacking in "independence." To me, this error was and is a vindication of an aphorism uttered a long time ago by the English essayist and polemicist G.K. Chesterton. All great heresies, he said, result from oversimplification. The journalist who hates, or is contemptuous of, politicians as a class (and there are more of these journalists than might be supposed) knows that there are crooks among politicians but forgets that there are also clergymen fooling around amongst the female choir; and, for that matter, that there exist some journalists not suffused with a perfect integrity. The journalist who brings in a scattershot verdict that politicians are, and are bound to be, a trashy lot then typically believes that for a journalist to know this or that politician really well is a suspect thing, in and of itself. This sort of journalist forgets that to be innocent of human sympathy with, and true human knowledge of, politicians is to be innocent of the important realities of public affairs, since inescapably it is public men and women who make and manage or mangle public affairs, not the other way round.

Nevertheless, some of the most influential journalists who have served in Washington in my time have had a kind of allergy to "the politician," who is merely elected, and an exaggerated respect, curiously, for the appointed bureaucrat—that is, on the level of the Cabinet. Such an eminence as Walter Lippmann, perhaps the most esteemed journalist of this century to date, and in many respects rightly so, was glandularly anti-politician. He infinitely preferred to chat things up with, say, an assistant secretary of state or an ambassador than with anybody in Congress or even with some of the politician-bodies who occupied the White House, such as Harry Truman. The error in this preference is almost incalculably large. Almost any one of the committee chairmen of the Senate and House, however lacking in couth and however colloquial in language, is so much more powerful in the true public life of this nation than any assistant secretary of state or ambassador that the contrast is ludicrous.

As to the presidency, its meanest occupant—meanest in the sense of current public disfavor—is never so short of effective power as not to be able utterly to dominate his Cabinet at any moment he might choose. He who got there by the public's votes is still, and always will be, king of the mountain—or, if one prefers to take an excessively melodramatic and harsh view of the evils of "politics," by far the biggest cock on the national dunghill.

7

Not often, for instance, has there been so striking a journalistic absurdity as in the case of Henry Kissinger, whose service as secretary of state to Presidents Nixon and Ford had the anti-politician national journalists gasping for superlatives to apply to this latter-day Metternich. Kissinger, whom I knew pretty well and liked very well, is an incontestably able man. But he never "made" our foreign policy—in Russia, in China, in Africa, or anywhere else. This was made, successively, by Nixon and Ford; it was *implemented* by Kissinger.

The same was true of an earlier secretary of state, John Foster Dulles. Otherwise well-informed Washington commentators created a legend that President Eisenhower was only a kind of amiable Daddy Longlegs to an incomparably puissant and brilliant Dulles, who "ran" both the State Department and the foreign relations of the United States. It was a pretty legend, but it was nonsense. Dwight Eisenhower, the elected head of the United States, alone ran those relations (he was, after all, not always out somewhere golfing and saying "golly" when he made a poor putt) and "Foster" was one hundred percent his subordinate and very well understood as much.

And wherever Eisenhower did bend a bit, it was not to Dulles but rather to the man who very nearly beat Eisenhower for the 1952 presidential nomination and totally bestrode the Republican party outside the White House until his untimely death in 1953, Senator Robert Taft the Elder. Once I asked Taft, who was ever suspicious that Eisenhower was "too European" and not concerned enough with Asia, if he did not fear that a Dulles in the State Department would frustrate Taft's cherished design to harden our line against communism in the Far East. "Nonsense," he said. "Ridiculous," he added, in his nasal Ohio voice. "I *understand* Foster; I can *handle* Foster." Here Taft turned his hand in the motion of a man shutting off a valve. Those who remember Taft's brief but unexampled career as Eisenhower's "Prime Minister"—a journalistic and perhaps journalese label that I invented—cannot doubt that Taft could indeed "handle Foster." And he did, if only via the Taft-Eisenhower accommodation that had been struck after the 1952 Republican convention.

It is, of course, hardly a tragedy that this nation and most of the publics abroad got the notion that three American presidents—Eisenhower, Nixon, and Ford—had to ring up somebody in the State Department to ask: "What do we do next?" It is, however, a regrettable circumstance, surely, and it proceeded precisely from the fantasy world in which some of our ablest journalists chose to live. Why they so chose is anybody's guess.

As to Walter Lippmann, I tried, in my admiration and affection for him, to make a believer of him, but I never got anywhere. He was a very shy and very private and, for a journalist, an amazingly sheltered man. He was haunted, I think, by fears that if he mixed with politicians he might run into brass spittoons on the sawdust floor or might encounter intolerably gauche minds. Despite his gift for trenchant and lucid prose, he was amazingly uninformed about the working realities of political life.

One evening at dinner I mildly reproached him for not having roundly denounced Eisenhower for running out on his old mentor, General George Marshall, in the 1952 presidential campaign. In that campaign Eisenhower had struck out of a scheduled speech a passage (written, as I recall, by publisher Arthur Hays Sulzberger of the *Times*) condemning the malignant demagogue Senator Joseph McCarthy for having brought Marshall's patriotism and personal honor into question. In no way whatever did Lippmann understand my point. He looked perplexed, a little hurt, and then said lightly: "Oh, well, I suppose it was a bit *caddish* of Eisenhower. But then, that's politics, isn't it?" "No, damn it all, Walter," I said, "it wasn't just 'caddish' and that isn't 'politics' as you put it. That is gutter stuff; and McCarthy is no more representative of politicians than the Mafia is equatable with the English Speaking Union."

To be sure, Henry Mencken, one of the greatest journalists of them all, endlessly damned "politicians"—but so did he damn Methodist bishops, with never a thought of being taken too seriously in a world he found mostly entertaining and also congenial to a pronounced talent for invective that was on the inside really cheerful. Actually, he was enchanted with national political conventions (and indeed, and by definition, with politicians) even in his tired latter years when I first knew him. He pretended to a great boredom that was transparently bogus. The frightful rockets loosed from his typewriter at the innumerable "boobs" he professed to find all over the political scene were never meant to be taken seriously. What he himself took seriously was not *what* he wrote but rather *how* he wrote it. He didn't give a damn if nobody followed his political advice; he cared very much for the good opinion of those who appreciated the skillful use of the English language.

At some convention or another—one at which I was still a fairly new boy and Mencken an old boy who had seen it all many times—I asked him, as myself a newly commissioned columnist, how he handled his hate mail. "Why?" he said. I explained that I had been getting a lot of that sort of thing from across the country on this or that piece and that unless a letter was hysterically abusive I tried to answer it. "No, no, no," he said. "Usually I just throw the damn things unread into the wastebasket. And if I don't do that, my secretary has standing instructions to answer all mail like this: 'My dear Sir, or Madam, you may very well be right. Sincerely yours, H.L. Mencken.' "

Mencken's contemporaries, such cape-and-cane grandees as Arthur Krock, David Lawrence, and Frank Kent, were never fooled by his tough-guy pose. They understood him for what he was—a satirist and a newspaperman only in a part-time and sui generis way. Nevertheless, the Mencken legend had on a following generation of American journalists enormous impact of a kind he never intended. Many a man who reached national journalistic position in the Fifties and Sixties had, some twenty years or so earlier, carried the *American Mercury* around in his raincoat on some college campus as a guide to what a Real Journalist was. Mencken meant only to make jovial mischief; to smash every icon in sight. What he did, quite unwittingly, was to create in many minds a doctrinal orthodoxy as solemnly held as the Nicene Creed.

But if some of the seniors in the profession felt it was not nice, and even naive, not simply to dismiss "the politicians" as frauds or mountebanks, some others in my own time have always known that the levers of power were in the hands of the chosen rather than the appointed in public life. This was true of the Alsops, Joseph and Stewart; of such as Tom Wicker and David Broder and Joseph Kraft; of Robert Novak and Rowland Evans, among a good many others. We in this latter set formed a kind of unstated, and even unconscious, freemasonry. While we all cursed "the politician" in moments of anger or impatience, we all knew that he existed, that he was necessary, and that, taken in the round, his was as good as any other profession. We never confused the Civil Service with the Ultimate Service.

At any rate, it has been mostly politicians and military men, along with some tough criminal lawyers, who have, from the beginning of my career, accompanied me as good companions in all the moments of passion, crisis, defeat, and victory of my long march across the serried fields of journalism. The three sets—politicians, soldiers, trial lawyers—have one quality in common. They are all combat types as distinguished from service-of-supply, rear-echelon, or zone-of-the-interior types. None among these sets is notably careful of tomorrow, the top politician being no exception, popular lore notwithstanding. And, by God, none of them is dull. None is over-ready to cry out for the medic or the chaplain, whether literally, in the case of the military types, or metaphorically, in the case of the others.

Journalism as I have worked in it, and in a way even lived in it, is a combat occupation unless one wishes to practice it as a sort of conscientious objector, by writing careful little pieces for the house organ of some blameless National Association for Something or Other. It is a combat occupation in the sense that in the areas of journalism where the action is, the indispensable thing is to accept risks readily in the awareness that all life is unfair and that some kinds of life are even more so. To practice journalism, that is to say, is to be willing and even eager to skip boiling the water that the natives are using— again whether literally or figuratively.

But to say that the journalist is one of life's combatants is not to say that he is a hero by any definition. He simply meets the preconditions of his work, of which one of the most imperative is that he not allow himself or his craft to become homogenized. Let that happen to him and before you know it he has set himself up as a Public Relations Consultant and bought himself a house in Larchmont. The great trick is to walk a waving line of avoidance. It is far too easy to slip into movieland and mentally become a character out of *The Front Page,* complete with a press card stuck in the hatband, and so to act out a silly caricature. It is also far too easy to react the other way too strongly and so to become a pompous member of one of any number of Establishments, if one is influential enough or widely read enough to attract the attention of such an Establishment—which always, of course, wants something.

I myself never had much truck with the "Hey Mac" kind of journalism, even though I was much exposed to that sort of thing in prewar New York, where there were still about a dozen surviving and strongly competing newspapers. I *did,* however, creep close enough to the "Hey Mac" school, while I was a reasonably senior editor in the Associated Press, to cook up a jape on Hey-Mac in order to make commuting to Scarsdale more comfortable than it would otherwise have been. I would enter the train at Grand Central prominently carrying a copy of *PM*, a left-leaning publication that was a kind of timid progenitor of such loudly dissenting current organs as the *Village Voice.* I took along *PM* for a very practical reason, and for no other, since I did not greatly admire it: no other commuter would crowd in beside me on one of those cane-bottomed chairs of the old Westchester line. The other—crowded—fellows all tightly clutched their copies of the *New York Sun,* the respectable man's evening journal of that day.

To say that consequential journalism is a combat field is not at all to say that melodrama of the Richard Harding Davis school is a part of it. Nor that God has chosen the journalist as his sole, or even primary, scourge of evildoers on this earth.

As to the first point, a little memoir of pre-D Day in England during the war may be of service. A colleague and I had been, with one day's notice, asked to "report at the Admiralty" at such and such an hour, and to come alone. This was along about the last of May 1944, and we knew, as correspondents who had long since been accredited for the D-Day assault across the English Channel, that we were about to be given marching orders. My associate and I were in my apartment in Knightsbridge in London with two young lady friends. We also had some whiskey, which in those days was hard to come by in England—except for "Ameddicans and tarts" as an English old-boy once anathematized me as we stood shoulder to shoulder in the blackout in the Strand competing for the attention of some cab driver.

My lady friend was an officer in the ATS, the British Army equivalent of our WACs, and she was also, as I knew, assigned to MI5, which was then understandably engaged with the most passionate intensity in trying to maintain security and prevent any military-related leak from an island almost literally sinking under the weight of the invasion gear already stacked on the coast facing France.

My friend's lady friend, however, was wholly unknown both to me and to my MI5 companion, and the two of us were being extremely careful about what we said. (It may sound silly now; it was not at all silly then.) My colleague, however, was in the first place of a deeply romantic nature. He was also pretty drunk. So he began to make remarks of a markedly lugubrious tone: "Bill and I are going somewhere soon; maybe we will get back; *maybe we won't.*" Things of that sort. While I had not the slightest fear of my own lady friend, I had the liveliest of concern about the effect upon my colleague's lady friend of observations that were about as subtle as a neon arrow saying, "This way soon to the invasion craft."

What to do? If I solemnly admonished my colleague not to "break security" I would of course break it myself, and in a jackass way at that. Finally, to the smiling and unuttered relief of my MI5 lady companion, I said to him: "Ah yes, the pity of it all. Hank, don't let's begin reading any continued stories in the magazines." (Some weeks later I ran across him in Normandy, neither of us having spilled any of our rich red blood.)

When one touches the second point here—that journalism

was not set up with primary responsibility to enforce the criminal code or even especially to assist the Church in its sublime mission to fight the sin and admonish and reclaim the sinner—one moves with the softest of tread upon the edges of the sacrosanct ground called Investigative Reporting. I myself was never much of an Investigative Reporter in the way such a journalist is currently perceived or with the methods that he sometimes employs—midnight meetings with shadowy informants in a cloaked if not daggered way, and the like. It has always been my professional view that the *public* malfeasances, or the malfeasances of public men, which the press has a positive duty to search out with all possible diligence, can be brought to light in nearly every instance without resort to methods that the press itself ought to and usually does denounce if they are employed by others.

By way of illustration, I needed no moonlight rendezvous nor any inspirational nudges from editors to help me deduce early on that at the turn of the Fifties, Senator Joseph R. McCarthy of Wisconsin was attacking the most fundamental concepts of personal liberty in what came to be called his "crusade against Communists in the State Department." No public figure in my time—and here I do not forget that many thought the Watergate episode of the 1970s was the public crime of the age—has done such tragic injury to so much. His immediate victims were people, individuals accused on the flimsiest of evidence or on none at all, of a kind of moral treason. But the ultimate victims included the Bill of Rights and, above all, that majestic Right not to be condemned without fair trial or traduced without hearing or recourse. And this was only the beginning. In McCarthy's wake, much that was institutional rather than personal was left in a walking-wounded state. For years afterward, the whole foreign policy of the United States was enfeebled by the unwillingness of a shell-shocked career Foreign Service candidly and without timidity to tell the president in Washington what was really going on, and why, in the outer world.

Next, in this litany of victims, an essentially decent and superlatively courageous administration was bloodied up so much, for no good reason, as to cause its chief, Harry Truman, to decide not to stand for reelection in 1952. In this spasm of madness, McCarthy managed the impossible by fairly successfully depicting as "soft on communism" the same president who was killing Communists in Korea—too fiercely to suit the American Left and for too long to suit an American Right whose early bellows to the president to "Get Tough" had oddly muted into the mutter, "Get Out."

And finally there was this: the very fact that McCarthy's endless "charges" were at long last shown as bankrupt put a curse that has endured to this day upon an inescapable if not widely accepted national need to take fair and nonhysterical measures against something that does indeed occur outside spy thrillers—actual as distinguished from fictitious subversive activities in the United States. These *do* exist. They *are* dangerous. They *must* be guarded against. There *is* a Wolf, even though in the Fifties we heard so many cries of a Wolf that never was. The single taunt "McCarthyism!" has aborted sensible and needed measures of national security—not phony cover-up national security, but the real article.

Now, I claim that I saw all this coming, in general and hazy outline anyway, though I hasten to add that I was not alone in this ugly vision. Unforgettably to me, two of my colleagues on "the McCarthy beat," Philip Potter of the *Baltimore Sun* and Murrey Marder of the *Washington Post*, saw the same vision. And so we set out as best we could, within the limits of an ideal of journalistic objectivity that was too rigid then as it is too relaxed now, to cry the alarm. Perhaps I had a better position than Potter or Marder in that for the Sunday *New York Times* news-review section I had sanction to write more or less editorial pieces. Moreover, I was published where most of the magazines were edited, in New York City, and Marder and Potter were not. I was asked by the now defunct *Look* magazine to write a piece on McCarthy. Joyfully I let McCarthy have it in what I believe was the first published mass-magazine attack upon his methods. What good, if any, it did amongst the wide public I did not know. But to me it assuredly did a power of good, as we used to say in Texas. My ulcer improved and, thirty pounds lighter than normal because of my months on the McCarthy beat, I even quit losing weight. It was the hardest assignment I ever had, in the sense of being the most draining, because for months I believed that the very best of the Anglo-American heritage was being destroyed in a country which, I hope I may say in no mawkish way, I love.

It was a time of an unhappy gathering of circumstances. Among these was the postwar weariness of an American people who had suffered less than they thought they had and far less than had the people of Britain, of whose gallant sacrifice I had such tender memories. This fatigue alienated Americans from any kind of "foreign affairs" that were not going wholly in our favor. Somehow, somebody had "lost China," meaning the Nationalist China of Chiang Kai-shek, but the national perception of this "somebody" was sadly amiss. We had never *had* China to lose. And, as a general whose name I cannot now recall finally in exasperation observed to one of the endless Republican-dominated Senate "investigators" of that monumental catastrophe to the West, if anybody "lost China" to the Communists it was Chiang himself.

The common American attitude at the time was an extraordinary amalgam. It was made up in part of an avid determination to get everything material in sight while the getting was good—an avidity common in what was endlessly called "the Home Front," but remarkably absent from those who had not long before returned from the real fronts, where deprivation of leg or arm or testicles had been rather more poignant than "Home Front" deprivation of gasoline or red-meat ration points. But this attitude, this national mood, was also made up of a curiously repellent naiveté, good and moral in aim and measurelessly and unconsciously evil in its implicit consequences: since the United States had "won the war" and was surely the world's spiritual leader, it concluded, any setback anywhere to its foreign policy hopes *must* be attributed to idiocy or malignancy in the home leadership.

I take some satisfaction still in an episode following my return from the war, at a time when assault war correspondents were sought out for the lecture circuit. Invited to address

16

a group of industrialists somewhere in the East (Washington as I recall), I gave a bit of a talk and then opened myself to questions. The first one, from an automobile manufacturer turned tank-maker for the war, was this: "Wasn't it American know-how that won the war?" "Well—yes," I said, "although American know-how had some assistance from about three hundred Allied divisions."

It was into this national mood of far too much conscious self-righteousness and far too much damned nonsense that McCarthy entered. He came in with the instincts of a puma on the prowl in that most savage of all hungers, the hunger of a basically insignificant and unworthy man for a renown for which notoriety will do very well as a substitute. Finally, he came in armored with what, sadly, is often more powerful than the armor of goodness—an impenetrable amorality accompanied by an uncanny instinct for smelling out the point of weakness in any man he encountered.

This strange X-ray vision into the psyches of others was very nearly infallible. To some of us journalists who were early onto him, acting, so to speak, as Investigative Reporters in an older school, he made threats: "I'll put you on my List"—meaning of "Communists" or sympathizers. He said that to me, but only once. "By all means," I said, "go right ahead." I knew he had made this thrust only half-heartedly in the first place, more or less just to keep in practice, because of my wholly unhidden admiration for Dean Acheson, the Truman secretary of state whom McCarthy was pleased to call "the Red Dean." McCarthy guffawed, in perfect good humor.

But he was not done with me, as he was never done with anybody who stood athwart him. Some weeks later, on an early version of "Meet the Press," he struck the blow home. To some rather innocuous question from Frank McNaughton of *Time* magazine, McCarthy responded with a bellow, and raged: "I have no respect for you or for *Time* and I will answer none of your questions." Then, to a fairly hostile one that I next put in, McCarthy responded with a dove-like coo: "I am *glad* to answer any question from my dear friend, Bill White." The man, as I have said, knew where everybody lived, or more

17

exactly where lay every man's point of pain. He knew that I couldn't care less if he denounced me, but that a public embrace from Joe McCarthy was going to make me very unhappy. As we left the broadcasting studio, he came up to me and observed with a wide grin: "I fixed you up back there, hey?" "Yes, Joe," I replied, "you fixed me up."

The McCarthy era is now long ago and far away but I confess that I am not unhappy in this remembrance of journalistic things past. There is more than one reason for this, and for these present animadversions. For nobody stole anybody's files, nobody contrived any leaks from a grand jury, that place where to me an accused person's rights come in ahead of the press's right to be informed unless and until an indictment is lawfully brought in. This is another and a longer way of saying that for my part I prefer the Old Journalism of, say, Murrey Marder of the *Washington Post* to some aspects of the New Journalism. I am *glad* to be an Old Journalist—a damned old one, to be sure, if it comes to that.

The media in general pursued McCarthy within the unwritten but terribly important rules of the game, that is, implacably but fairly. This was true in radio and television as well as within the press. (There is a big difference between an Edward R. Murrow and a Daniel Shorr.) So did the Senate of the United States. Rightly agitated men there, such as Senators Fulbright of Arkansas and Flanders of Vermont, wanted to censure McCarthy out of hand. The intention was right; the method was wrong. For a condemnation without trial would only have created a McCarthyism at another level but not really of another kind. I remember myself urgently asking Lyndon Johnson, then the Majority Leader, to move at once against McCarthy. "Later," said Johnson, "later."

"The timing is not right," Johnson went on. "Right now, the country is in hysteria. As majority leader I have no intention whatever, at this point, of opening a high school debate on the subject—Resolved that communism is good for the United States—with my party arguing the affirmative." Then he added: "In due time, but *with due process*, the Senate will act." And so, of course, at length it did. Some years later in London I told this story to Hugh Gaitskell, the British Labour party leader. "Exactly so, exactly so," he said. "I have on my desk just now a report from a Royal Commission recommending an easing of the laws against homosexuality. But I have no intention whatever of opening a high school debate on the subject—Resolved that homosexuality is the very best thing—and having my party take the affirmative. All in good time; all in good time."

I tell these stories to make the point that there is no God-ordained requirement upon journalists to be automatically hostile to public officials; sometimes the two sets can and ought to walk, each in unimpaired dignity and integrity, upon a common path toward a goal of common decency.

Supreme Court Justice Felix Frankfurter once observed to me that he discerned a "confessional quality" in my work, both as a journalist and as an author. When I looked a bit perplexed and troubled, he added: "There is nothing at all wrong in that." I never knew exactly what he meant, though I trusted that he intended the remark to be somehow congratulatory. For he was too good a friend and far too mannerly a gentleman to have inadvertently said to me at my own table anything that he might have calculated would upset me. Whenever he wanted to do that sort of thing he never hesitated about it and was never the least bit ambiguous. I suppose he may have meant that behind the somewhat bleak realism and sophistication with which I confronted the world of my work, there lay the bruised idealism of a young man who had come up the hard way from the Texas back country.

CHAPTER TWO

IN MY OWN little sandy town in central west Texas, people didn't care a damn about the legendary Sam Houston, and not too much about the Alamo. To them the Texas Republic was in their collective memory as antiquely unreal as, say, Sparta. To them "the" war was "the War Between the States." A nonconformist bloc of one—my father—always loudly called it "the Civil War," even though his father and four of his uncles had fought with the Confederacy, as his distant Tory ancestors had fought in this country for the British king. But no matter. He could get away with this and other outrages upon our town's consensus not because he was poor-but-honest but rather because by local standards his "connections" in the Deep South were impeccably right. You couldn't beat the Mississippi Delta for "background." For the Delta had historic associations with England—by blood ties, by romantic recollections of the Confederacy shared by many in Britain, and, coming down to earth, by all that cotton trade so long carried on across the Atlantic. In short, my part of Texas in the long ago was in truth a kind of unwitting small British colonial settlement.

As a correspondent for the *New York Times*, I found, in Salisbury, Southern Rhodesia, my town's cultural counterpart in the last days of colonialism in Africa. Take away the differences in accent and grant such minor variations as more tea-drinking in one place than in the other, and white Salisbury was the old home town: the same quietly desperate dedication to doing what was both undoubtedly right and incontestably dull. The same careful division of sheep and goats; in neither place blatant nor cruel, but in both places resolute. The same excessive homogeneity in which nothing and nobody was alien or even really different. The same quiet and absolute assurance that we are right and the Others are wrong. Even the same kind of vaguely Victorian wooden hotel with its toilet facilities (in those days my part of Texas called it "the water closet," too) as inconvenient and draughty as possible. Salisbury, when I last saw it in the Fifties, was more British than the British—and so was the area of Texas in which I grew up. In high school we studied English history fully and American history fitfully, if at all. We shot off our fireworks not on the Fourth of July but on Christmas Day. In school we almost never sang the "Star Spangled Banner," but every day we sang "America" to the tune of "God Save the King." We also sang "The Bonny Blue Flag," in honor, of course, of the Confederacy.

Central Texas's provincial capital, Waco, was the first Big City I ever saw—possibly about forty thousand people then— and in my imagination it is still the biggest, my fifty years onward—in New York, London, Paris, Berlin, and others— nevertheless and notwithstanding. The trip to Waco, 110 miles distant from my home, was the first I ever took on a train. Shrieking through the night at the blinding top-speed of 40 miles an hour, its steam whistle blowing half in arrogance and half in a sort of mourning wail through one sleeping village after another, this train was, as I thought, taking me from one world to another. And so it was.

Arriving in Waco in the early morning, in a cavernous railroad station bigger than Grand Central, Penn Station, Charing Cross, or Euston would ever be in my future, I saw my first skyscraper—all twenty stories of it, as I recall—and for the first time heard newsboys hawking a newspaper. I saw my first streetcar, and my first "foreigner." He was a Greek; he owned the restaurant in which my mother and I had breakfast while she inquired for directions to the Waco "Cotton Palace," a fair that once a year brought some of central Texas to its metrop-

21

olis in a regional carnival, carefully policed to see to it that gaiety retained a proper measure of sobriety.

A satisfactorily old colonial "family background" was about all the small confort we had. So I was perforce a poor boy on the make, although just as the phrase "on the make" did not then carry the harsh and brutally ambitious connotations it does today, being "on the make" then did not mean that one was excused from the obligations of generations of Anglo-American gentlemen, stretching back to the mid-seventeenth century, to "play the game." (This phrase was used, and used, and used in my youth.) When I went to the University of Texas at the age of sixteen I was seen by my father as a man (*boys* did not go to college in his time and in his view). And a man of sorts—a self-supporting man—I had to be. I didn't have much in my locker but an overgenerous measure of personal pride.

This, in my case, meant a certain standoffishness, a trait that in all my professional life has served me well, since standing off and taking a good look at men and issues helps any journalist to avoid a too-facile acceptance of what may turn out to be the shoddy—in men, or issues, or programs, or whatnot. Pride helped me most of all, as it happened, in my association with professional politicians and professional soldiers. Contrary to the stereotype, at least that of the politician, the great ones in both these professions do not really take into their confidence, on a level of mutual respect, any man who has his working heart on his sleeve and is too eager to stick out the glad hand of fellowship. Perhaps the politicians don't like this sort of thing precisely because they themselves have to do so much of it. The great soldiers don't like it—General Eisenhower being the only exception to this in my acquaintance—because they tend to a certain taciturnity, anyhow. At all events, the most valued political friendships among civilians of my career in journalism were made in the Senate (a training ground also of presidents) and were made entering every relationship with reserve and letting it warm up only as it might. The same was true of my work as a war correspondent.

The best illustration that comes to mind involves the British Guards. I saw something of them in the war, at a time when I was the only American within hailing distance, and to call them casual and notably detached would be a profound understatement. To begin with, they didn't believe in introducing anybody to anybody, perhaps because they all seemed to be cousins, anyhow, and all seemed to have gone to the same school before Sandhurst, the British West Point. (I once heard a subaltern, a second lieutenant, call his commanding general "Ricky," to his face. "Ricky" was General Sir Richard O'Connor.) When a member of the Guards absolutely had to make introductions he did so in a kind of strangled drawl impossible to understand or to render in print. I stood my alien ground without pain—and thereby made some of the warmest friends of my life among these foppish, languid officers whose bravery in action could only be called gaily suicidal. They had a deep suspicion of outgoing or talky people of whatever sort; to my surprise I found that they didn't really like Winston Churchill, for example. "Feller talks too much." That about summed it up. One could imagine General Omar Bradley, USA, saying much the same thing.

They got on my back a good deal, of course, usually with the old familiar line that the trouble with Americans was that they were "overpaid, overdressed, oversexed, and over here." To this I replied with a dainty anecdote about the Guards officer in the War Office whose ATS aide came to him in tears to announce that she was pregnant by him. "Oh, Sir," she said, "I suppose I shall have to throw myself into the Thames." To which he manfully replied: "Good old *girrll!*"

Now for the other side of the medal: a certain standoffishness has been all very well professionally, but in my personal life it has caused me a lot of wholly unnecessary pain and of what is now called "alienation." ("Alienation," as often as not, is simply a pretentious word for a stiff-necked loneliness; but then, increasingly we live in a world that complicates things wherever it can.) The plain truth is that some journalists—this one for certain and others I will not mention because no one has a right to undertake such judgmental prying—sublimate the lonely self with a kind of guilty relief in what would appear to be the most gregarious of callings, a

23

calling in which, in the cliché, one meets so many interesting people and situations. Some who are notably non-team players (and such men were unpopular in the two vast and somewhat bureaucratic collectives in which I spent a lot of my professional life, the Associated Press and the *New York Times*) take to drink. Others take to drink and also to independent ventures in unsupervised personal writing, as I did, partly simply to escape the too-possessive bonds of "team play" that more and more pervade newspaper work. Now one may occasionally see not simply a double byline but even a triple one. How a committee of two, or even three, can write *anything* I have never divined, though obviously such committees can and do.

Wisely or not, I settled upon a course of professional apartness even before I had my first newspaper job. When I turned up at the University of Texas, not exactly a ragged waif but certainly no member of the affluent set there, I had already decided that I was going to be a journalist, but a journalist all on my own. First off, as a freshman I got a variety of highly nonprofessional jobs—wiping the dishes in a girl's boarding-house for my meals, feeding white rats in some arcane university laboratory experiment, and delivering the town's morning newspaper on a bicycle. This was all for the excellent reason of necessity.

I went on in this fashion through my sophomore year. In that year through great good luck I drew a stimulating professor of English who could and did write salable short stories that people actually read. I thought of him as a latter-day genius; and he was good, at that. His course in English composition (I suppose it would now be called "Creative Writing") so fired me up that I pitched heartily into my assignments and he gave me a job as a kind of teaching assistant; specifically, I was to recommend to him grades for the class's compositions. By this time I was aloft; the white rats and the dish-wiping faded from memory. And I was solvent withal, since my total monthly expenditures scarcely went above forty dollars. Now established, in a way, I looked into the School of Journalism, but found too much togetherness therein and so withdrew before actually taking any course, save one in journalistic ethics.

Some of my friends worked on the campus newspaper, and one indeed was its editor. I hung back from volunteering for the staff because I was getting on for nineteen years old and felt that I would rather be a professional without serving any apprenticeship as an amateur. Someone, somewhere, told me there might be a vacancy for a cub reporter on the city's evening newspaper, the *Austin Statesman*, and I went down and somehow got the job. I began at ten dollars a week, no overly-generous sum even in those far-off days, and worked twelve or fourteen hours a day, six days a week. I covered at one time or another, and sometimes simultaneously, such diverse places and events as police headquarters, the criminal and civil courts, Rotary Club luncheons, and raids by sheriff's deputies on moonshine stills in the cedar brakes surrounding the city. Add City Hall and county politics to the list, too.

In these early days, I saw sights strange to the eyes of a boy who had perhaps become a man too soon. Among other things, I formed a lively dislike for policemen in general, granted some very decent exceptions. I was, and am, a law-and-order man, but with the stress heavily upon law and considerably less on order. I never enjoyed watching wretched drunks being tossed around in the tank at the city jail. Nor did I feel myself to be on a noble mission when I went out into the hills to see some poor old moonshiner flushed out like a lame partridge and triumphantly "brought in," along with a Mason jar or two of the fearful rotgut, later cheerfully nipped at by the avenging authorities—and myself.

Still, I met and got to know well some wonderful types, one of them an ancient justice of the peace (or committing magistrate) named Tannehill, who was a direct descendant of an officer who had fought under Sam Houston in the Battle of San Jacinto, the climactic action by which Texas won independence from Mexico in 1836. Old Tannehill, though compelled every two years to "meet the voters," nevertheless maintained a sturdy independence, verging upon the openly contemptuous, from the electoral process of that time. He filled me up with the kind of Texas lore that I have always liked the best. That is, the iconoclastic kind. He alleged, for example, that his revered

25

ancestor had claimed that General Houston, perhaps the pre-eminent hero of all Texas, had refused to go out and do battle with the Mexicans and had consented to do so only after subordinate officers beat him with their swords. I did not and do not now credit this tale (I have friends who descend from Houston himself and I ask them to linger over this line). Nevertheless, I gloried in old Tannehill's "oneryness" in telling it. "Onery" means cantankerous: colorful without trying to be, "independent as a hog on ice," and nonconformist in the highest degree.

The people I have liked best and enjoyed most, both as a man and as a journalist, however humble or exalted their place, have all been as onery in their way as Judge Tannehill down there in Austin nearly a lifetime ago. I think here of my own father, of Harry Truman, of Lyndon Johnson, of Robert Taft the Elder, of Sam Rayburn, of General Terry Allen, of Winston Churchill. And, among others, of the most grouchily reticent and stealthily generous bartender I ever met. He was a man known to me only as Louie. He ran a saloon across the street from Rockefeller Center when, before the war, I worked in the Associated Press in that antiseptically gleaming pile.

But, to return now to the old, old days in Austin. The beginning of the making of this journalist was about as hard on the spirit as, say, basic training in an infantry training post in wartime. Whoever got "beaten" on a story was flung psychologically into the city editor's guard house. Whoever scored a "beat," conversely, was awarded another stripe on his sleeve—which, of course, had about as much real meaning (except to the man so honored) as that epic transmutation in boot camp from Private Jones to Private First Class Jones. Nevertheless, it was all very satisfying at the time, just as it was memorably humiliating to be punished by banishment to two weeks of covering the Chamber of Commerce. All the same, the harsh disciplinary consequence of losing on the "beat" front, along with the meager but nevertheless valued reward for some triumphant "scoop" (say a two-dollar-a-week raise), were toughening to the fiber of the young journalist, if not quite significant enough to be described as character-building.

26

Indeed, the process of training a young journalist in the Twenties, as I saw it anyhow, could without too much fancy be analogized with the method of an army officer candidate school of a later time. To be sure, the physical obstacle courses run at Fort Benning by potential second lieutenants were not required of cub reporters seeking to elevate themselves into general-assignment men, the aristocracy of any city room. But psychological obstacle courses there were in plenty, not least of them being the extreme likelihood of being abruptly shifted off some well-trodden news run or beat, where the undeniable boredom was to some extent offset by one's knowledge that one had at least *that* particular job licked. I remember being lifted up from the press table at the City Council under orders to hare up to the county jail to see (and shortly write about) the first dead man I ever looked upon. He had hanged himself by his old-fashioned suspenders. He was the first, but not the easiest forgotten, of a long file of the dead, in disasters, in electric chairs, in warfare, that has passed before my eyes in all the years since.

The unspoken journalistic tradition of my early days in the craft required one to be cynically tough on the outside, however untough he might feel on the inside, and in a curious way that separated him, like a newly arrived alien on Ellis Island, from all other occupations, certainly from what was then only a nascent form of "public relations." The term then for the practitioner of this endeavor was "publicity man"; and, as penurious, raffish, and somewhat ragged a lot as we newspapermen were then, we nevertheless affected and actually felt a grand haughtiness toward such operatives. The dignified word "journalist" was not in common usage then and certainly rarely denoted young men and women who wrote for the daily papers. A "journalist" was generally perceived, if somewhat vaguely, as a pretty learned fellow, fastidious in dress and deportment, who did long thoughtful articles for such periodicals as the *Saturday Evening Post* or, better yet, some literary quarterly issuing from the precincts of a university, or perhaps the *Literary Digest*. (I recall with pleasure and undimmed amusement—and here I jump years after my cub period in

Texas—the reply given to me when in New York I telephoned a high executive of the *Literary Digest* in 1936 to inquire how it was that his publication had forecast a sure victory for Alf Landon over President Franklin D. Roosevelt in 1936, FDR having carried everything but Maine and Vermont. "Why," he explained, "something must have gone wrong." I told this later to James A. Farley, who had managed the Roosevelt campaign and who on the eve of the election had advised some of us correspondents in the Biltmore Hotel that Roosevelt had a genuine chance to sweep every state in the Union. "Yeah," said Farley, champing industriously on the chewing gum that was his substitute for any other stimulant, "sure looks like something *did* go wrong.")

To be sure, the journalism schools in the old days were already doing their best to "improve the image" of newspaper work, but they were not getting very far with this campaign. This fact was brought home very often to all "on the streets" and "on the sheets"—two phrases commonly used by reporters of themselves. Shopkeepers looked upon us with gloomily speculative eyes if and as we asked for credit. Businessmen thought we were poor risks, anyway you looked at us. Corporation lawyers (though never criminal lawyers) had an even more glacial view of us. So, for that matter, did the very business officer on the paper for which we worked.

The Puritan Ethic, of whatever shade, did not prosper among us. For my own part, the infinite distance between my career and real respectability was made clear to me, without unkind intention, by my own mother. A gently bred southern lady with one son who was a university professor (highly satisfactory on the social scale) and another well launched in business (well, reasonably satisfactory), she was nearly all her life unable to conceal her perplexity that her youngest son did not only consort with *reporters* but even was one himself. I think, indeed, that she never got over her distress at my sadly errant choice of occupation until, a highly mature "boy" indeed by that point, I had won the Pulitzer Prize—in *letters*, that is. To her, newspapers were to read, not to work on. And in my young days as a journalist this was the view of a very large, if not actually dominant, part of society. All this did nothing whatever to make disconsolate those of use who were "on the sheets." We enjoyed our odd-man-out status—indeed, we romanticized the devil out of it and it did us not the least bit of harm. To the contrary, the absence of true acceptability within the generalities of our communities was compensated for by our warm associations with what we considered the elite of the cognoscenti—"real" writers, nonconformist professors, trial lawyers, lobbyists, bootleggers, prostitutes, and some Texans so aristocratically well placed that the prevailing middle-class values repelled them.

And there were other compensations. A friend and early colleague, Hubert Mewhinney, and I conceived a daring plan to exploit our outness in such a way as to both find pleasure and relieve the heaviest of the pressures applied by those to whom we were constantly in debt. I was the first to put the scheme into effect. A haberdasher had written me a wrathful letter pointing out, correctly, that I had owed him forty dollars for three months and must now pay up without delay. I worked out a reply to this effect: "My dear Sir: I have a letter from you that appears to be a dun for a debt. I say 'appears' because in the first five lines I note at least four misspellings and five errors in syntax so grave as to put the whole meaning of your letter in some doubt. Will you please clarify all this and so oblige me?" This put off the time of reckoning for a couple of months, and by then I had enough money to pay off. Mewhinney, too, seized upon this counteroffensive tactic and used it for years.

Still, such jollifications were far from frequent in my days as a young journalist. Life was indeed real. It was indeed earnest. At times it was indeed grim. When I went from the *Austin Statesman* to cover the state capitol for the Associated Press, I entered a world seething with competitiveness, competitiveness as absurdly venomous as anything pictured in the most melodramatic newspaperman movies.

Leaping the gulf between covering local politics, from city hall and county courthouse, and covering statewide politics involved a quantum jump, a difference more in kind than merely in degree. It did not take me long to find that the competing interest-group pressures put on around city hall were, relative to those up at the state capitol, mild and benign. Texas, even in these late Twenties of which I write here, was too big, too diverse, too rich in many senses, and spiritually too distinct from the rest of the nation, to be merely a state. It had, after all, once been a sovereign republic, owing little to the United States of America that had not been amply paid off in its contribution to the other and larger Republic's successful—and slightly "imperialist"—war against Mexico. Texas, in short, was a state only in a legalistic sense and was in truth a confederation that ran its own foreign policy when it chose, as it had certainly done in Woodrow Wilson's time by sending its own unofficial expeditionary forces into Mexico after the bandit (Texan view) or revolutionary-reformist (Mexican view) named Pancho Villa.

In short, Texas was not centrally and locally governable in the way that most states were. And my journalistic life up at the capitol was in consequence, and quite fortuitously, an early introduction to the demands of national journalism that I was later to enter in New York and Washington. The politicians of East Texas had their own fief; so did those of West Texas and, most of all, those of South Texas. Over this sprawling—and brawling—political terrain the governor could not be parochially oriented; he had to balance off one section against another, pretty much as the president of the United States does. More than a score of distinct ethnic cultures made up Texas, and the Anglos whose venturesome forefathers had made the state in the first place were able to keep on top only by a policy of muddling through, by giving ground here and there as occasion demanded, and by seeing to it that no governor ever gathered to himself any more power than his quotient of guts and brass could contrive. This was so because the almost excessive pluralism of the state made it impossible for *any* governor to be truly representative of a whole whose separate parts invariably exceeded its sum.

Now, I do not allege that as a correspondent who had not yet reached the age of twenty-one I discerned this complicated state of affairs in any but the dimmest and vaguest way. But I did get a small bite of the truth, so to speak, a bit that would serve me later as a national correspondent. And I had a splendid time reporting on an amorphous mass of earnest do-gooders, small-time easily-bribable types, and brilliantly able big-time rogues: such, unforgettably, as the *patrone* of a slice of Mexican-oriented South Texas centered upon a county called Duval. This magnificently insouciant worthy, a state senator named Archie Parr, was not without reason universally called the Duke of Duval. He voted his Mexican-Texan *vaqueros* en bloc, never making the slightest secret of it, and was critically powerful in any close state election. On one occasion when the Duchy of Duval had returned about three thousand votes for one candidate and precisely one vote for another, I asked the Duke, out of irresistible curiosity, who the devil had been the one voter who had gone against his wishes. He replied, with the calm of a man telling you the time of day upon your request, that it had been his wife. Damn it, he observed, he never *had* been able to control her.

All the same, I was not unhappy when I was transferred from Austin to Dallas as night editor of the AP, even though I was soon to discover that being that kind of editor mostly meant taking a big pencil and cutting down big dispatches from the main trunk wires to much shorter dispatches to go out onto the smaller wires radiating into the various provinces of Texas. The memory of all this made me deeply sympathetic years later when, as executive night editor of the AP in New York, I jumped from my chair in alarm when, from a desk half a block away, I heard a shout from one of my subordinates, Norman Lodge, who was "filing the South wire"—that is, cutting big ones down into littler ones as I myself had had to do in Dallas. "Jesus Christ!" Lodge screamed, flinging great handfuls of ticker tape into the air, "Where does it all *come* from?"

Dallas, at any rate, was a fairly brief interlude until my transfer by the AP to Houston as correspondent, with never again another wire to "file." In Houston, whose enormous innate energy was mixed, in an implausible amalgam, with a spirit of cheerful and convivial indolence, I was for the first time in my working life freed of all sheerly routine chores. The management that had sent me to Houston had intended that I should be in but not necessarily of that city, should be available for special assignments over the state on what were, at least relatively speaking, the big stories.

CHAPTER THREE

THE BIG STORIES turned out to be of mordant and melancholy qualities—celebrated murder trials, a hurricane now and then along the Gulf Coast, and a series of grisly executions at the state prison, where thirteen times I stood within a few feet of an electric chair in which some poor devil was being hurled into eternity. I have relived those scenes in many a nightmare, but not again, God be thanked, in this book. In fact, my Houston tour turned me, for its duration, into a murder and/or robbery trial expert.

It was a curious kind of specialty, into which I had been briefly introduced in my cub days back in Austin. The wife of a friend of mine from the University of Texas, Rebecca Bradley Rogers, became a national figure as the first coed "bobbed-hair bandit" in the United States. For reasons that nobody ever really discovered, she drove up to a little bank in a little town, stuck a little pistol into a cashier's face, and made off with quite a lot of money.

Rebecca was small, demure, excessively shy, and not really even pretty; but by the imperatives of our craft she became, of course, not only "the bobbed-hair bandit" but also "the *beautiful* bobbed-hair bandit." My friend, Otis Rogers, a recent law graduate from the University of Texas, undertook to defend his wife himself, notwithstanding the professional axiom that counsel to the accused should have no emotional involvement with that accused. Otis was every bit as conventionally buttoned-up as his wife had only appeared to be. Nevertheless, in this supreme crisis of his private life he threw aside the almost painful decorum in which he had always walked when I had known him at school. He became in her behalf an advocate whose reckless charisma (a word we didn't know much about in those days) would not have shamed Wild Bill Fallon or, to be more contemporary, a Washington friend of mine, Edward Bennett Williams.

Hard put to it because everybody knew Rebecca had indeed robbed the bank and because she herself did not deny it, Otis Rogers took two courses, one impersonally scientific and the other unstintingly emotional. He pleaded her not guilty by reason of temporary insanity, showering the rural jury with such exotic terms as "dementia praecox." And when it came time for his closing speech to them, he took—this mild owlish little fellow perfectly type-cast for the role of a timid book-keeper—the most desperate and audacious gamble I was ever to see in a courtroom, considering the intimate nature here of the client-attorney relationship. He told the jurors that if they elected to find her fully sane they had no choice but to find her fully guilty as well—and armed bank robbery was then a capital offense in Texas. "Should you so find her," he shouted, "then go and hang her high as Haman and I shall come and cut her down and bury her with the last of my dreams!" He got her off. And in that moment I came to think of the practice of criminal law as a theatrical form, complete with all the traditional tragicomic elements.

I recall, too, the trial in a little town called Sinton of a middle-aged woman accused of killing her husband with a draught of poison. I was on hand with two or three colleagues I had become accustomed to traveling with on such assignments, riding the circuit more or less as some judges do. I was telegraphing my pieces by Western Union back to the AP headquarters in Dallas, where they were put on what we called "books," or multi-copy blocks, by a junior editorial employee named Marvin Brau. Brau had read all too well the AP's all-to manifold instructions, one of them cautioning us against profanity in our dispatches. The trial in Sinton reached its climax with the testimony of a neighbor that over her back fence she had seen the accused widow standing over the prone and writhing body of her wretched husband; had seen the widow dash a blue bottle to the ground, and had heard her cry out: "My God! What have I done?"

I naturally made this testimony the lead of my piece and sent it off to Dallas. Good old Marvin Brau recoiled from the word "God" and dutifully struck it out of my dispatch. In the papers that came in from the cities the crucial line thus read, "My, what have I done?" Not unnaturally, my colleagues, the prosecution and defense attorneys, and even the judge himself, did not let me off this one. The judge, in fact, was the most merciless of all. "My goodness," he said to me in an exaggeratedly mincing way, "what have I done—dropped my watch?"

While it would seem perverse and callous to say that I enjoyed being a journalist at murder trials, there is no denying that it made a welcome change from covering, say, the progress of appropriations bills in the state legislature. The most intense courtroom melodrama I ever saw—more so even than Dewey's prosecution of Tammany boss Jimmy Hines in New York, long political shadow though that trial threw—was a murder trial in Austin in the late Twenties.

One of the most brilliant legal scholars of the century in Texas, John Brady, a judge of the highest court of criminal appeals, had gone to a homecoming football game at the University of Texas in Austin and from there to a personal disaster. He had far too much to drink at the game and, returning from it, decided to go by the apartment of his mistress, Lehlia Highsmith—and in broad daylight at that. Brady was of the cream of the Texas establishment, a good ole boy too elevated and too aristocratically aloof to be called one. He was, moreover, the leading Catholic layman in all Texas. He was white-haired and enormously handsome in a ruddy sort of way; but he was also elderly and Miss Highsmith was young. At her apartment he found she was not alone; a young man was most indelicately upon the scene. So this, the most widely respected judge in Texas, pulled an ordinary knife from his pocket and stabbed the girl to death. To Texans, he had been a sort of combination of Charles Evans Hughes and Oliver Wendell Holmes. And here he was, not only a murderer—the episode took place in front of a dozen people at the apartment house—but a man who had killed a *woman*. Now ensued a courtroom contest, in a dim and shabby old stone building that was then the county courthouse, the like of which I have never seen since.

The prosecutor was a young district attorney named Henry Brooks. He was the son of a distinguished former law partner of John Brady named Victor Brooks. Henry Brooks had grown up calling Brady "Uncle John." Nevertheless, Henry Brooks, reared in the most Calvinistic integrity, declined to disqualify himself from the prosecution. On the contrary, he went after Brady with controlled savagery from start to finish, and Brady, facing God-knows-what punishment at that point, watched Brooks, savagery and all, with a patient and seemingly almost paternal pride in the obvious professional skill of that young man. Nor did the old man flinch or turn away when young Brooks, ending his formal summation to the jury, picked up from counsel's table the knife with which John Brady had taken a life, hurled it point downward into the table and, precisely quoting what Brady had admitted he had cried out to the girl, shouted the terrible line: "I told you I was going to kill you; and now, God damn you, I'm going to kill you!" Not a muscle moved in Brady's face. His equally patrician and elderly wife, sitting at his side, looked without expression at Henry Brooks.

Three of the best criminal lawyers in Texas had gathered in Austin the instant they read of Brady's arrest. There was Dayton Moses, who among other things was counsel to the Texas Cattleman's Association, a brief which, then as now, carried a subtle and special cachet. (Moses, by the way, was a partner of another Establishmentarian lawyer named George Christian, father of George Christian, Jr., who would become the tough-minded and laconic press secretary to President Lyndon Johnson in his last troubled years.) There was Lon Curtis, often called the biggest small-town lawyer in Texas. Finally, there was Samuel Dickens. This was a free-spirited trio, each of whom had many a time fought one another in many a case in many a courtroom. Now they had come together, as they told me in a suite at the Stephen F. Austin Hotel the night before the trial opened, "to save John."

Privately, they had no special brief for him, partly because they all had a deep affection and respect for Mrs. Brady, and partly because "John had been such a damn fool." They freely allowed me, a young reporter, to sit in on their council of war that night. All of them drank plenty, but none of them was ever mastered by whiskey. (Come to think of it, I do recall that Moses, in closing at last for the defense, was swaying slightly and gripping the rim of counsel's table so hard that his knuckles were white.) The ultimate motive in that hotel suite that night, then, was to save not a man named Brady but simply a client. Through all the years since, I have forgotten few details of that evening. All three of Brady's lawyers were in philosophic but totally calm despair. One of them, I remember, at one point went to the window of the eighth floor suite, looked out and pointed downward and said: "Of course, we all know what John *should* have done about this damn business!" "No, no; wouldn't do at all," said another. "John's a Catholic, don't forget."

Suicide thus having been ruled out by these tough old birds, each of whom, in the old Texas expression, would have charged hell with a bucket of water, they had another drink and, refreshed, approached the problem again. Manifestly, they could not possibly defend Brady by denying that he had done what he obviously, visibly, and admittedly had done. They decided to use the defense of temporary insanity, though they well knew the immeasurable risk of trying to tell an ordinary jury that one of the state's most celebrated intellects was crazy. How tricky this path was came later to be seen when young Henry Brooks, for the prosecution, brought out proof that, on the night before the ill-fated homecoming game at the university, Brady at a gathering with friends in the Faculty Club had read at length from original Greek manuscripts.

At any rate, insanity it was to be: but insanity very, very temporary, due to an excessive intake of alcohol. This was the weapon of Moses, Curtis, and Dickens when they faced Henry Brooks on behalf of Brooks's "Uncle John." So potentially dangerous to the defense itself was this weapon that they spent endless days in selecting a jury of twelve men. Between them counsel for the defense knew something about practically everybody on the venire of two hundred men that had been assembled by the sheriff. Before they were through with their questioning—now by Moses, now Curtis, now Dickens—counsel knew *everything* about every prospective juror, short of such details as his conjugal relations.

In that drab and pokey old courtroom, smelling strongly of the jailhouse disinfectant that wafted up from the basement cells, everybody knew everybody else, and yet everybody didn't. For the very judge on the bench, Judge J.D. Moore, was, like Brady, an Irish Catholic in a community then utterly Protestant in culture and ethos, and yet was in another sense wholly unlike Brady. For, like counsel on both sides, the accused—murderer or no murderer—was a member of the elite of Texas, and the judge on the bench was not. The judge chanced to be an outsider, socially and professionally, sweating to try this *cause célèbre* fairly and firmly, but unsure of himself among the haughty dukes of the legal realm who were contending nominally at his feet but actually over his head.

More was on trial here than a man of distinction and graceful living destroyed at the bottom of a whiskey bottle on a single afternoon. A judgment beyond that of guilt or innocence had to be made here, by lawyers and judge, if not by jury. The ultimate question was not just what was to be done with a man who had committed a murder. It was not what was to be done with a Texas gentleman who had killed one of his own kind (such things, after all, were not so very novel) but rather what was to be done with a Texas gentleman who had killed a woman.

This was the staggering poser that confronted Moses, Curtis, and Dickens. Which of them precisely must confront it would depend on which of the three was at the top of his form at the high moment of decision. None of the three, as I said, was himself notable for temperance in living. Their plan of counterattack upon the prosecution was thus flexible in the extreme, fluid from hour to hour and day to day. They dropped innuendos that the young district attorney, Henry Brooks, was perhaps motivated by political ambition, but they held such suggestions to well this side of the insulting. After all, they too had known Henry's father, Victor Brooks, and any one of the three of them might well himself have been an "uncle" to the boy Henry.

For all their exertions on their client's behalf, however, they never once showed any real warmth for John Brady the man. For to them Brady had crossed an ultimate line, not because of the act of homicide but because of the sex of the victim of that act. When one of them had suggested on the night before the trial's opening that Brady should simply have jumped from a high window, he was in fact speaking for them all.

But no matter; for their client John Brady, Moses, Curtis, and Dickens went the very last mile with a kind of wild, hopeless élan that I have seen among long-blooded infantry troops. They brought in their alienists to testify to the frightful effects upon human conduct of too much alcohol and to how these effects were summed up in the phrase "temporary insanity." Brooks, of course, brought in his alienists to contradict them. The jury understandably became somewhat lost in all this professional jargon, as Moses and company had intended they should. Nor were matters much clarified by the neutral testimony of the one expert witness who came forward not to say whether Brady had been sane or insane but only to define authoritatively some of the operative terms being hurled about.

"Dr. Gilbert," asked Moses (or perhaps it was Curtis or Dickens), "just what is real drunkenness?"

"Ah," replied the fastidiously eminent Dr. Gilbert, "I should say that drunkenness is the temporary loss of the power of self-criticism." Even Brady smiled.

With such strange and formidable rhetoric rolling about in its largely unsophisticated head, the jury at length slouched off to deliberations that were to prove too much for it. In the end it was hopelessly deadlocked. In due time Brady was retried, in a second trial removed from Austin's supercharged atmosphere to Dallas, where he at last got a sentence of four years.

Henry Brooks was philosophic in defeat. Moses, Curtis, and Dickens were, as Winston Churchill would later say in a different connection, magnanimous in victory. "The Brady problem" had been solved, anyhow, and not a single leading trial lawyer in Texas, on either side, had been professionally humiliated before his peers. Their professional successors contend mightily today in both law and politics. And now and then, at the conclusion of some particularly hard test at arms, they may rest a bit and temporarily lose their power of self-criticism.

That lawyers on both sides of a case, and even judges, had no hesitation in forgathering after working hours with a journalist, whom one might suppose an outsider, flattered me in these early days. It turned out, however, to be a kind of special association with the criminal bar and bench that persisted in my career in other places and circumstances. It was never a question of my consciously setting out to get along with such characters; I simply had a strange empathy for them and so (or so I have always thought) had they for me.

It may be that somewhere hidden in me was a vagrant wish that I had become a lawyer myself, as my father had wanted me to be. It may be that my father's almost religious reverence for the Law and for the courts and for Justice as the highest of human aspirations, which he had instilled into me from my earliest recollections, made me into what might be called a courthouse nut. Whatever the reason, I have had in all my professional life a special feeling for judges. And the higher the bench the higher the respect—a respect that transcended my feeling for, say, presidents or prime ministers. I have seen presidents appoint to the federal district bench men whom I knew to be barely deserving of the term mediocre. I have felt able without self-consciousness or impertinence to call a good handful of justices of the Supreme Court by their first names. But nevertheless a hidden awe, not so much of them as of what they represent, has persisted in me. Some of them have been friends: Felix Frankfurter, William O. Douglas, and Abe Fortas among them. But with none of them have I ever felt free to mention any case before the Court, not even after it has been settled.

I have rarely been more embarrassed, for example, than I was one night in the Brazilian embassy in Washington when Chief Justice Earl Warren sat down beside me in the post-dinner men's brandy session and began to tell me chattily the "inside story" of the Supreme Court's historic anti-school-segregation decision, reached under his leadership. Somehow, I felt it grossly improper even to dare to listen to his cheerfully volunteered tale of how a chief justice had gone about among his colleagues appealing and exhorting and even arm-twisting in his determination to have the court come out with a unanimous decision. I had supposed, even though by then I had been around Washington a long time, that the in-camera deliberations of the loftiest court in the world should be, and were, utterly secret and utterly sacrosanct. So much for the naiveté of a journalist who was by that time an old pro. Or was it not really naiveté but rather the intractable, the unalterable attitudes that had been drilled into me as a boy in Texas in a time so long past?

The Texas phase of my work, and the journeyman phase, drew to their close as the first truly national crisis I had known and reported on had its agonizing beginning—the Great Depression, heralded by the stock market crash of 1929. In Houston, already a great industrial city though still clinging resolutely to its wistful vision of itself as just a good old bayou-washed southern town, I had literally heard the factory gates clang shut: for example, at the oil-field tool plant that later became the seedbed for the improbably vast fortune of Howard Hughes. I had seen thousands of men walk out into despair.

At "Mister Jones' Hotel" I had attended one of the most gallant occasions I shall ever see. "Mister Jones" was Jesse H. Jones, the impenetrably tough financial genius who for a time held Houston in his hands and kept it somehow alive, as later he was to assist the country's survival through the Reconstruction Finance Corporation in Washington. Gathered for dinner at the Rice Hotel was a company of the broken financial elite, men who had made millions in oil or cotton or shipping and who now stood, nearly all of them, on the brink, if not over the edge, of bankruptcy. Stoutly they drank the good illegal whiskey that still came into Houston up the Ship Channel from the world's nonprohibition ports. At the end of the dinner they stood together and, grinning at each other like the sinewy old pirates they were, loudly sang a popular song of that period, "Brother, Can You Spare a Dime?"

And I myself—quite comfortably situated at sixty-five dollars a week in a good apartment that cost me, furnished, forty dollars a month, and able to breakfast daily in the best places in Houston for about thirty-five cents—knew a poignant feeling of helpless and guilty brotherhood and pity that I should not know again until nearly twenty years later, among combat troops in the Second World War. For Houston, an inland and artificial seaport, lay upon the natural line of withdrawal (the route of the coastwise freighters) for the Depression casualties of my own kind of men—the journalists—who were falling back in disarray from the shambles of a collapsing New York press.

The darkest days came when the *World* folded in New York. No newspaper, not even the *Times*, had symbolized to newspapermen such high professionalism, such grace in despair, as that magnificent publication. (Miss Madeira of the Madeira School in suburban Washington, to which my daughters went in due season, adopted for its soprano battle cry the slogan "Function in disaster; finish in style." The *World* had tried as long as it possibly could to do the one; to the end it never failed to do the other.) Men nationally distinguished in journalism when I had been a cub came off the freighters at Houston in those days, their hands shaking in the embarrassment of the proud and the hopeless, and made their way to the *Houston Chronicle*, where I had my office as AP correspondent, seeking work of any kind. And, failing work, which was simply not to be had (notwithstanding that the *Chronicle*, for all its crusty conservatism as "Mister Jones' paper," had practically broken itself with its patient, stealthy generosity to "the editorial side"), these shabby refugees had to ask for "loans."

I made as many of these as I could, feeling all along that something was indeed out of joint when such men as those of the *World* were out of work while I was living it up, by the measure of those Spartan days, at the advanced age of twenty-two. Earlier, I had thought of George Cottingham, the managing editor of the *Chronicle*, and Emmet Walter, the city editor, as flint-hearted types, silently cheering on the supremely flint-hearted old man in the White House, Herbert Hoover, while he deliberately starved out the American peasantry. Cottingham I had seen in this light, I suppose, because he never spoke when a grunt would serve. He glowered impartially upon everything and everybody falling within his field of vision, and he took pride in sauntering out of the office with hands in pockets whenever the paper was about to put out an Extra, as though to say *I am too damn big to be at all concerned.*

But I changed my mind about Cottingham when he offered to put up five thousand dollars of his own far-from-vast savings to start the ball rolling for a Save-the-*World* fund among newspapermen; he asked me to put a story about it on the AP wires. I changed my mind about Walter when he flatly refused to fire one of his criminal court reporters put under indictment for bootlegging in a moonlighting way.

And I changed my mind about Herbert Hoover many years later when I got to know him in something closer than the mere occasional press-conference relationship. While writing a posthumous biography of Senator Robert Taft the Elder, I called on Mr. Hoover and found him one of the kindest and most humorous—yes *humorous*—politicians I had ever known. I recognized in Hoover the very kind of man so many millions of us have been, are, or will be—a warm personality encased in a rigid outer shell from which he was psychologically unable and emotionally unwilling to break out. That high, stiff collar of his was more nearly his cross than his trademark.

The Houston experience taught me that knee-jerk responses and judgments in life and especially in journalism (I claim to have coined the term "knee-jerk" in reference to politics) are not merely unfair, they are puerile. The experience with Hoover (who was, at the time I talked to him about the Taft book, in Washington helping "that fellow named Eisenhower" reorganize the federal bureaucracy) was moving and memorable. And as the lesson applied to journalism, I understood fully for the first time the dangerously instantaneous image, so apt to be meretricious, that the press, and not just the tube, may contrive and perpetuate.

Finally, I noted that a legendary Texas hero, old Cactus Jack Garner, could be, for all his bluff and engaging qualities, as savage and pitiless an adversary as William T. Sherman ever was in his march through Georgia down to the sea. I met Garner when he was Speaker of the House during FDR's first term. I was freshly up from Texas, reporting for the AP. He was in a cluttered little hideaway office in the Capitol, with Mrs. Garner in attendance upon him, as always. He never cared for any Johnny-come-lately and this was immediately made clear to me. In fact Garner told me that if I ever wanted any news about him or his office I could go ask one of his two old Texas cronies in the Washington press corps, Bascom Timmons and Mark Goodwin. This was the insult deadly to any journalist, new boy or not, and I got up from my chair and said, "Mr. Speaker, with all respect, I will like hell go to any other reporters for news. You can keep your damn news, sir."

He grinned, his white eyebrows dancing up and down, and said to Mrs. Garner: "Looks like we've got a buck here." Whereupon his manner totally changed and he went to a cabinet and took out two hotel glasses and a bottle of bourbon whiskey. He filled both glasses almost to the brim—no water here—handed one to me, and said, "Son, let's strike a blow for liberty." This was at about ten in the morning, early for me but about midday for old Garner. He habitually got up before five in the morning and worked his way through a bottle of whiskey before nightfall, with no perceptible effect on his speech or deportment. He only got redder and redder in the face as the day went on. He also chewed upon a great quantity of cigars. These habits he gave up on the occasion of his ninetieth birthday in his home town in Uvalde, Texas. "Got to thinking they might be bad for my health," he told a birthday caller, Lyndon B. Johnson. It was Garner, as head of the Democratic party in the House of Representatives, who more than any other man managed to convince the nation that President Hoover, who was quite powerless against a worldwide economic storm he never made, had somehow consciously set in motion himself the hurricane that swept through the lives of the people.

When I had finished my talk with Hoover about Taft (and the old gentleman had been splendidly wasteful of his time in helping me), he sighed, looked out the window with unshed tears in his eyes, and said to me: "I always thought Bob to be such a promising young man. I hope you will deal *justly* with him."

I never forgot that day; just as I have never forgotten that, when Harry Truman opened his unpretentious presidential library out in Independence, Missouri, Herbert Hoover was stoutly on hand to wish him well, though the almost perpetually grinning and outgoing Dwight Eisenhower was not. No Republican ever had more to forgive the Democratic party for than did Herbert Hoover; no Republican ever got from the Democratic party such immense gifts of help and kindness as did Dwight Eisenhower.

CHAPTER FOUR

I FIRST "went East"—the great beckoning light to all provincial newspapermen of my era—only months after Franklin D. Roosevelt had been inaugurated in 1933 and was assaulting the Great Depression with innumerable recovery and relief bills that a frightened Congress was passing on the double, sometimes using a rolled-up newspaper on the House floor as the surrogate for a bill not yet actually printed.

Washington then was a sort of crazy mixture of a sleepy southern town (hardly a city, except in the eyes of such newcomers from the hinterlands as myself) and a vast, yeasty pit of intellectual ferment, imported largely from the Ivy League, and mostly from Harvard. Felix Frankfurter, apart from his duties in the Supreme Court, undertook a self-assignment as dean of this remarkable College of the New Deal, whose professors, in both senses of the word, were by some sour types called "Felix's Happy Hot Dogs." And though dogs by any definition they were not, hot they certainly were—afire, that is, with several grades of reformist zeal to do something about the terrible wasteland that the economic collapse had made of this country and of the lives of so many of its people.

Grade One amongst these worthies, as I classified them, was made up of men whose lively compassion was nevertheless accompanied by a robust anti-Marxism and a determination not to see the Roosevelt Administration eradicate Tradition along with Travail. This grade was embodied by such men as

Jim Rowe and Tommy Corcoran, early members of a celebrated Brain Trust, who tried very hard to live up to Roosevelt's expressed wish for White House assistants with "a passion for anonymity" but who in their happy Irish exuberance and liking for people never quite achieved this most difficult goal.

Another set of the academic whizzes down from the ivied halls thought Tradition had quite run its course, and a good thing, too. These set up their central lodgment in the Department of Agriculture, heretofore one of the stuffiest bureaus in Washington, where the saturnine Lee Pressman settled in as a youngish sort of éminence grise of the Far Left of the New Deal. I sensed, after a bit, that where the Rowes, the Corcorans, the Harry Hopkinses, and so on wanted to put the national train back on the track with a fairer shake for its occupants, the Pressmans really wanted to derail the whole damn thing, blow it up, and bring in another model altogether.

Thus, inevitably, I suppose, I made my friendships among the Rowes, the Corcorans, the Ben Cohens, and their ilk—friendships that have happily endured for a lifetime—and with that extraordinary man named Lyndon Johnson. At that time, Johnson was nominally "secretary" to a rich, relaxed, and somewhat playboyish congressman, Richard Kleberg, a member of the King Ranch dynasty of Texas, whose federal salary would, I suppose, have paid part of his club bills. The nominal "secretary," however, was the congressman-in-fact most of the time. And with the matchless mixture of audacity, persistence, compassion, and a kind of cold gambler's calculation that would become his lifelong persona, Lyndon Johnson was cajoling, extracting, and emotionally extorting for the needy in Kleberg's district prodigious sums from federal bureaucrats who winced automatically when the telephone rang and Johnson's drawling Texas voice loudly announced that "Congressman Kleberg's office" was calling.

I had been sent to Washington by the AP as what was called a "regional correspondent," meaning that I was to look out mainly for news of Texas and vicinity; but my territory, though disappointingly limited in geography, was from the first pretty wide in scope. For Texans were very big in all of Congress, and

Garner, of course, held the vice presidency. My Texas connections soon led me, journalistically, far beyond the limits of the Rio Grande and the Red River alike. As I have said, I met Garner early on, along with Johnson and Sam Rayburn, who would later be Speaker of the House but who even then, in the autumn of 1933, was a powerhouse as chairman of the committee through which he and Roosevelt set out to bring the more brash and monopolistic of public utilities and Wall Street barons to their knees.

Rayburn, Johnson, and to a lesser degree even old Garner, tight-fisted though he was personally, were more or less in the Rowe-Corcoran-Cohen school of reform, being careful of the baby while gladly throwing out the bath water—the bath water being too much ancient privilege in too few hands. I suppose I can say that in a small way I became a minor-league Boswell of this confederation of fundamentalist Protestant southerners and Irish Catholic Yankees, even before that confederation ever knew itself to be one. This was an Austin-to-Boston arrangement nearly three decades before John Kennedy and Lyndon Johnson made the big one in the 1960 presidential election.

If you don't "know somebody in Washington," whether you are a reporter or a lobbyist, or for that matter a newly arrived president fresh from some statehouse boys' school and innocent of the Federal City's (sometimes real but more often fancied) unique wickedness, you would be about as well off to stay in, say, Toledo, Ohio. I myself was fresh from a counterpart of Toledo, but I did not remain that way very long. For, long before leaving Texas, I had been inaugurated, without putting in any kind of application and without knowing even what was going on, into one of the most powerful clubs in the United States, the old-boy network made up of alumni of the University of Texas. Whatever the shortcomings of that institution, it was then, as it is now, immensely muscular in the political affairs not only of that state but also of Washington. As a reporter and correspondent in Texas, and earlier as an undergraduate, I had had little patience with that club and certainly had never sought its assistance or followed any of its subtle

directives in my work. Nevertheless, for reasons I do not understand, since I was an extremely free thinker in those days,
somehow the truly old boys of the old-boy network had decided that I would do. It is conceivable, I guess, that this was
because I was innately simpatico with so many lawyers, who
practice a profession that occupies a special place in Texas.

Again, it may simply have been because the old-boy network
rather likes mavericks. Too, I was by this time pretty well
known in Texas journalism and, in the context of Texas, had
been successful at it—and success is never undervalued by the
old-boy network. For whatever reason, metaphorical letters-
of-credit on my behalf had somehow gone up to Washington
before ever I set foot in it, not only to such Texans as Garner
and Rayburn but also to non-Texas friends of theirs who were
among the movers and shakers in public life.

So I cannot truthfully say that I arrived in the capital like a
character from Horatio Alger. When I first met Lyndon
Johnson and set up with him a lasting entente cordiale that
survived many strongly stated political and ideological differences and endured mainly on simple personal friendship,
I was actually (and ironically, considering where he was
headed) a more established figure than he was. Partly through
him, but in fact more because of others senior to him, I soon
"knew somebody in Washington," and no mistake about it.

Johnson's boss, Congressman Kleberg, was about to lose
some of his Texas patronage appointments (though characteristically Kleberg himself was unaware of this looming
threat) because old John Garner was preparing to lay claim to
all the patronage of Texas. Garner was simply bored, as vice
presidents are sure to be once they have looked around, and I
doubt that he cared much of a damn about the patronage
business except that he thought it might give him *something* to
get his teeth into. But to Johnson, or so he told me, this was a
classic example of that "arrogance of power" of which he
himself was much later to be accused, as president of the
United States. It was a shameless raid upon the property of
innocent Texas congressmen, and was being conducted by a
Texan, at that. I myself did not look upon this as exactly a

storied atrocity in political warfare. But as a reporter I did see in it substantial news interest to the people of Texas, my journalistic constituents. My piece turned out, however, to mean a good deal more than that to me.

First of all, it made the national wires of the AP, which had been more or less closed to me since I had moved north as a regional man. Secondly, it caused old Garner to draw back from an unpleasant uproar in his home state and elsewhere. Finally, it was a Washington Secret (meaning no secret at all) that this cocky and successful attack upon the most powerful Democratic politician in Washington short of Roosevelt had been pulled off by a congressional secretary named Lyndon Johnson.

The matter came to the ever-attuned ear of FDR himself, whose affection for Garner had at no point been overwhelming, and FDR marked that young fellow Johnson down as a man to be watched. Johnson, in short, became a Roosevelt protégé before ever he won his first elective office, and some interesting things began to happen to me as well.

The first thing I knew I was invited to the White House for a party otherwise given over to the notables and squires of the press business. There I met that extraordinary lady Eleanor Roosevelt, first in the routine "receiving line" and later on the dance floor, to which she had fallen flat on her face, after lodging one of her high heels in a crack on an improvised platform from which she was directing the festivities. As she fell I darted forward to help her, and in a tenth of a second she shook her head in an emphatic negative. She meant, I learned later, something to this effect: "No, don't do it; otherwise the rumor will be all over the country either that I got drunk and fell down or that I suffered namelessly grave injuries the nature of which are being kept from the public." Whatever else I didn't know, I knew a real politician when I saw one, and I joined there and then a small minority of correspondents who thought her a more instinctively perceptive politician than her distinguished husband ever was.

I began, after the White House affair, to know more and more Somebodies, though I honestly cannot recall having worked at it, and by now I was regularly "getting on the national wire." My boss in Washington, Byron Price, was one of those executives who ran his shop by mirrors, never looking sideways at anybody and laying waste to the myriad rules of the AP up to the very point of no return. One day he called me in and announced that if it was all right with me he was taking me off the regional run and putting me on general assignments as a feature writer. Mind? It was an unexpected parole, since far too often the "regional run" had meant writing such stirring stuff as "Senator Thomas Connally announced today that. . . .

My boss in this new job, Frank Weller, was a talented, kind, and bibulous type who looked like an Indiana dirt farmer gone to seed but who was capable of good, even distinguished, prose. We adjourned from the office one day to the bar of the nearby Raleigh Hotel and spent too much time therein. We both still had pieces to do that day and as we returned to the office, rocking a bit in the heavy weather we had brought with us, we ran flat into Byron Price. He was somehow unseeing; but I did think I saw him shift his cigar from one corner of his mouth to the other before continuing on his stately way into his private office.

The feature writer's job was, by AP standards of that time, a liberated one, subject only to Weller's far-from-urgent assignments or directives, and I ambled pretty much wherever I pleased and, amazingly enough for a new boy, saw pretty nearly anybody I pleased, short of the president. I got caught up in the bravura, if not in all the dogma, of the First New Deal. Though the glamour was "Downtown," in the Executive Department, the halls of Congress became my favorite places because they were less structured, were still innocent of "press secretaries," and in the end were so pleasantly disorderly.

If one senator or representative wouldn't tell you something that you wanted to know, you could always find another who would. Moreover, the lofty (and sometimes precious) bureaucratic promises to "remake America," such as came from so perfectly decent a fellow as Rexford Guy Tugwell, tended after a bit to jade, especially as put against the exultant and none-

51

too-literate tallyhos of the congressional Democrats as they endlessly chased the scarred and hapless old Republican fox through the corridors of the Capitol.

When I got too tired of rhetorical inflation Downtown, to be sure, I could always go to see Harold Ickes, who from his den in the Department of the Interior was an impartially curmudgeonly growler of the bald epithet. He was perhaps the Henry Mencken of the Roosevelt Establishment until General Hugh Johnson of the National Recovery Administration (Blue Eagle) came along in the role of Old Iron Pants, with oaths and maledictions hot enough to strip a cavalry saddle down to the blanket and pommel. Harry Hopkins, who would become Roosevelt's most intimate of advisors and at length a world figure in his own right, was another pleasant acquaintance, though this was while he was still occupied with Relief, and long before he entered the White House to live there as a war companion of Roosevelt, scarcely less elevated in fact, though not of course in form, than Winston Churchill.

I found all this—the widening circle of powerful political figures with whom I was on terms of a certain casual intimacy—a somewhat intoxicating business, but not one that had much to do with my personal life. This I lived in modest circumstances. I belonged to no Washington clubs in those days (the very thought of such a thing would have frightened me) and along with some of my colleagues I ate my lunches often in the form of five-cent hamburgers at a dark and scrofulous little beer joint which, along with others of no very different sort, lay huddled just at the feet of the gleaming and majestic Capitol, looking down upon Pennsylvania Avenue. If there was something of an anomalous feeling in lunching at times with the mighty in some Cabinet officer's elegant departmental dining room and returning within hours to the rather grimy little apartment I occupied in a shabby-genteel (but mostly merely shabby) part of downtown Washington, I do not now recall it.

Already, back there in the early Thirties, Washington journalists were being treated with a privilege that may well have been too marked, by a Roosevelt establishment all too keenly aware of the sweet uses of publicity. And anyhow in those Depression days it was not good form to live splashily in Washington, even for those who could afford it. Many, myself included, took street cars, not taxis, as a matter of course, even though one could ride in state from downtown to the Capitol for twenty cents. A nickel tip evoked no snarl from the driver; a dime, his earnest thanks.

The air was full of an honestly dedicated national effort, springing naturally from the painfully obvious fact that this country was in the very devil of a fix. A journalist's understandable temptation was to busy himself solely with the Executive and Democratic legislative architects of the New Deal, since in those days they really ran everything and went only from strength to strength, while the poor old Republicans, enormously and routinely outvoted in Congress, had perforce to occupy themselves mainly with faint, far-off cries of "waste" and "regimentation."

Nevertheless, as a journalist I for one felt a perverse sympathy for the Republicans even though as a private person I thought them rather guiltier of benighted error than I was later to think. I tried, therefore, to keep up Republican as well as Democratic contacts, there being after all that ingrained duty to objectivity, among other things. Moreover, though privately I was a convinced New Dealer, I had enough orneriness to question this dogma within myself from time to time, as well as an embedded determination to be even-handed as a reporter.

This devotion to a principle which is now under considerable attack in the New Journalism—an attack which to a point has something to be said for it—troubled me greatly during the formation of the American Newspaper Guild in Washington and New York. The publishers were arguing that this would turn out to be nothing less than a labor union—an argument in which events did prove them largely right—and that men writing and editing the news could no longer act with disinterest, certainly not on the multifarious labor issues of that time, if they themselves were to become a part of the union side of the tug-of-war. The rebuttal to this was that editorial workers' pay was ridiculously low. As indeed it was—so much so that sometimes the managing editor of a newspaper was paid less money than the composing-room foreman.

In this set of affairs a great journalistic star of those days, Heywood Broun, came down to Washington from New York to organize the Guild in the capital. I attended the meeting and, influenced decisively by the consensus there that we were forming a professional association and not really a union, I became a charter member of the first Guild in Washington. I let two of my older and far more experienced colleagues in the AP talk me into joining a committee of three to call upon Byron Price, our Washington boss, with the bad news. We all hated the mission. We all immensely liked and immensely respected Byron Price, who was as thoroughly decent as he was thoroughly traditional, the very type of the ex-infantry officer who cared almost desperately for his men but was shaken to the core at the very notion that they might seek to challenge his ultimate authority.

Our Committee of Three entered Price's office with far less than revolutionary zeal for the downtrodden workers of whom Heywood Broun had spoken so grandly the night before. We were aware of several facts that tended to limit our enthusiasm. The first, as I have indicated, was our sure knowledge that Price was as fair and humane an executive as could have been found in all of American journalism, even if he was strongly attached to the chain-of-command concept. The second was that we knew, as those things are known among men working closely together, that Price had a special liking for all three of us—a circumstance, it occurred to us post facto, that had led to our nomination to this mission the night before in the Broun caucus. Moreover, it did not escape us in the morning-after of that caucus that Broun, while urging us all to get in there and fight, himself had a multi-year contract at twenty-five thousand dollars a year from Roy Howard of Scripps-Howard, while none of us three had any contract at all and nothing remotely equal to Broun's income. Finally, we knew that we were making an enormous break with an honored newspapering tradition which had always genuinely, however foolishly, turned up its nose at mere money and at the form of "job security" that was high on the Guild's list of demands. We knew, too, that we *could* wind up by losing such "security" as we already had—by getting fired on the spot. It should be remembered that this was the infant Newspaper Guild we were forming and nobody could have any assurance that its founders—or "fomenters" as the publishers liked to put it— would not wind up very short of allies among their own colleagues.

All these concerns have a kind of gas-light fragrance about them now, of course; then, they were very real. So the Committee of Three—W.B. Ragsdale and Richard Turner, both later distinguished seniors on *U.S. News and World Report*, and I— more or less tiptoed into Price's office and scuffed his rug good and proper before getting down to cases. A gentleman to the soles of his shoes and a paternalist from the bottom of his heart, Price looked at us in white-faced sadness and perhaps with some controlled anger. I sensed then, I *knew* then, that this man who truly loved his profession felt as he would have felt as a company commander in the First World War if his men had suddenly pointed their rifles at him instead of at the Germans. He could hear the distant knell for the kind of profession he had known. I thought that he and his grief were dated; I also felt like a dog.

I noted, too, that the loudest clamorers for "Getting Tough with Management," who had dominated our caucus the night before, were shunning the precincts of Price's office on this morning of the great confrontation. They had become suddenly quite busy with other affairs. This circumstance did not leave me with any sense of apocalpytic revelation; I had already learned in my earlier, Texas days that there was no necessary correlation, in life or journalism, between the most belligerent rhetoric and the will to act, not merely to talk, at personal risk. From way back I remembered how, when I had been a small boy in my little home town, a half-dozen hoodlums had pursued a frightened black man up Main Street for some supposed offense. He had run to my father's justice of the peace office, or more precisely cubbyhole, for shelter.

The most stentorian leaders of this small and ugly mob demanded in unlimited violence of voice and manner that "the nigger" be turned over to them; else they would come in and get him. "Come right ahead, you *blaggards,*" said my father, in his soft Delta accent, drawing a Smith and Wesson revolver from his desk drawer. Nobody came, least of all the most bellicose of the lot of blackguards.

I do not suggest, of course, that my colleagues in the matter of Byron Price and the Newspaper Guild were to be equated in any way with those louts of my youth. There is, however, a point of congruence, though certainly not an analogy, between these two wholly dissimilar episodes. That point (one with which in my earliest days in the Senate and House press galleries I was already familiar) is that among politicians, soldiers, or really any and all sorts of men, those who approach matters with the greatest vehemence are least likely to approach them with effective *action.*

At the time, the truism was important to me primarily in my work as a young Washington journalist. My understanding of this human reality helped me a great deal, even as a newcomer, to smell out and identify politicians who were going to *do* things as opposed to politicians who were only going to *say* things, however gracefully or forcefully. It is mistakenly supposed that spell-binding ability is immensely important in politics. To be sure, when the capacity exists *along with the capacity to get things done,* passionate rhetoric almost never does any harm and may do a great deal of good—sometimes, and in some circumstances.

At all events, here we were with our brand new Guild, entering upon a kind of phony war with Management—phony in the sense that, while the Committee of Three remained in being, we were not terribly active. Price on his side remained a Buddha-like figure, usually hidden behind the smoke screen of his cigar. Nothing much happened; nothing much on our side, that is, because the New York Guild moved quickly to dominate the whole Guild scene nationally. The New Yorkers used our Washington charter group as a sort of showcase—or, as politicians would put it, a sort of store-front subheadquarters—which they could point out to provincial reporters as an activist body down there in the thick of the biggest activism of all that was New Deal Washington.

I did not stay long in the Committee of Three. My tour of duty in Washington, in this first phase, was suddenly terminated from on high; that is, by orders from the AP's general headquarters in New York. Price called me in one morning to say that the general manager, Kent Cooper, urgently required my services in the big city, and without delay. As I recall it, I was given a whole three days (to Price's apologetic and affectionate regret, I was happy to see) to move myself and my household gear to the North. I was not asked by Cooper whether or not I wanted to make this journey; in those days things were not done that way in journalism. One asked not the reason why.

I assumed that I was going up to be even more of a feature writer than I had been in Washington; and this expectation somewhat softened the jarring impact of New York, which I had never seen before and whose subways and els both enchanted and frightened me. When I had found an apartment out in Queens, near beautiful downtown Jackson Heights and not a thousand miles away from the ambience of that fictional Queens where Archie Bunker lived much later, I found my way into the Manhattan offices of AP and at length up to the aerie of Kent Cooper.

Cooper, an imperious old boy to whom "employee-employer relationships" meant that everyone did as he said, and without any nonsense, announced that he had made a wonderful opportunity for me. Henceforth, he informed me, I was to be executive editor of the AP photo service, with God-knew-how-many competent, and much older, professional photo editors under me.

I gasped and tried to protest—Mr. Cooper, I know nothing whatever of photographs or photography. . . . Mr. Cooper, I had never in my life even taken a snapshot with a Kodak Brownie. . . . Mr. Cooper, I was a *news* man and a writer. And so on. All this did me no good at all. Cooper grandly waved away all my disclaimers; told me that here he was about to make me

57

an executive, at age twenty-eight or thereabouts, and that anybody who didn't want to be an executive was a hopeless damn fool. What *he* wanted, he said, was somebody with good news training and *detachment* from photographs.

My mind was reeling, understandably I think, for Cooper seemed to be saying that his greatest desire was to have an executive editor for the photo service who knew nothing of photos, cared less, and would be much happier without the title and with about a third of the pay that would go with it. A bit of light broke when I learned in our conversation that Cooper had just bought a new and very expensive system called Wirephoto without telling his board of directors and that he wanted to launch it with a splash. Why it was supposed that I was the man to provide splash I never did know. I had never thought of myself as a splashy type.

There was nothing to do but to go downstairs and set about being executive editor of the photo service, whatever that was. I still remember a distinct chill emanating from my highly professional—and, as it turned out, nominal—subordinates. The only useful thing I ever did was to keep on top of the national and international report, page by page, as it was brought to me by copy boys, and to make quick domestic and foreign assignments for the camera crews to go out to cover this or that disaster or other event. I also spent, or authorized the spending of, a vast amount of the AP's money. I remember, for example, putting eight chartered photographic airplanes over New England, at one time, during its great hurricane of 1938.

Cooper beamed with pleasure when, upon descending from his suite above, he saw this example of the executive at work, and never uttered a syllable of protest at what it was all costing. Nevertheless, I kept at him, as often and as diplomatically as I could, to defrock me and send me back to the news side. Sometimes he seemed to be all but in the mood to do it, gazing at me as at some implausible species of man, but then he would veer around and announce that I was the man for the photo service job. I did not delude myself that he really thought me to be any great prize as a photo editor; it was simply that I was calling his judgment of men into question and this he could not abide. He went to extraordinary lengths to resist such a challenge. For illustration, not long after the coronation of George VI of Britain, I happened to be standing by Wirephoto when our London bureau offered a photo of the new king making his first address to the British Empire, as it was then called. The editor immediately in charge, Al Murphy, an old and perhaps parochial New York hand who loved to cover Easter Parades in front of St. Patrick's Cathedral, and who may have been just a little bit of an Anglophobe, snapped to London: "Forget that one!" Aghast, I countermanded his order instantly, and felt a fatherly tap on my shoulder. I looked around and here was Kent Cooper, murmuring: *"That's* why I need you here." This brilliant stroke of editorial judgment on my part kept me yoked to the photo department for three months more, until at long last I was able to break away.

It was the only journalistic job I ever wanted to lose. And to lose it took a bit of doing. By this time, Byron Price, too, was in New York, having been appointed the AP's editor-in-chief. He cast somber glances at me on many occasions during the seemingly endless time I was trying to get demoted. On the other hand, though, he gave me from time to time a certain form of negative, or perhaps passive, support on those occasions when the senior AP executives were summoned to Cooper's offices for general conferences. At one of these, Cooper, still infatuated with having obtained Wirephoto, passed from hand to hand a photo of something that had happened abroad. The print was rather like one of those ambiguous blobs shown to the nation on television in the early days of space exploration, accompanied by enthusiastic commentaries from the scientists: look here, a lake; look here, a mountain, and so on. Price, who had been through these exercises before, affected to be busy reading a newspaper, wholly hiding his face; he did not put out his hand to grasp the photo when it came his turn. This small, unverifiable act of heresy so heartened me that when it came my turn to look at the picture I observed to Cooper that for my part the thing might as well have come over by slow freighter.

It was a measure of the conviction of Kent Cooper that Wirephoto was little less than a gift from the gods that he tolerated this remark with nothing worse than a brief scowl. Nevertheless, the incident perhaps did lead to my liberation from the photo service, though not quite in the way for which I had longed. Not long afterward, Cooper transferred me into another big job (I speak in the context of AP life) as general night editor. In a way this was a disappointment, in that I had wanted to go back to writing, an activity that Cooper did not hold in the highest regard. All the same, I had at least got back into what I considered real newspaper work, into something I understood, something where no longer did I have to issue orders to men who thought of me as some kind of top-management pet.

Though as general night editor I had to give orders to much older men (my principal deputy editor was fifty-seven), at least I felt I knew what the devil I was doing when I issued them. Still, there was some awkwardness in it for me. I had been brought up in a family operated on somewhat military lines, my father serving as senior officer present, and the youngest son—myself—being by definition the most junior officer of all. This did not mean that the senior officer was unkind or dictatorial. It did mean that when a man some thirty years my senior, in age and in service on the general news desk, made a news decision of which I disapproved, I did not find it easy to put in a veto. Yet I was very often in a pickle. For if anything went wrong for any reason anywhere in the world with our coverage during my trick of duty, it was I who had to carry the baby—upstairs to Price's office and, in severe crises, right on up to Cooper's. Price rightly would not accept the alibi that some other George had did it; and I never offered it. Cooper was usually off dreaming of an ever more imperial AP.

So I didn't put in the veto as often as I should have— generously assuming, of course, that I was right in my judgment in the first place—because to me thirty years' senior was in some sense thirty years' superior. A lot of my colleagues never guessed this then, and a lot of people are never quite going to believe it now. But any man who grew up in a heavily

60

Anglo-American home, and especially one still remembering and honoring Royalist, Stiff-Upper-Lip England as mine did, will understand.

I remember years later taking Newbold Noyes, editor of the *Washington Star*, to the house on N Street in Georgetown the day before the inauguration of 1961 to meet President-elect John Kennedy. Kennedy was still making up his Cabinet, casually giving orders over the phone to men who had been eminent while he was a Harvard undergraduate, and Noyes was looking very thoughtful. "Don't you think he'll have a little trouble in directing men much older than he?" he whispered to me. "Why don't you ask him, Newby?" I suggested, and Newby did. Kennedy looked astonished, smiled understandingly—he *was* an understanding man, whatever his faults—and replied: "Good God, no! Why should I?"

Still, I don't wish to make much of the difficulties of the age-gap (there's a perfect journalistic term for you) during my service as AP's general editor. For among all the things that did go wrong, the two most ghastly could in no way be charged to any associate of mine.

The first mishap involved the Japanese invasion of China while the Communists were trying to take it over. The AP had a new man in Rome, and on the basis of some conversation he had with some monsignor or another, he sent in to the New York cable desk a dispatch strongly implying that the Pope was blessing every bomb that fell on China so long as it hit a Communist. The cable desk put out this absurdity and somehow in the ceaseless flow of copy over my desk (all major dispatches were to clear my desk before going to the wires), it got out and got printed all over the world.

The resulting flood of Catholic protesting mail to AP—all of which descended upon Price, who was in every acute situation the final It—had the building aquiver. When my desk telephone rang I knew very well who was calling and that somebody up there was going to be very put out with me. I went to Price's office, spread my arms, shook my head—and said nothing at all. "All right," Price growled, "get on back to work." Thereupon he dismissed his secretary for an indefinite leave, got in a fresh box of cigars, and sat down at his typewriter. He stayed there, taking time out for eating and sleeping, for about three days, and eventually there emerged what we all called the Price Letter. I could not possibly reproduce this extraordinary document, which was sent unchanged to every protester from Cardinal to communicant, in each case freshly typed and addressed.

In that letter Price somehow accomplished several impossibles. He admitted the AP had been wrong, but suggested that since the offending dispatch had been datelined Vatican City, any open and public retraction by the AP now might be read by some as suggesting that Vatican City itself had been the irresponsible informant. This, he said, surely would be gratuitously insulting to His Holiness. On and on went such specious but ineffably gracious reasoning—and Price, and the AP, got away with it.

Again, there was the Case of the Broken Faith. When the Spanish Civil War broke out, our correspondents on both the Loyalist and the Insurgent side (these terms were of my coinage, under a directive from Kent Cooper to find a nomenclature as objective as possible) took the customary pledge to send back nothing in code in their dispatches. In a perhaps regrettably clandestine way, we nevertheless had instructed our man with the Franco forces to drop in a certain word in a dispatch (what the word was I do not now recall) when and if Madrid should fall, since such an event would signal the beginning of the end. In those days a "bulletin" was a hot dispatch of a single paragraph to introduce a story of moment. For the truly transcendent stuff we used what we called a "flash," a single terse phrase—for example, "Major earthquake hits Lima"—to alert newspaper editors of very big news indeed.

On one more or less somnolent night, New York time, Madrid did fall and we got the coded word. In his excitement and his zeal to beat the opposition, a rewrite man on the cable desk dashed off a flash reading: "Madrid falls, says coded dispatch to AP." A copy boy dropped my flimsy on my desk while another copy boy was dropping another flimsy of the flash on our main trunk wire. I leapt from my cell with a hell of a yell, to quote an irreverent limerick, and ran to the trunk wire that fed most of AP's associates in New York—British, French, Japanese, and other news agencies—in the hope that here at least I could scratch out that damning phrase "says coded dispatch to AP" before the operator had punched it out on the tape. I was too late. The AP had not only violated its undertaking with Franco but had been caught—or rather had caught itself—doing so. Little was made of this, however, and I did not even have to go upstairs to Price again. It is a pretty good bet, of course, that the Falangists never kicked out our correspondent now they had got what they wanted in the capture of Madrid.

Aberrations of this sort aside, I got along pretty well and was reasonably happy on the big news desk, one of the consolations being that I had no routine work to do—no copy editing, for example. Another was a certain sense of self-importance that I neither quite acknowledged to myself nor quite denied myself. After all, I was not yet thirty years old and the power lay in my hands to plan out each night the basic pattern of what national and international events the AP would cover, and to some extent how, by whom, and at what length they would be covered. Each night I prepared what the AP called a budget message, which went out to many hundreds of news editors, telegraph editors, or managing editors of individual newspapers, briefly outlining the major news stories to be expected during the night, in descending order of the importance attached by AP (which here meant me) to each.

We received hundreds of our member newspapers daily. AP called them "members," by the way, because AP was a cooperative and a nonprofit association, or, in the end, a publishers' club whose franchises were eagerly sought. The idea was drilled into us that we were unsoiled by commerce, whereas our principal competitor, the United Press, was plainly and openly in business. UP called its papers "clients"—and called AP "Rocks" or sometimes "Grandma" in its intra-service coded messages. "Rocks" referred to a long-dead AP head named Melville Stone. The Hearst organization's competitive network, International News Service, called us "Apathy." AP, for its part, was loftily above such flippancakes as "Rocks" or "Grandma" or "Apathy." Our code word for UP was "Levit;" for INS it was "Epitoe." Whoever dreamed up these enigmatic non-words I never knew.

At any rate, from the newspapers coming in from across the country I kept general track of who was doing what to whom competitively as between AP, UP, and INS. It was a nightly race for the front pages of America and that was one of the factors that kept the dust off my assignment. Of more interest to me personally, though, was the visible evidence every day that a large proportion of the newspapers of this country were displaying the morning news almost precisely as I had described it in the nightly budget message. Dispatch No. 1 on the budget message was almost always the most heavily featured in the papers, Dispatch No. 2 the second most heavily featured, and so on.

While this pleased me, it also made me wonder if journalism was not becoming altogether too homogenized when a twenty-nine-year-old man in New York could pretty well lay out much of a nation's front pages in advance. I do not suggest that some great philosophical revulsion arose in me. I was far too attached to the Service, as we all called the AP, for anything quite so heretical as that. All the same, a seed was planted here. For the first time I began to wonder whether I wanted to be an organization-man journalist for the rest of my life, even in so decent and respected an organization as AP.

I think I got to looking at us as journalists did outside—say, those on the irrepressibly irreverent *New York Daily News*, who laughed a lot in print and still managed to do an entirely creditable journalistic job. One night I decided that while being a news executive was infinitely preferable to that awful executive editorship of the photo service, I had had enough of it. Again I began a campaign with Kent Cooper to be demoted. Plainly and simply, I wanted to get back to writing my own pieces.

This time around, the task of unjobbing myself from what Cooper steadfastly regarded as the only important sort of career, that is, a managerial one, was not half so difficult as it had been when his beloved Wirephoto instrument was involved. Helpful, too, was the circumstance that, while I never let down the executive side in public in its running and often bitter quarrels with the office activists of the Newspaper Guild, still in my rather rare encounters with Cooper I had never pretended to share his passionate resentment of the Guild.

Nevertheless, shortly after I became night editor I quit the Guild. This was partly because I was then in a managerial, or at least quasi-managerial, position and thus in an anomalous one, too. Far more important to me, though, it had become impossible for me to stick with the Guild for two other reasons. The first was that the Guild had long since abandoned any pretense of being a professional association or even a union confined to professionals. Telephone operators, clerks, and other wholly noneditorial members now far outnumbered journalists. In the second place, the leaders of the Guild in New York, and in other cities here and there, were taking up violently partisan and ideological positions which seemed to me to outrage any rational standard of objectivity and to hand over to the publishers a weapon of shattering impact. How, they asked with undeniable force, could reporters publicly proclaiming their partisanship on various political issues be trusted to write disinterestedly on just those issues?

For me, and for others, the end of the road came when some of the Guild's leaders sought to apply a litmus test on the issue of the Spanish Civil War. The Loyalists were good guys; the Insurgents were not only bad guys but Fascists as well. This view was not without its merits, but it had some demerits, too. If Nazi Germany was helping Franco, as indeed it was, Soviet Russia was helping the Loyalists. This unremarkable conclusion of mine, which I venture to say is supported by subsequent history, forced me to leave the Guild.

I do not wish to imply that I ever held, or hold now, the notion that newspapermen (I speak here of those supposed to report the news and not, of course, of those entitled to write editorials or columns) should be innocent of convictions. Nor do I believe that the practice of objective journalism in the

65

reportage and display of news should be like cutting up a boarding-house pie, so that each claimant at the table gets precisely the same size slice. A humorless (which is to say proportionless) and fatuous "objectivity" was never in my mind and is not now. All the same, there is much to be said for the proposition that it is a fundamental obligation of the reporter to keep his own private opinions to himself in his pieces, leaving it to those authorized to editorialize to do so openly, and hoping that in time he himself can qualify for that undeniably more attractive side of the profession. This in no way excludes interpretive or "in-depth" articles so long as a commitment to fairness underlies them. The Supreme Court once observed that while it could write no definitive description of pornography as distinguished from free expression, every sentient man and woman knew damn well that there was a line to be drawn. So it is in the matter of objective reporting.

If I have dwelt too long on this subject, I submit in my defense that it is a vastly important one to the public, ever growing more so; and, secondly, that it is a subject much involved in the career of this journalist. For in departing from the Guild I had to part, in a way, from men with whom on the whole I was most agreeably at home, and enter what is now called the Establishment, of which I was in most ways far from fond. I never had any use for men in the executive or sub-executive level who were always yammering at the Guild for the purpose of currying favor with management. I had as little use for the Guild extremists who were always climbing some secular cross and seeking martyrdom. This was a martyrdom in the name of job security; nobody active in the Guild in the Thirties was going to be fired, however incompetent he might be, and everybody knew it. For my part, I was painfully in the middle, a lonely position that was to be mine for nearly the whole of my subsequent career as a "moderate."

My second and final break away from AP officialdom was certainly not harmed by this posture, since my refusal to rah-rah for management came naturally to me and naturally did not please the Top Floor. My release was certainly not deterred by the small service impieties which, executive or not, I felt

66

compelled to commit from time to time to show that I was no True Believer. On one occasion, for example, Kent Cooper ordered to be posted in the general news and city rooms an admonition against the use of AP telephones for private calls. Under this, I wrote: "Moreover, members of the Staff are hereby directed not to use AP pencils in future to write personal notes." This did not amuse the upper level; I noted that my advice was sought there less and less frequently, though no outright rebuke was directed at me.

Then there occurred what might somewhat extravagantly be called the Rudolph Flesch Affair. Flesch, who had come out of nowhere so far as I knew, somehow convinced Kent Cooper, along with a good many other high brass types in journalism, that writing came down in the end to a System. This, of course, was *his* System: he became, as I believe, the first man in history to apply the techniques of the efficiency expert to writing. Flesch had it figured out that certain words had more oomph than other words; he had identified these jewels of communication, and one needed only to buy his System to find the efficiency and productivity of one's word factory, so to speak, immensely increased. There was more to this farrago, including, as I recall, an arbitrary proscription on any sentence longer than nine words. But what I have said about it is enough, I hope, to indicate both its sensitive appreciation of the English language and its remarkable effrontery.

Kent Cooper, who would have been a tremendous entrepreneur in any other line of work and was only too enthusiastic about progress, and not a born Philistine, eagerly came forward to buy Flesch's system. It became his new pet project. And while I should say here that the powerful drive of this formidable man did much good for AP in many other ways, he characteristically demanded from his associates enthusiasm for Flesch's system equivalent to his own. When Cooper flattered me by sending me the prospectus for this extraordinary "system" and inviting comment, I replied that in my view the English language could not be thus packaged, and that what was wrong with AP writing was not that it lacked a Ten Commandments but rather that it was too shackled already.

67

That did it. Cooper approved without further hesitation a formal request I had finally made for a transfer back to a writing job. He sent me to the New York City Desk, which in his view amounted to replacing my service colonel's eagles with the brass bars of a second lieutenant. As for me, it was just fine.

CHAPTER FIVE

AT THE CITY DESK I was put on general assignments, which meant that I soon got to know a New York City I had not known before. It meant, too, that I was the senior staff correspondent for the night side—that is, for the morning papers— doing what in the trade we called the "night lead." The only stories with which I had to be involved were national in interest or scope, and occasionally even international. Moreover, I had the backup help of the tapes of the old City News Association, which swept New York like a vacuum cleaner, with incomparable dullness of expression but incomparable fidelity to those details that help put life into a news story.

Too, the City Desk had "stringers," men reporting more or less on a piece-work basis, in the boroughs outlying Manhattan and on Long Island. In a word, a senior AP correspondent had the benefit of a vast amount of other fellows' leg work, particularly in such teeming but alien places as Darkest Brooklyn. These stringers were not only useful; they often brightened the day. When, for example, a grisly story called "Murder, Incorporated" broke ("Murder Incorporated" being the inevitable journalese epithet for a horrendous syndicate of killers), much of the subsequent police action was centered in Brooklyn. Reporting on the telephone to me on some development or other in this story, our Brooklyn stringer read to me a list of the newly arrested, a list that included the striking name "Pittsburgh Phil." Why, I asked, did they call him Pittsburgh

Phil? "Well, you see," said our man in thick Brooklynese, "he just happens to *look* like a guy from Pittsburgh."

The charm of the City Desk job was that it moved me about in a kind of zany way from a "Murder, Inc." story and the offices of police captains, to the long decline of Tammany Hall, to on-ship interviews with world celebrities (we used to go down the harbor in Coast Guard cutters to meet the incoming liners), to covering the visit of King George VI and Queen Elizabeth, in my world's last glowingly bittersweet summer, that of 1939. As a reporter, and sometimes fortuitously in a more personal way, I met with all manner of people and encountered and wrote about many of the most notable events of the late Thirties. I interviewed and then talked privately with that wartime Pope Pius who had earlier been the Vatican's Secretary of State, Cardinal Pacelli.

At a reception in New York for King George VI and Queen Elizabeth, I had the privilege of having a drink in the king's party—and the unforgettable experience of seeing the queen firmly nudging him and emphatically shaking her head in the negative when he was about to accept a third highball. I was to meet that shy, stuttering, wistful, and deeply gallant man again, in wartime England, and to see again the Queen put down her Scottish *nae* upon him when the third highball—served in the big, American style—was passed around.

New York was then a lovely place—not in the ladylike sense of the word, but in the deep sense that it stirred an enormous, unspoken affection for the incredible richness of its pluralism, for the superficial rudeness and basic kindness and tolerance of its polyglot masses and high-toned classes. Here, except perhaps for London, was the great beating heart of the world in nearly all its aspects: finance, the arts, the theatre, communications—everything, that is, except an adult appreciation of the true nature of the menace rising in the east from Hitler and, for a time, from Stalin.

Indeed, it was this general unawareness in the United States that a war of scarcely conceivable ferocity was surely going to break over the head of a nearly naked England, and an England moreover that under Prime Minister Neville Chamberlain had debased itself before Hitler, that really brought George VI across the Atlantic. Nominally, if I remember correctly, he had come over to give a touch of "class," as New Yorkese would have put it, to the 1939 World's Fair. Actually, as he was always faithful to the elliptical advice for the defense of the realm often given him in privacy by such shadow-minister counselors as Winston Churchill, the king's mission was infinitely more grave. He was in search of the comradeship—and more importantly the help, once the storm broke—of the one part of the English-speaking world that had outgrown in riches and power all the other parts put together. I hesitate to claim, across the long span of years since then, that I sensed something of all this—in fact, I am embarrassed to do so. But I have set out in this book to tell it as it really was. And so I do say that I *did* sense it, by that intuitive process that I have earlier claimed for myself in other journalistic connections.

So much is this so that standing there in Flushing Meadows in the Borough of Queens in the City of New York I felt proud of a hitherto long-forgotten episode that had occurred years before, while I was still down there in Dallas, Texas, filing a little wire trimmed from a bigger one in the AP regional office. It was the night Adolf Hitler ascended to the chancellorship of Germany, a brawling, seemingly hysterical little man whom my big boss in New York, Kent Cooper, was even much later to dismiss as no one of consequence—just as, right up until September of 1939, he assured us all in the senior staff in New York that talk of war was sheer nonsense.

In Dallas, I took the copy about Hitler that was pouring in from a trunk wire from the East at better than sixty words a minute and put it, intact, on a state wire running at less than thirty words a minute. Something, of course, had to give. What gave was a whole complex of stuff that our member papers regarded as sacrosanct—stock-market tables, baseball boxscores. I threw all this into the wastebasket, deeply violating my operator's sense of a routine almost divinely ordained, and remained deaf, if apprehensive, when the papers out on the line tried to break into the teleprinter's recital with such queries as "How about the wool market report?"

71

I knew, however dimly, that a truly historical watershed was being crossed in a Europe which I had never seen, and I was determined that Texas papers should have all they could get on the subject, even if they didn't like what they were getting. What I myself got was nearly my discharge from AP. It was the hardest weather I was ever to meet in that Service; but it was worth it to me.

As I watched the king, slight and self-deprecating, in Flushing Meadows that day in 1939, I pretty well lost my interest in the stories like "Murder, Inc." that had been engaging much of my attention. I began then to have a passionate concern with world affairs; I became a little bored with the City Desk and all that. As matters turned out, this was just as well. For on the September day on which Neville Chamberlain at last announced that Britain was going to war with Hitler over Poland's rape, I became, in a most unceremonious way, a member of the foreign staff—at New York HQ—of the Associated Press. Higher authority came rushing to the City Desk, took me by the arm, hurried me across the great general news room in Rockefeller Center to the Foreign News Desk, sat me down before a radio and said: "Write it, quick!" The radio was on and Chamberlain's weary voice was announcing Britain's declaration of war. I wrote what we call in the trade a "running story," quoting directly from the prime minister as much as I could, under a dateline thus devised: "London (Via Radio)."

I was told it was a temporary assignment to the foreign staff. As it worked out, it lasted quite a long time, for shortly the foreign news editor, an utterly audacious North Carolinian named J.M. (Buddy) Roberts, created for me the title of war editor. What this meant in practice was that I had two jobs. First, I was the principal rewrite man on the Cable Desk, putting the major shortform cablese stuff into what was designed at least to be better prose at fuller length. Second, I wrote under my own name a rather long nightly interpretive and semi-editorial roundup of all the principal war news. We called this the "Night Lead Undated International," and Roberts, who thought the byline "William Smith White" was a bit more "interesting" than my old byline of William S. White,

72

insisted on the full treatment. This was to give me some slight problem later in England, while I was sitting around the AP London office waiting for D-Day. I occasionally pitched in to help write a routine piece, though I had been assigned by New York—with others, of course—specifically to cover the D-Day assault. The British Ministry of Information published a daily "Impact" sheet telling what stories the New York papers were playing up and who had written them. On that sheet my name invariably came out as Smith-White, the British assuming that two such common surnames could hardly coexist unless conjoined by a hyphen. My American colleagues did not let me rest easily with this situation. One of my old friends, Gladwin Hill, went so far as to write notes to me as "Smythe-Whyte." Hill, a transplanted Bostonian, was always in a way spiritually attuned to the famous Tea Party. He was vastly indignant with everything about Albion. "Good God!" he would exclaim in getting off a London subway: "*Look* at that damn sign: '*Alight here for the Whipsnade Zoo!*' "

On the Cable Desk in New York, with London and all that yet a good way in the future, Roberts and I had a long, mad, and mixed fling with the news of the early war—that is, the phase before Pearl Harbor and our own national entry into the struggle. Roberts was, plainly and simply, the very model of what in the old days a newspaperman was supposed to be, Objective to the point of being almost wholly detached from the issue of who was right and who was wrong about anything, and passionate about only one thing: to be *first with the news*, to "beat the opposition." I, as his deputy more or less, was, from the moment of Chamberlain's speech to the world (giving belated and exhausted fulfillment of the British pledge to Poland's borders), emotionally involved far more in the struggle itself than in the struggle between AP, UP, INS, and the *New York Times* foreign service. I always sensed that Roberts saw in this a regrettable frailty on my part; all the same, we got along very well together.

Under one of my hats, the one labeled "Chief Rewrite Man," I did my best to be objective, though this was surpassingly hard at times and never more so than on the day on which

I had to assemble a hundred fragments of frantic cablese—from our correspondents with the British Expeditionary Force in France, from London, and elsewhere—and knock together a long account of the evacuation at Dunkirk.

Roberts, who always believed that in so vast an event as the Second World War the field dispatches should be merely the raw materials for his writers in New York to work over, was so pleased with my piece that he sent it upstairs to Kent Cooper. Cooper, who had most reluctantly accepted the fact that a war really existed, was not deeply enchanted until the managing editor of the *Baltimore Sun* telephoned him to commend the AP's job on Dunkirk. The story, he said, was "like a modern *Iliad*," a comparison I recognized to be highly empurpled praise of what I had put together. But I confess that I was not unhappy that the commendation, however exaggerated, had penetrated to Upstairs. Roberts was simply and unqualifiedly delighted. He was a magnificent editor in that he loved those he believed to be good writers—a category in which he was kind enough to put me—and the success of my Dunkirk story elated him.

I was not elated when Kent Cooper paid one of his rare and stately visits Downstairs to the Cable Desk to give me an absentminded pat on the back after he had mulled over the signal from Baltimore. For I was wholly unable, then or later, to see the Second World War as primarily an opportunity for the exercise of journalism, AP-style or otherwise. To me Dunkirk was, as it would remain, a moment and signal of the greatest grief I had ever known, apart from personal grief over the loss of someone I had loved.

It required no ingenious insight to see that this disaster was one of the gravest in all the history of warfare and that England was now to be in a position of extreme peril unlike any she had known since the Battle of Hastings.

Thus, when Cooper made his little speech of compliment to me, dwelling on the fact that his AP researchers had found we had "swept the field over the opposition" on the Dunkirk story, I was of no mind to jump up and down for joy. "Don't you feel very good now, White?" Cooper demanded. "Oh," I said, "so-so,

I guess." "Jesus Christ!" Cooper exploded, "I don't like men who just feel so-so. What the hell is wrong with you?" I think it was probably at this point that he gave up on his long project of making something out of me. Certainly, the incident planted the germ of what was to grow into a fairly active suspicion on the part of AP's general manager that White lacked a certain detachment from the news item called the Second World War and needed careful handling lest he become too pro-British.

Cooper was among the hardiest of all that hardy band of isolationists, or noninterventionists, and in order to sustain that position he was, like his close friend Colonel Robert Mc-Cormick of the *Chicago Tribune*, subtly compelled to find something very wrong about Britain, British character, British military operations, and whatever else British. None of the old isolationists—not Cooper, not McCormick, not anybody else among them—was a monster, and none of them could shut his eyes to the bald fact of Nazi aggression or his ears to the screams of anguish that arose from the victims of German genocide. They all simply, and somehow piteously, wanted us to Stay Out of It; and one could not honorably Stay Out of It unless he could convince himself that the moral posture lay in "a plague o' both your houses."

Roberts pretty well looked the other way in all this. It was not that *he* was an isolationist or that he was without pity; it was simply that his whole being, his whole ethos, was enrapt with the old-time newspaper view that the Story was the Thing. I, though, was in a pickle. As chief rewrite man I had no call to "editorialize" in my work; German actions in what became Occupied Europe required no semantic additive to speak their message to the world. Moreover, the phase of the Phony War now set in and for this time a comparative lull set in over the Cable Desk.

But the self-restraint I practiced under this hat was by no means easy to come by when I set out each night to function as war editor and to write my nightly "interpretive" of the war news, a piece, by the way, that I often heard read intact on one or the other of the national radio news networks. It appeared also in hundreds of newspapers.

In the Undated International I was fully as "pro-British" as Cooper had ever suspected me to be, and this without apology or ever looking over my shoulder. Colonel McCormick wrote in from Chicago to Cooper to denounce me as a British stooge. Look, he said to Cooper, that fellow White even uses *British* terms like "Near East" and "Far East" when everybody knows that they are to the *West* of Chicago. All the same, nobody in AP ever interfered with me in my Undated. I think Roberts served as a kind of unguent between me Downstairs and Cooper Upstairs. Moreover, I suspect that even Kent Cooper began to question some of the assumptions of his isolationism.

For one thing, certain activists in the Newspaper Guild (we never heard the term "activists" in those days, of course) were busily promoting a thing called the Popular Front that was designed, even if they did not know it, not only to keep us Out of It but also to do nothing, in the intermediate stages of the war anyhow, to help prevent the destruction of Britain. I say that it was thus "designed," not on the basis of guess or rumor or an enfevered fear of communism, but by direct knowledge. It so happened that Earl Browder, then the ostensible, and possibly the real, head of the Communist party U.S.A., had indirectly sought to recruit me not into the party but into the Popular Front. My reply was that I was otherwise engaged. I had formed, in my own small way, a William Smith White Committee of One to Aid England. This, I knew, was a small thing indeed next to the prestigious William Allen White Committee to Aid the Allies; but small though it was, it was my own. (By the way, I am not, and never was, as the saying used to go in Senate investigations of other matters, related in any way to the William Allen White family.)

Now, if Kent Cooper disliked the British, to the extent and in the context which I have already indicated, he disliked the Newspaper Guild "activists"—or nonactivists, for that matter—far more. But many of my friends in New York and Washington, and most of my colleagues on the Cable Desk, were Popular Fronters, openly or at heart, and as displeasure at my Undated International abated, if only slightly, in the AP Establishment on the Right, it mounted rather heatedly from my working associates on my left. To describe the experience as searing would be going too far. Nevertheless, it *was* hurtful, for I both liked and respected these men on my Left, and it all made me even more of a loner than I had been. (Few loners wish to be; it is only that by genetic accident or body chemistry they cannot help being.) All the same, I simply could not go along with the notion that since Britain undeniably had a "Class System," a full quota of snobs, an undue love of aristocrats, and unfair rewards for the Old School Tie, it was therefore about as evil as a Nazi regime engaged in wholesale murder in search of "racial purity."

(I did not then realize what the Old School Tie really meant to England in the desperate hours. Later on I came to have a profound respect for that Tie, and even for Colonel Blimp. After all, a man named Winston Churchill wore such a Tie; and so did some other, unknown men who did so much to save both England and us. The contributions to Allied victory of the essentially Old-School-Tie British MI6 and American OSS in bamboozling Hitler were matchless. As for Colonel Blimp, how many would weep with rage if his number should now burgeon in the England of the present? I knew some MI6 types in England. I later met a fellow called Dick White—no relation— who turned up the traitor Kim Philby. I knew some Colonel Blimps, too, particularly in the Guards, and my regard for them was and is unapologetic.)

The season of comparative calm that we knew on the Cable Desk in New York during the period of the Phony War came to a most lurid end, of course, when Hitler's armor and Stuka dive bombers brushed with ease past France's supposedly impregnable Maginot Line and drove to whimpering surrender a far larger—yes, far larger, far more "professional," and far better armed—French Army. Again AP was "out in front," to use the language that was common to us on the desk, under the compulsive force of the Cooper theory that not merely frantic but above all *successful* competition was the name of the game.

The redoubtable Buddy Roberts, who had much the same

view (though in his case it was not made of purely mercantile considerations), saw to it that we should remain out ahead of the Opposition. For illustration, we had with the main French forces an old-time correspondent, John Lloyd, whose dispatches invariably were redolent of a simple, bleak realism and were put in the most gracelessly honest of laconic prose. One day as one of his pieces from the field came across the Cable Desk, one short take at a time, the ever vigilant Roberts, who read every word of every line that came into and went out of our New York HQ, noted that Lloyd had begun each one of five successive paragraphs with the cablese sentence: "French, if fight on. . . . " Translated, this read: "The French, if they fight on . . . . " Lloyd's material, of course, had to pass French field censorship.

Roberts was the kind of man who never balked at the highest jump. Earlier in the war he had fully established such a persona. He had somehow struck up a friendship with Hendrik Willem Van Loon, the Dutch writer then resident in New York, and had learned that Van Loon had certain enigmatic contacts with "people in Holland." One night, then, Van Loon called Roberts at the AP office and uttered a single declarative sentence: "Roberts, the Nazis have invaded the Netherlands." With that Van Loon hung up. Roberts, not one to bother about the fact that from none of our own staff sources and from no other sources had we heard of any such thing, sat down at his typewriter and sent out the flash: "Germans invade Holland." Van Loon turned out to be right, of course; otherwise we should very shortly have had a foreign news editor whose name would not have been Roberts.

This was the kidney of the editor who was reading those "French, if fight on . . . " lines. He called me over to his desk, quietly said, "Look at these paragraphs, Bill," and asked, "Is it clear to you what John Lloyd is telling us?" I said it was, and wrote out a bulletin, under Lloyd's byline, beginning thus: "The French Army tonight is in its last retreat before surrender." I then took the rest of Lloyd's dispatch as it trickled in and fleshed out this outrageous gamble. Well, not quite so outrageous as might appear. For Roberts knew Lloyd and I

78

knew Lloyd and we reckoned that for no reason would he begin five paragraphs in precisely the same way unless he had for us just the message we thought we had got.

Roberts and I usually worked from about noon to about eight in the evening, which was past midnight for our correspondents in Europe, and then knocked off to leave the Cable Desk in more junior hands until the morrow. This is just what we did on that night of the John Lloyd Dispatch That Never Was. We went across the street from Rockefeller Center to Louie's Bar, Roberts as calm as any Bret Harte gambler and I definitely on the nervous side. When we parted for the night, for the regular Saturday and Sunday off, Roberts casually observed to me: "Better leave your home phone off the hook this weekend." I did, and I was glad that I did. For when Paul Patterson, publisher of the *Baltimore Sun* and a member of the board of directors of AP, read his paper Saturday morning and saw the pseudo-Lloyd dispatch, he telephoned Kent Cooper in great agitation to say that he knew damned well that no such dispatch had ever passed the French censors and to demand to know what in the hell was going on. Cooper, Roberts and I learned later, set in motion what in journalese would be called a citywide search for one J.M. Roberts and one W.S. White but was unable to reach either. We spent a restless weekend, or at least I did, until our dispatch was fully confirmed—sometime on Sunday, as I recall. When we entered the AP office together at noon on Monday, walking tall, as they say in the movies, the interoffice phone on Roberts's desk was urgently buzzing. Kent Cooper was on the wire with a hearty "Well done, fellows." We learned from his private secretary that he had been trying earlier to reach us for the less amiable purpose of firing us out of hand. Now, of course, he was one of those many fathers that Success turns up.

The truth of the business is that day after day we were under Cooper's lash to be ahead, at all times, not only of the United Press, our chief news agency competitor, but also of the *New York Times* and *Chicago Daily News* foreign services. Not a week passed that we did not cut some corners very fine; we told no lies but we spared no effort to put into the war news those qualities cherished in the trade—"color," "impact," and all that. Had there been in existence a journalistic Canon of Ethics, and had it been monitored with considerably more care than are the Canons of the Law and Medicine, we should have spent half of our time before some skeptical board of inquiry.

I recount this tale of our flying trapeze act on the AP Cable Desk not in a spirit of confession but only in candor. After all, Roberts and I had the excuse that Higher Authority was pushing us to the last limit. Cooper designated one of the most senior of the older AP news executives, Thomas O'Neill, to keep up a minute-by-minute log on all big war stories. O'Neill sent Upstairs a running report as to precisely where the minute hand and even the second hand stood when such-and-such a bit of cablese arrived on the Desk, as to precisely what minute and second it cleared through our rewrite mill, and at precisely what minute and second the equivalent bit of news cleared through our United Press opposition. (This latter information he obtained through some sort of covert operation, through some informant inside the UP, about which I never had any knowledge.)

If these were exhilarating times, they were hard on the nervous system. I never relaxed until the hour came nightly when I could cease my labors as a rewrite man over other men's copy and sit down in something approaching a calm state of mind to write my own Undated International. With this piece—as my own—I tried to lower the temperature a little, as is the old privilege of newspapermen acting as editorial writers rather than as reporters pushing hard to "take the play."

All the same, the view of AP's top management that the Second World War was first and foremost a journalistic challenge wore upon me more and more during my months on the Cable Desk. Though it was not for me to instruct my seniors, I myself was unable to forget that a great many people were dying in a great many places, and was unable, too, to suppress the inner certainty that before long my own country—and countrymen—would surely be involved.

Memoirs that salute the author's geopolitical foresight, humane feelings, and the like, have never much appealed to me, and I am trying to avoid such self-service while trying also to tell what happened to me and why. Right up until the day Hitler invaded the Soviet Union most of my colleagues pretty well retained the view that the one unspeakable thing would be for the United States to intervene in what, in a marvelously convenient phrase, was called "this senseless slaughter."

On my side, I felt that President Roosevelt was moving much too slowly, rather than too fast, toward intervention. I felt that the isolationists in Washington, and most particularly such professional "anti-war" senators as Gerald Nye, with his "merchants-of-death" investigations of munitions makers that helped to keep this country naked of arms, were profoundly, unforgivably, wrong-headed. I thought the Western world owed much to an England that was standing alone against the Nazis, and that was sometimes assaulted by Soviet-made steel falling from Nazi bombers over the Thames Estuary in the days of the Hitler-Stalin Pact.

I therefore set out in my war roundups quite consciously and with no sense of guilt for violating Objectivity (since under this hat I did have a certain unstated and undefined editorial license anyway) to support the idea of American intervention in any way I could. This Undated International piece, or so I was told by the AP's promotional people, was perhaps the most consistently read feature put out by AP. In a word, it reached many millions, at least on the hypothesis that most of the people were reading their morning papers. I thus felt entitled to assume that to some extent, however small, it was helping to shape public thinking. And I was obliged to recognize that, accepting the validity of this assumption, a very big responsibility was falling upon one journalist named White. I could not sustain any degree of genuine impersonality, so I did not try. When, for example, Hitler at last struck at Stalin, it seemed to me that if ever there was a time for a separation of the men from the boys, that time was now, while the illusion of the Popular Front lay in ruins for all sensible people to see.

I now began an internal transmutation of myself from a journalist writing about war to a conscious prospective armed participant in the struggle. No doubt it was a romantic notion, possibly fed in part by the fact that my ancestors had been in combat in every war in American history, albeit on the "wrong" side in 1776 and again in 1861, but I felt under a special sort of obligation. Having recommended that my countrymen involve themselves dangerously, it began to chafe me guiltily that I was sitting in New York under a 3-B deferment as a war editor.

CHAPTER SIX

THE JAPANESE ATTACK on Pearl Harbor made the chafing intolerable. Acquaintances at the headquarters of the First U.S. Army on Governors Island offered me a captaincy in Intelligence by telephone on the morning after the disaster at Honolulu; but that was not for me. If I was to enter the service I wanted to earn some form of combat command, however lowly. Here, then, I set out upon the most quixotic enterprise of my life, an enterprise somewhat embarrassing to me in retrospect but not one I regret all that much, either. I approached my draft board in Queens with the idea of enlisting in the infantry as a volunteer officer candidate. This proposal was not well received, perhaps because I had been assigned by the board to that category called "indispensable to the war effort," or some such having to do with my profession. More likely because the board was too busy to care one way or the other.

I told Roberts what I was about and received from him an incredulous and quizzical look that wordlessly said that I was a most unusual damn fool. An old friend and colleague, Gayle Talbot, was more forthright. "Good God," he said, "you are thirty-five years old and doing more here than you could possibly do on any battlefield. After all, this is not some war where Teddy Roosevelts charge up San Juan Hill." This latter observation hit home. I had not forgotten my father's amused memories of what he thought of the conduct of Teddy Roosevelt ("that fella with all those *teeth*") in the Spanish-American War.

Nevertheless I persisted in my plan to enter the infantry. The draft board in Queens, perhaps bemused that some slightly over-aged idiot was trying to get *in* where so many were trying to get out, dragged its feet for four or five months after my application for a reclassification to 1-A so that I could go into the volunteer officer candidate category.

In the meantime, my work went on pretty much as before, though I had to put up with a good deal of wit from my colleagues, some of whom would from time to time mutter within my hearing a line or two from one of the popular war ballads of the time: "Buckle down, Winsocki, buckle down," or "He's 1-A in the Army but he's A-One in my heart."

At last the paper work was cleared by Selective Service and I went before a kind of preselection board at an army installation in suburban New York. There I was quickly cleared except for the fact that I had high blood pressure. However, the Army of the United States in those days—days when we and the Royal Navy were losing one Pacific bastion after another and things were not going all that well for the Allies across the Atlantic, either—was not too choosy about its recruits. It was all right so long as a medic could look into a rookie's ear and not see a beam of daylight. I was instructed to go into a small room and sleep overnight and return in the morning for another blood pressure test, which I passed.

I began to accept the eternal veracity of the old service joke that there were two ways of doing anything—the right way and the army's way. For now there came still more paper work. I was ordered to Houston, Texas, for induction as a private, my papers being stamped with the large initials VOC. At the induction station in Houston my ardor began to cool further when a young woman typist filling out one of those interminable army forms objected to the fact that my middle name was simply "Smith," and loudly sniffed, "Smith! Hell of a middle name that is!"

I felt additional chilling premonitions, or bad vibes as the saying now goes, when my levy of "inductees" was marched off in a straggle down to a Houston railroad station while the sturdy male patriots of my native state uttered cat calls at the whole lot of us from the streets. The troop train itself, innocent of any air conditioning in this summertime of 1942, did nothing to improve my morale. It was incredibly hot when we left Houston (whose climate compares unfavorably to that of the erstwhile Belgian Congo, on the evidence at least of my own experience in both places) and it got no cooler during the long night ride down to Fort Sam Houston in San Antonio.

At Fort Sam, there was yet more "processing," the high (or low) light of which was my experience with a clerical sergeant who was taking down my personal particulars for inclusion in my army file. When he asked me what I had been doing in civil life I told him I had been war editor of the Associated Press. He had not heard of the Associated Press, but presumably informed himself of it by reading from one of a number of manuals he had with him. He then asked me what a war editor did and I told him just to forget it. What he put down I shall never know. (Two years later in London, as a habitué of the Junior Officers' Club in South Audley Street, I knew a mess officer, a young second lieutenant named Rosenthal, inevitably called Rosie. "Rosie," I asked him one night, "how did you come to be a mess officer?" He looked thoughtful for a moment and then said: "Well, when I was drafted the sergeant asked my civilian occupation and I told him I had been a banker. He typed 'baker' on my file and after I had got out of Officer Candidate School and some character was looking for a mess officer, the word 'baker' on my papers happened to strike his eye and no doubt he said, 'That's just what we want for a mess officer.' ")

By the time I got through processing at Fort Sam and was sent, again by troop train, to Camp Robinson, Arkansas, which lay steaming in the bottomlands of a turgid river, I had reached two conclusions. The first was that I had been ridiculous not to take that commission from Governors Island. The other was that nevertheless, by God, I was going to make it as an infantry officer or die in the attempt. As it happened, I very nearly did the latter. The basic training was fierce at Camp Robinson, particularly for VOCs, whom the training cadre of noncoms soon identified—and never forgave for their unworthy ambition. Matters were not helped by the fact that I was in my mid-thirties while most of my comrades were in their early twenties or even late teens. All the same I held on, to my astonishment even winning the designation Expert on the rifle range.

At last the day came when I was called before the camp's board of officers to determine whether I was to be recommended for officers' school at Fort Benning, Georgia. My appearance was a trial, indeed. I had been issued an excessively beat-up set of fatigues. I was dirty from the rifle range and had had no chance even to wash my face. I was talking to a board of officers two of whose six or seven members were semiliterate. And I was ordered to disassemble and reassemble a Browning automatic rifle—blindfolded. I had never mastered breaking down and putting back the BAR even in the full light of day. I utterly failed the blindfold test and in the bluest of blue funks I stood wretchedly before my superiors thinking disconsolately that it had all been to no purpose—all the chivying and harassment and hardships, the aching bones and muscles, the lot.

But then came a most unexpected rescue. One of the members of the board, a major whose name I never knew, intervened. "Private White," he said, "sure has failed this weapons test; but tell you what. He has leadership qualities." I heard with amazement what the major went on to say. The day before, he recalled, each man in our little band of VOCs had been given a detail of men to command in a simulated battle. As I marched forward with my men I was ordered by a training lieutenant to take them into a gully down which one of those 1942 wooden "machine guns" was leveled. I knew this was to enter a field of enfilade fire and so I refused the lieutenant's order and ordered my troops instead to flank the gully. This was the right reaction, bearing on an officer's primary obligation never to put his men unnecessarily into a hopeless position. This had convinced the major that I had "leadership qualities."

So I escaped in the narrowest possible way the ultimate indignity of being returned to civilian life as unfit even to aspire to the lofty commission of a second lieutenant. I thankfully left the officers' board and returned to the drill field. The next day, I collapsed in that same field and several days then vanished forever from my life. It turned out that I had contracted spinal meningitis, though I did not know this for some weeks. When I came back to a hazy consciousness, it was to be told that I had maintained a temperature of 107° for eight days. I learned, too, that during this period a funeral detail had measured me for a coffin and a Roman Catholic chaplain attached to the hospital staff had administered to me the rite of Extreme Unction. Though I was not a member of that church, my family religious affiliation for many generations having been Presbyterian, I had nevertheless worn the letter "C" for Catholic on my dog-tags because I had taken in a Paulist church in New York some preliminary instruction in the Catholic faith.

It may be that at some point I had actually "died" in the clinical sense; there must, I suppose, have been some reason why the senior medics at the hospital had summoned the burying detail. In any event, something had saved me, and as my mind grew clearer and I was told more and more of what had happened to me I thought I could cloudily recall some fugitive vision of having passed, without fear, over some shadowed frontier of some indescribable sort. I do not wish to dwell upon this point, partly because it is both so intensely private and so vague in my recollection, and partly because I claim no kind of theological knowledge or aptness. Nevertheless, the experience had much to do with my later life, as did the harsh and all too palpable experience in my brief career as a soldier in the Army of the United States. I had never been irreligious, except as a college boy in a milieu in which to profess atheism, or at least agnosticism, was the done thing, but I had never been very religious either. But religious I now became in intention (not, I am afraid, in practice) because I had learned that I, at least, could not stand up to life without a faith that there was something better, higher, and finer than I could possibly find in this world.

In my memory of the army hospital at Camp Robinson in Arkansas, the dark element is largely erased, as for that matter is the dark part of my participation in combat, by the memorably comic aspects of life in the ward. Next to my bed was another private, named Dekker, a farmer from Illinois who by some insane draft board decision had been inducted and by some equally insane army decision put into the infantry, in the face of the most manifest evidence that he was at least forty-four years old, was totally inept physically, and was far from bright. Dekker, who had been in my training company, had somehow installed himself in the hospital during my period of blackout, and when I came around to consciousness the poor devil attached himself to me just as he had when we were drilling together. In those earlier days he had never said anything whatever to me, or to my corporal instructor, except that he wanted to go home. Now, in the hospital, he would waken each morning to take up his refrain, "I want to go home," just as the medics and nurses started to make their morning rounds.

I had, before my illness, taken it upon myself to suggest to my training company commander, a man named Way, that it was preposterous for such a tragic fellow as Dekker to be held in a military service in which on no account he could ever perform. Way, a decent type, had agreed; but then he had shrugged and said: "Well, White, it's up to the medics; that's the army for you." Of course, he had then briskly and even brusquely dismissed me, embarrassed at having held such an intimate discussion with a private.

In the hospital Dekker provided a black-humor kind of relief. Every morning the entire ward took up the cry along with Dekker: "I want to go home." I spin out the tale at this length because it illustrates a point that ever since has had a distinct bearing upon my work. As a journalist I have always believed that extreme antiwar people (I speak of the pacifist-at-any-price people) are short on human understanding in assuming that men are invariably brutalized by military experience. Perhaps it ought to be so, but it simply isn't. Those men in the ward at Camp Robinson, some of them very ignorant and some of them actually loutish, were all of them kind to Dekker. More to the point, men I knew later in combat almost invariably had sensitive, generous instincts, even touchingly so, to a degree I had not met in civilian life and have never met since. Why this is the case I do not pretend to know; perhaps war strips men of all such nonessentials as pretense, overactive ambition, and arrogance or intolerance. Like death itself, it is indeed a great leveler.

My stay in the Camp Robinson hospital was long; I had been carried into it in the blazing heat of August and I left it in the chill of November. During most of this time I thought little of journalism, being urgently occupied in staying alive. In the open ward, I kept getting viral pneumonia and was in poor shape to withstand it, since I had gone down from about 175 pounds to 113.

My discharge from the army was automatic, since a VOC was automatically dismissed if he did not make his commission within a specified period, and that had passed, but it was obliged to wait upon an army medical regulation that no man could leave a hospital unless he had shown no fever for three days running. Again and again, I passed this test two days running and then flunked it on the third. Meanwhile, I was going a little crazy, to put it bluntly. I had, first of all, a great desire to get out and get to doing something useful again, since I knew that I had lost the whole object of the exercise, namely, to be commissioned for combat. The hospital's commanding officer thought he could get me a captaincy to oversee his sergeant-clerks, intending to be kind but succeeding only in being unintentionally insulting. My second problem was that I had reached the settled conclusion that unless I could emerge soon from that hospital the army was going to kill me by obtuseness. I needed a private room to avoid continuous reinfection by pneumonia. As a private, I could have no private room. I settled the matter once and for all by doing the kind of thing one always has to do now and then in the army. I juggled the books, so to speak. One day when, after two days of no fever, I could feel its flush as the nurse approached on Day Three, I covertly shook down the thermometer and had a reading *below* normal.

By this means I emerged from Camp Robinson, went in my flapping civilian clothes to the railway station, and booked a stateroom, no less, back to New York. I took a bottle of whiskey with me, both because I wanted whiskey and because I needed to eat a great deal if I was to get any weight back. In New York, I returned to the AP and went instantly back to my old job as war editor. If I felt slightly ridiculous at the way my martial career had ended, I was aware that I had learned a lot I would never have learned otherwise. That would be of use within a year's time or less: I had learned at least some of the techniques of military survival.

Upon reporting back to AP in New York I got a commitment from management that if and when I was restored to full health I could go to London as an assault war correspondent accredited to the forthcoming D-Day operation, however distant that operation looked at the end of the year 1942.

The qualification "assault war correspondent" was highly important to me and did not involve mere theatrics on my part, if I must apply that term to my late exertions as a VOC. I had no intention whatever of going abroad only to fall into another kind of Cable Desk, rewriting other men's copy in Europe. I knew, of course, from briefings I had had from a staff colonel called "Cappy" Wells (sent to New York by the Pentagon to keep in touch with me and with my counterparts at United Press and Hearst's International News Service) that once the invasion was well launched, a Supreme Allied Headquarters would be set up where the Big Picture of the war news would be processed, as now it was being processed in New York. Of this, I wanted no part, simply because I knew that, while ultimately New York would only reprocess what was first processed at Supreme Headquarters, once American war correspondents were in the field reporting to an America now itself at war, nobody at either European Theater HQ or AP HQ in New York would trifle with their dispatches—as I had, God knows, trifled with the dispatches of others before Pearl Harbor changed the rules of the game.

Having got my assurance, I worked along philosophically enough, if restlessly, in New York until the early spring of 1943. Then, quite suddenly, on a date I certainly ought to remember but do not, I was summoned to a medical office, attached, if I recall correctly, to First Army, and there given shots for a dozen kinds of disease. Then, a bit later, I was instructed spectrally by telephone to report to a pierside in New York. On a Sunday night it was. There lay a dirty little freighter, one, I learned later, in a convoy of a hundred and ten going to England. The vessel had a name I don't remember, something totally undistinguished, such as, say, the Oscar T. Brown. When the high, bulky old New York cab pulled away from pierside, its radio softly calling out that Lucky Strike Green had Gone to War, I left a world I was not to see again soon. I carried my duffel bag aboard and eventually found somebody who knew that I was supposed to be there. I was directed to the ship's sick bay—the whole vessel was packed with food, whiskey, and also some hush-hush gadgets designed for the British Admiralty—and told that here was my "cabin."

We sailed about midnight from a darkened harbor in the most stealthy, almost guilty, way possible—no bands playing, no sad relatives to cry farewell. The only sound was the ship's radio, linked to the Yankee Network, over which some crooner was proclaiming that he was going to buy a paper doll he could call his own, a doll that some other fellow could not steal.

"Security" seemed to me a bit weak all around, since nobody had asked me for any sort of identifying document. And it turned out that the captain was an *unnaturalized* German alien, a hot Nazi for all any of us knew. At that time, the Merchant Marine was combing the bars and brothels for ship's officers, for the North Atlantic run was still exceedingly chancy, and casualties to cargo ships had decimated the available officer and crew classes alike. Our valiant skipper I saw once in a seventeen-day crossing. For days he remained comatose from whiskey in his locked cabin while his deputy, a first mate who had had his head knocked about during a career in the prize ring, would sometimes entertain himself by shadow-boxing on deck.

If ever there was a hapless ship it was ours. The "security officer" put aboard by the army turned out to be a second lieutenant who, like my friend Dekker down at Camp Robinson, had no enthusiasm for going to battle. This fellow stayed in his bunk behind locked doors. The navy gunnery officer, a cheerful Irish ensign from Chicago, confided before we left the outer harbor that three of his crew of five or six were *hors de combat* after their shore leave in New York, stricken with what service medics called influenza whenever officers were involved and "the clap" when enlisted men were involved. (This was not really a class distinction but only a matter of considerateness. In the army at least, and I suspect in the navy, too, officers stricken with venereal disease had, according to the book, to be put before a court martial for conduct unbecoming and so forth, whereas enlisted men did not.) My ensign friend told me, in a quite casual way, that he was very short of hands to handle our exceedingly light armament, which amounted to small ack-ack guns, and asked me whether I knew anything of such matters. I told him I had qualified on the machine gun in the army and would pitch in to help stand a watch whenever he might ask, and so I did.

It was not reassuring, either, that our ship, alone of all those in the convoy, trailed no barrage balloons above it. Somebody had forgotten this detail, and as I have said the captain's attention was elsewhere. Finally, there was the fact that we were carrying high-octane aviation fuel. Since the convoy was at times proceeding in close file, this posed a problem. "Let this damn thing so much as rub the stern of that ship ahead," the first mate told me after we were several days out from New York, "and this damn thing goes up, boom."

In short, it was a most feckless voyage across the Atlantic, though our ship, possibly by the operation of that mighty truism that God looks after idiots and drunks, was never fired on. Other ships in our convoy were hit; twice we saw one go down in the far distance. All the shooting we experienced was on our side. As we entered Scapa Flow our ensign ordered an open fire on an emerging submarine; it turned out to be a sub of the Royal Navy and it never bothered to return our piddling assault.

Now the distinct shortcomings, one way and another, of this voyage might be supposed to have made it quite unsettling. Oddly enough, it was nothing of the kind. One felt—I think we all felt—that Disaster would not demean itself by striking so absurd a target as our ship. We made it safely to port in Scotland with no harm done to anybody aboard and, in my case, with a growing and entirely serious conviction, sown in the Camp Robinson days, that the United States and its Allies, if they were anything like us, would urgently require the Providence of God to survive, let alone to win. Indeed, though I know it is unfashionable to say so, I most earnestly believe that the Allies did have the help of such a Providence for what I believed then and believe now to have been a far from ignoble cause.

I gained twenty-five welcome pounds on that voyage and cleared the very rugged Scottish wartime Customs and Immigration Office in the best health I had known for many months. I took the Flying Scot (the British ran some splendid trains all through the war) from Edinburgh down to London and found, in the vast human sprawl under the great clusters of barrage balloons that hovered above the ancient tiles and chamber-pot chimneys, the warmest city I ever knew, rivaled only by New York City of the Thirties and early Forties. The fact that some of my old Undated Internationals from my Cable Desk days had been quoted occasionally in the wartime London press, and that this appeared to be known within the British Ministry of Information, did me no harm. In truth, I met few strangers in England even in my first days there. And I met an astonishingly large number of warm friends among what were supposed to be those very reserved island types.

My accreditation to the British armed forces was accomplished quickly. I needed plural accreditation because the luck of the draw would determine whether I went over on D-Day with American or British forces. The thing was actually determined, when the time came, by the toss of a coin with an AP colleague named Roger Greene. Greene called it right and elected to go with the British; I drew the Americans, though I later served also with the British.

Whereas the American military in England were inherently suspicious of the "security" of those correspondents who had been tapped for D-Day, the British were either trusting or—

perhaps more likely—more skilled in hiding their mistrust. In dealing with secrets, they seemed to adopt the theory of Poe's "The Purloined Letter." Figuratively, it appeared that they tossed their Most Secret Documents (it was "Most Secret" to Them and "Top Secret" to Americans) on top of the nearest chest of drawers.

From the beginning and through the long months while so many of us were more or less just sitting around and awaiting the The Day, I got a vast amount of the kind of information useful to a journalist as "background" though he can make no immediate public use of it. An ostensibly civilian member of Parliament, who was in the cloak-and-dagger business as a brigadier in mufti, told me a great deal of what was going on within British counterintelligence. A Royal Air Force friend told me how the British had "teased" the Nazis by sending out a squadron of Lancasters to drop wooden bombs on a wooden mockup the Germans had set up to divert RAF attacks on Hamburg. "Why?" I asked. "Why not, old boy? Can't you see those Jerries scratching their heads and trying to work out what the crazy Englishers are up to now? Think of the time they are going to waste on the business."

Again, a Grenadier Guards officer showed me, on a car trip to York, the precise table of organization by which the British were running two battalions of tanks round and round on a kind of belt because they knew a Nazi agent, Swiss by birth, was being allowed to operate there. They wanted him to report to Berlin, as indeed he did, that a previously unknown British armored force of at least divisional strength was being raised in the North of England.

I was often in a comfortable/uncomfortable position—comfortable because I appreciated being trusted, and uncomfortable because any journalist is troubled by knowing things he cannot print. Before I had been a week in England I was casually invited for drinks and intimate conversation by the chief of all British censors, a one-time fighting admiral named Thompson. I was amazed by the candor with which he would discuss almost anything. On one occasion, for instance, his other guest was a War Office official who told me the highly classified details of the scope of both British and German casualties in the battle for Crete. The Germans knew what they had suffered but they could not know the wasting sacrifices of the British at Crete.

They, the British, treated me as a member of the family, so much so that had Colonel McCormick back in Chicago known the full truth he might this time have been able really to get me fired. Even some in-house doings concerning Winston Churchill were told to me by a British friend of high station, as they say over there, before I met the prime minister. There was, for instance, the occasion when the leadership of the Conservative party became intolerably worried about the old gentleman's large daily intake of alcohol and drafted three most reluctant members of Parliament to call upon him to remonstrate. They went to 10 Downing Street, rang the bell, and were admitted by Mrs. Churchill. That it was she and not he pleased them enormously but she cut them off by saying that whatever their business might be it was surely with the prime minister himself. Churchill shortly descended in his favorite "siren suit" and demanded to know of the delegation what they meant by coming to disturb him. They scuffed the carpet a bit and finally said their mission concerned his health. "Ah, yes," said Churchill, "my health. You may go back and tell them this: I eat what I please, when I please, and as much as I please. I drink what I please, when I please, and as much as I please. My only exercise is in going up to bed. Goodnight."

Churchill was far more than a great war leader; he was the very embodiment of the best of the Cavalier tradition. By his life, public and private, he threw back into the teeth of Cromwell's ghost the harsh, pietistic inhumanity of its unforgiving moralisms. He was quick to pardon almost every flaw or shortcoming except cowardice and cant. (Looters of bombed-out houses who took away only food and liquor received automatic clemency from him.) In an indescribable way he was not only London's wartime morale but also wartime London's morals, granted that these latter were perhaps a bit on the flexible side.

The mood was for living one day at a time. And if a touch of hedonism crept in, as it surely did even with the prime minister himself, not even the sternest of padres, Church of England or Roman Catholic, was disposed to sermonize. Men and women clutched each other in the nighttime for more than the obvious reasons; the endless blackout was no darker to the human spirit than were the pitiable rations of both food and cheer that were available to even the most fortunate of Britons.

I know, of course, that many millions in Europe, perhaps most tragically of all in Poland, underwent far more dreadful things than did the people of Britain. But it was the people of Britain among whom I lived; and one of my most lasting regrets as a journalist is that the people at home in the United States were never really informed by the members of my profession what it was like over there. I suppose it would have taken a Victor Hugo among the corps of correspondents to do a proper job of it; but among us there were no Hugos. Ernest Hemingway might have done it; but that wonderfully theatrical writer was obsessed by the military side of things and seemed to lack recognition of anything or anybody merely civilian. To the end of his life, I think, to him the bell tolled really only for the human being in uniform.

For me the winter of 1943 amounted to something close to a pause in my career as a journalist. I was formally attached to the London Bureau of the AP for the purposes of administrative paperwork, but I was more in it than of it. As war editor in New York I had held a higher rank than anybody in the London Bureau, and though this circumstance did not impress me, it was an embarrassing bureaucratic anomaly, almost an act of gaucheness in an office that—unhappily like all AP offices, in my time at least—was as strong on pecking-order protocol as the Foreign Service of the United States.

So I kept more or less out of the way, spending a good deal of time at the Officers' Club in South Audley Street and a great deal of time in a purely sociable way with British friends, military and civilian. Only rarely did I go out on anything resembling a real assignment; and when I did it was to accompany the prime minister's party whenever he traveled on anything definable as a military mission. Churchill, of course, fancied himself as a warrior-statesman, and he liked to think of himself as intimately in touch with His Majesty's Forces. The fact is that he not only ran the War Office; he also so enjoyed the company of his generals and admirals that they sometimes wished he were not quite so keen. And he made an occasion of it whenever and wherever he could "get out among the troops."

One memorable such occasion (memorable at least to me) was along in the late winter of 1943. Churchill had called the Dominion prime ministers to London for a conference of a nature never publicly defined except as "military." When the discussions had been completed in Downing Street, I was invited, along with a few British war correspondents, to "go into the field" with Churchill and his retinue of Dominion PMs. The party went by automobile from London northward to some point, now forgotten, where the War Office had arranged a demonstration of very spartan training in which troops were crawling forward under streams of live ammunition.

Churchill was in an expansive mood, building morale among the visiting representatives of what he still defiantly called the Empire though everybody else called it only the Commonwealth. His party of prime ministers followed him through a break in the ranks of troops, as necessarily did my British colleagues and I, in an order of preference chosen by the Old Man himself. One might have thought that Prime Minister Mackenzie King of Canada, the source of the largest troop commitment to the European Theater from among the Commonwealth nations, would have pride of place, but this was not be be. Churchill loudly directed Prime Minister Smuts of South Africa to walk arm in arm at his side and left King to follow along some paces behind. The whole affair had an almost comic, and in some way touching, air of an old-fashioned headmaster taking his pupils out for a nature walk. That Smuts was the favorite pupil was made all too apparent. Churchill, I was told later by a staff officer who was very close to him personally, was indulging himself in sentimental memories of his own experiences nearly half a century earlier in the Boer war in which Britain's chief adversary was Field Marshal Smuts.

Indeed, Smuts always had enormous influence with Winston Churchill, and no visitor to Downing Street was ever so royally entertained except perhaps for Prime Minister Menzies of Australia, who also had a special relationship with the king's First Minister. I had also heard it said in the War Office that while Franklin Roosevelt could say "no" to Churchill only because Roosevelt represented so much more latent power, Smuts could say it, notwithstanding the relative insignificance of his country in terms of power, without evoking the slightest displeasure from Churchill.

It certainly seemed a reasonable assumption on this day of which I write. Churchill, extravagantly attentive to Smuts, at one point raised his swagger stick toward a detail of crawling Tommies and said loudly: "You know, Marshal, the science of infantry has become infinitely complicated since we were young." Smuts—in whom I detected, though I had only the slightest of acquaintance with him, no sentiment whatever—grunted, shifted the cigar in his mouth, and said in a tone of plain boredom, "Yep." There were some snickers back down the line of toiling prime ministers; but Churchill was lordly deaf to this.

Onward he persisted with his military mission, taking the whole of his retinue into tank formations, into company command posts, into wherever he could poke his round, beaming face, and introducing his visitors to officers and men alike. That is, he introduced those of his visitors whom he considered to be of suitably senior rank. Toward the remaining prime ministers he only waved, muttering the names of their countries but not their own names. The very last man in the line was Roy Huggins (later Sir Roy) of Southern Rhodesia. He never seemed to come to Churchill's notice at all except on our last stop to chat up the troops. At this point, Churchill, after presenting Marshal Smuts and "Mister King," seemed to collect himself, pointed to Huggins and said: "And Mr. Higgins of Northern Rhodesia." Huggins, game to the end, replied: "No, Sir. Huggins. *Southern* Rhodesia." Churchill loftily took note of the mild rebuke. "Ah, yes," he murmured, "Southern Rhodesia it is, isn't it?"

On we walked, on what seemed an endless day, and a day

whose end Churchill was clearly not anxious to see, since that would mean he would have to stop acting like a serving officer and go back to being just the prime minister in London. At our last halt on the mission, the army had arranged a demonstration of a new flame thrower to which Churchill now proudly directed attention, like a tour guide happy in his job. This monstrous affair stuck its snout in the direction of a concrete blockhouse and cut it in two in seconds. "Jesus Christ!" Churchill exclaimed. Mackenzie King, who was quite proper, was visibly affronted by this language. Everybody else looked amused. And the military censors in our party frowned sternly at the press contingent, saying without words: "Don't print that."

None of us had the least interest in printing that, or anything else about the mission, for that matter. None of it was of news value, of course. But like other missions it did provide some insight into the complicated character and personality of Winston Spencer Churchill, whose deep devotion to the past and its people and traditions marched abreast of an almost futuristic engrossment with science-fiction weaponry. He would try almost anything novel in that line; and he always coddled those he called "my profs"—men who were engaged in weapons research and development—whether they had come from Oxbridge or from red brick universities.

Fiercely and arrogantly combative in war, he was also soft of heart and nostalgic. I once saw him standing alone in Green Park in London—he had drawn away from the couple of anonymous men who were his bodyguards—openly weeping while the band played "Land of Hope and Glory." He did not even wipe away the tears when he turned from the scene.

It would be difficult to assert that my random travels in the prime minister's party in the long twilight time before D-Day had any significance in the journalistic sense, in the sense of "hard news." Certainly I never cabled home any of the essentially impressionistic stuff that I stored in my mind. Still, I think that what I saw and heard of him in these unbuttoned circumstances could be said to have been useful to my job. Specifically, I learned enough of Churchill, I believe, to gain a pretty good grasp of the real nature of his substantial and then-unreported conflicts with Franklin Roosevelt over grand strategy. History tends at times to adopt false clichés no less than does journalism, and one of the hardiest of these is that Roosevelt, widely seen as an Anglophile, had no differences with Churchill except over means to ends. First of all, FDR was far from an ardent lover of Britain, if only because some of his forebears had bitterly dueled with Britons in the China trade, and tales of English duplicity had been absorbed by him from childhood, as can be seen in some of his private papers at the Hyde Park Library.

Secondly, and much more importantly, FDR and WSC were profoundly different types as human beings. Roosevelt was the product of an essentially nationalistic Anglo-Dutch American squirearchy with only a somewhat limited feel for history. Churchill was the scion of an ancient aristocracy which had European history in its very bones. Roosevelt's view of the war was a comparatively short view and therefore an oversimplified and overoptimistic one, illustrated by his tragically wrongheaded insistence that the Allies adopt the war cry of Unconditional Surrender. Churchill went along with this proclamation only in distress and under duress from his stronger American partner. He knew the Germans well enough to understand that they thought very literally and would assume that the Allies meant what a German would have meant in uttering such a war aim: the utter and abject humiliation and debasement of a defeated enemy, if not in fact his extirpation. Churchill knew that Unconditional Surrender was going to throw the Germans, if the war's tide turned against them, into paroxysms of maddened resistance, and would thus cost Allied lives, as indeed it did.

In the last months before D-Day, British acquaintances in both the Foreign and War Offices quietly and carefully put to me, and undoubtedly to a good many others, the thought that Roosevelt's sunny belief in Stalin's being really not such a bad fellow was dangerously generous. The fountainhead of this thought—which turned out to be absolutely true, as witness the partition of Germany and a Cold War resting upon Stalin's broken pledges—was of course at No. 10 Downing Street. As an American correspondent reporting to "An American at War" (as Byron Price back at AP headquarters in New York had exhorted all of us to be, once the shooting started for this country), I wanted to believe that Roosevelt was right, but I was unable to avoid the conclusion that he was dead wrong. This attitude sprang from no British machinations, no invitations to weekends at English country houses, but strictly from reportorial instinct in a man who had had limited but fairly instructive exposure to both of these statesmen.

Whenever and wherever I saw Churchill in England I saw a man who demonstrably didn't give a damn for personal popularity or for what was then liberal-chic and who had, as Roosevelt had not, the great good sense to know that human perfectibility is only a phrase to be found in a dictionary. In Churchill, moreover, I saw a man who knew Stalin to be nothing better than a mass murderer who, through fortuity, happened to be engaged in killing Nazis. In Churchill, as in Roosevelt, I saw a man of great vanity; but their vanities were of two very different sorts. Churchill's vanity never encompassed a yen to have subordinates fighting each other so that the master might feel free of any possible challenge. Roosevelt's vanity was in a sense insecure; Churchill's was so solidly set in hereditary rock that he needed nothing to bolster it.

When Roosevelt profoundly disliked someone he could be less than objectively just. Churchill, on the other hand, was almost totally unswayed by personal dislike when it came to estimating men. To illustrate: for complicated reasons—perhaps that he had an American mother, perhaps that he talked with a certain floridness, a lack of that reserve of which the upperclass English are very proud even when they don't have it—the prime minister was never popular in that most aristocratic of all British military forces, the Guards. He knew this, or so I was told at any rate, just as he knew that *he* personally detested General Sir Bernard Montgomery, later Earl Montgomery of Alamein. He was capable of making harsh witticisms concerning Montgomery, a man who on my own experience was easy to dislike, but he never denied that

Montgomery was a good general. The maintenance of this attitude required a good deal of generosity, for Montgomery was almost everything that Churchill loathed: a Puritan, a "Cromwellian" (a term that to Churchill was a powerful epithet), a teetotaler, and a somewhat humorless headline-hunter to boot.

Having all this background in my mind, I was more than usually interested when asked to go along when the prime minister went on one of his missions to review a daring military innovation—the merger of the Coldstream, Grenadier, Scottish, Irish, and Welsh Guards into an armored division. I could only assume afterward that he had decided to do a double job of a pretty subtle kind. I thought he wanted to tell the Guards that if they didn't like him he could easily live with the fact, so long as they did their job. And I thought he was concerned to make it very clear to this elite outfit that his widely known personal distaste for Montgomery—a distaste even more vehement within the Guards themselves—was on no account to be interpreted as any lack of prime ministerial respect for Montgomery's professional competence as a senior commander.

The meeting did not go entirely smoothly. The divisional commander, General Sir Richard (Ricky) O'Connor, met his country's leader in less than martial costume—in a sweat shirt bearing no badge of rank, hatless, and in tennis shoes. In this outfit O'Connor, a small, shy man, climbed onto a half-track with the prime minister to ride through the ranks of Guards. In no way disconcerted by this extreme informality, Churchill, waving his big cigar about as though it was a field marshal's baton, announced in a loud voice: "O'Connor, I have to tell you that Montgomery thinks very highly of you." There was a short silence and then O'Connor responded: "Oh, dear, I do hope he is right." Churchill only grunted.

I recall these experiences concerning Winston Churchill as strangely heartening breaks in the gloomiest and longest winter I ever spent, and in a way the idlest one that as a journalist I had ever known. In some curious sense, those of us who were ticketed for the D-Day operation were somehow

progressively isolated from the large corps of American correspondents in London who were going about the business of
running news bureaus and sending back home dispatches
about American air raids over Germany and Occupied Europe.
Our numbr8those who were going on the assault across the
Channel—was tiny in contrast to the vast number of correspondents in England.

For us few there was too little to do and far too much time in
which to do it. For a while I was supposed to be profoundly
involved in "planning," as I had been originally designated
chief of AP assault correspondents for D-Day, but there was
really no "planning" to do. How could one plan for the un-
knowable? Anyhow I was soon shorn of my title because I
made myself so scarce in the AP's London office. The AP man
ultimately put in charge of all of us who crossed over was Wes
Gallagher, who later became general manager of the AP, and
made a very good job of it, too.

In one way or another, in short, it became harder and harder
to bear the inactivity and the sheer lonely waiting around. By
about March of 1943 the Junior Officers' Club had become a
home away from home, and the locus also of much probing
about, some of it positively comic, by American Counter Intelligence officers to find out who Knew Anything among the
correspondents or was likely to Break Security. The fact was
that nobody knew anything and that even if anybody had
known anything there was no possible way in which he could
put it into any dispatch, even on the ludicrous assumption that
he might want to. For this war commanded our total alle-
giance; I never knew an assault correspondent who did not
believe it right and just; and I never knew one who would not
have been desolated at the possibility of being sent home in
disgrace. General Eisenhower, and I suppose perhaps even far
less senior American officers in the European Theater of Operations (that "ETO" whose insignia was popularly called the
Spam Ribbon), had the power to expel any correspondent at
any time. So far as I know such a thing never happened; so far
as I know such a thing was never even contemplated.

In truth, Eisenhower and all the other American commanders I knew had a rather good relationship with the press, at the base of which was the assumption that we were all on the same side. A good deal of journalistic griping at "the Brass" went on, of course, and some of "the Brass" affected to find correspondents something of a nuisance. On the whole, however, there was no problem, mainly because Eisenhower from the onset of his appointment as supreme commander established no restraints upon reporting that were not eminently reasonable, and lesser commanders followed suit.

CHAPTER SEVEN

AS SPRING CAME to England in 1944 I knew, along with a good many others, that the plunge across the Channel must be launched within a space of weeks, not months. I had had no hot tip from somebody in the military, but had simply observed that it was plain that the Day *had* to come soon if only for reasons of troop morale. In a London hospital with a broken arm—I'd been hit in the street by a British army staff car in the blackout—I met at least half a dozen American officers who were there for reasons most vaguely mentioned. Actually, they were there for covert psychiatric review, to determine whether they were going to be sent home rather than across the Channel. The long wait, the eternity of the blackout, and the still-frequent German air raids on London (no longer much reported in the American press, I gathered) had been too much for some. The general atmosphere was pretty well described in a much-repeated parable wherein a sergeant went to his company commander demanding medical help. Asked what his problem was, he replied: "I get these damn butterflies all over me all the time, Sir." With this, the sergeant vigorously brushed the sleeves of his blouse. "Goddamn it!" shouted the captain, "Don't brush them off on me!"

When the summons then came at last, it was almost anti-climactic. A man in civilian dress came to my apartment in Knightsbridge one evening toward the end of May 1944 and quietly said: "They want to see some of you correspondent chaps tomorrow morning at the Admiralty. You will see some of your friends there but you are to go there alone—everyone is to go there alone." Accordingly, I hailed a cab the next morning and rode to the Admiralty like any man going to his office. Inside, a sailor took me to a large room in which a good number of my colleagues—my memory now says about twenty, but there may have been more or less—were seated. One of them I did not know at the time; he was Ernest Hemingway. Hemingway had brought with him an imperial quart of gin, which he mounted on a table in front of him.

We were briefed for the coming assault by a hulking and bearded commander in the Royal Navy. He told us how many thousand tons of steel would be laid down by the grand Allied fleets and by American and British aircraft; but he never told us where any one of us was going from the Admiralty building. He did make an observation about the possible strength and durability of the beachhead, which was, as we all certainly hoped, to be raised up in France. It ought, he said, to be consolidated within a few days—"if everything goes tickety-boo."

From the Admiralty we were taken by automobile very quietly, one small group at a time, to various ports on the east and south coasts of England. I wound up in Poole, far down to the south. The AP had arranged for its two senior assault correspondents, my old friend Don Whitehead and myself, to do a sort of tandem job. Whitehead was to go across, land, and stay there; I was to go across, get as much of a look as I could within a fairly short time, and then return by Coast Guard cutter to England to file my story at the Ministry of Information, the clearinghouse for outgoing dispatches. The theory back of this was that if "something happened" to either of us, the AP would be "protected" by the other. An immensely complex arrangement for getting correspondents' dispatches back to England had been set up by the Supreme Command's press officers, this involving specially marked bags which, as it was said, were to be carried back by returning logistical ships. AP, largely on the advice of the canny Whitehead, a veteran of action in North Africa, preferred its own way.

At Poole, I was under escort (as were all correspondents) and quartered in an undistinguished old tub in something approximating polite ship-arrest. On the morning of June 5 a British sailor burst into my cabin and shouted, "The Invasion's on." I asked him how he knew and he replied: "Radio." I told him that he was talking nonsense, basing this on the undeniable facts that I was going nowhere and that the weather was thick and heavy. I learned later that my own outfit, the AP, was responsible for that premature announcement that D-Day was at hand. Back in England the following August on leave, I got filled in. One of the young women teletype operators in our London office, under pressure, as always, from AP to "be first with it," had been practicing punching out a flash. She forgot and left the tape in her machine, which always cleared through the censors at the Ministry of Information. The regular war communiqué from the Soviet Union routinely cleared both the AP office and the MOI on its way to the United States and had done so for so long that everybody in both offices had long since quit reading it. Our young operator's flash tape was sent through her machine behind the Soviet communiqué and so got out on the air, first in the U.S. and then in Britain and, I suppose, everywhere else.

The curious thing about the episode was that June 5 had indeed been fixed for D-Day. Eisenhower deferred the assault at the last minute because weather conditions were so ghastly. He gave the signal for us really to go on the sixth, though the weather was still very bad, because he had no choice. The eastern side of England was all but sinking under the weight of Allied men and weapons; tactical surprise at least was most earnestly hoped for by our high command; and, finally, it would have been impossible to rewind that vast juggernaut, so long coiled and ready.

We knew for a fact that we were going only when the aircraft friendlies, American and British, began to fly over us, shorn of the familiar national markings—the star for ours, the circle for the RAF—and bearing the insignia of Supreme Allied Headquarters.

A great deal of what happened next is gone from my memory; indeed, a kind of haze lies over my recollection of both the hours before dawn, when we set out from Poole, and D-Day proper. If given the assignment to describe anything in much detail I could not possibly comply, as I have learned much later some of my colleagues in that memorable event could not now do. I have only random recollections: of the dark silhouettes of what seemed to be thousands of war ships in the Channel, with here and there a monster of a battleship wallowing like a leisurely whale; of Allied aircraft crossing overhead with no answering fire from any German aircraft in my vicinity; of small fires springing up on hundreds of small assault boats as infantry officers burned their last orders as we approached the landing on the French shore.

I did not know where I was when my Coast Guard cutter landed. (At some time I do not now recall I had transferred from the old British vessel back in Poole to this fast, fifty-foot American boat.) I do know it was on a steeply rising beach crowned by high grassy hillocks over which German artillery was lobbing screaming shells with devastating effect. Our men were having a hellish time getting ashore, some wading shoulder high in the wild surf and some sinking and drowning. God knows how much equipment went to the bottom. The cutter had no armament to speak of beyond twenty-millimeter popguns; she was designed as an escort and not an assault vessel and her main mission was to pick up American casualties from the water. There were heavy casualties there, heavier, I should estimate, than on the beach itself.

When the cutter turned about to make her return to England I went with her. I reached England, as I recall it, some time after midnight, on June 7 that is, and made my way in the blackout to the Ministry of Information. There I saw a madhouse, and I myself went madly from desk to desk to try to get my own copy moved without delay. The wire editors there were snappish but I was finally able to learn that the stuff had cleared to New York. How much of it was printed and where I do not know. Whitehead's piece, a brilliant job as always, had beaten me back to England; he had used the bag-and-ship arrangements set up by Supreme Command itself and, by God, they had *worked*.

I felt both cheated and let down—deflated is perhaps the better word. I was a man who had waited so long for the transcendent news event of his life; had written of it on a portable, steel-clad Hermes typewriter through the heaving seas back to England, only to feel that perhaps fate had tossed his copy, the fruits of all his labor and all the dangers he had met, out into the void of the night.

To descend rapidly into a more prosaic mood, I also made up my mind to learn a lesson—which, characteristically, did not take me all that long to forget. The lesson was that no dispatch was worth a damn unless it got to its destination; that a correspondent no less than a military unit had a need to protect his line of communication that all but approximated his need to stay alive. My friend Whitehead, a Kentuckian who always approached the war and its challenges, journalistic and otherwise, with a laconic absence of romanticism suitable to his mountain heritage, never once failed in this regard. Long before he began to write a piece he had already meticulously traced its way mentally to the most secure transmitter in any given area at any given time.

I stayed in England a few days after my return there from D-Day—seeing, by the way, what I had not seen before, the arrival of Hitler's V-1 weapon, the unmanned "doodlebug" flying bomb. (The V-1 was ravaging England frightfully in the days shortly after D-Day.) After a good deal of paper work and rushing about here and there, I picked up my second set of orders, which was to recross the Channel with the British. As it turned out, I actually went over with elements of the Canadian First Army, an outfit that by the measure of its size and fire power was in reality only a corps but that in deference to Canadian pride was always called an army.

This time we set out while doodlebugs were falling near, but never onto, our marshaling area. As usual, these were hitting the surrounding civilians, as we ourselves embarked for the other side. We landed somewhere on the Cotentin Peninsula, more or less between Bayeux and St. Lô, and headed toward Caen. We met and merged with Montgomery's Second British Army, with which my AP colleague Roger Greene had landed earlier. Greene had had no respite since D-Day, whereas I had

had that hiatus in London between the crossing and the re-crossing of the Channel. (This break a cherished friend, later killed in Germany, Peter Lawless of the *London Daily Telegraph*, was fond of saluting as "White's time of splendid license!") Greene, in a word, was pretty well knocked out by fatigue, so I volunteered to go in on the third and, as it turned out, decisive British-Canadian assault to break into and liberate Caen.

Many things of importance depended upon this assault. Its success was absolutely vital lest the British arm of the Allied pincer (the American First Army forming the other arm to the southward) be broken by the Germans and possibly even neu-tralized. There was moreover the awkward fact that the British field commanders had been informed that Churchill, in a fit of premature rejoicing, had announced to a happy House of Com-mons in London that Caen, the first grand objective of the invasion, had *already* fallen. It was thought to be highly desir-able to make the Old Man's report to Commons stand up.

Montgomery had called Allied correspondents back to his headquarters to tell us that this time, the third go at Caen, he was "going to give the other chap a bloody nose," and inciden-tally to assure us in many repetitious phrases that he was a loyal member of "Eisenhower's team." I thought this latter observation was directed to me, as the only correspondent in American uniform at the press conference, but when Mont-gomery demanded, "Have I given you a good story?" Bob Cooper of the *London Times*, my jeep mate on occasion, draw-led the single reply: "No, Sir."

When the forward assault force moved out to "give the other chap a bloody nose" we were all pretty tense. It was a heavily fortified city with much masonry; the approaches to it were as full of German mines as a field is full of turnips, and the Germans had massed the best divisions they had in France to stand athwart the British advance. They had also sealed in the city's civilian population, which I believe was then about two hundred thousand, in order to keep the narrow little bridges across the river Orne free for a Nazi withdrawal. Bursting into the city was a nasty business in two senses: the British had very heavy casualties; and moreover they were compelled, in

110

the heavy artillery barrages that had to be put in to support those of us on the ground, to kill a great number of the civilians of Caen.

I returned to the press camp from the action at Caen with the belief that I had a "first" on the most important French city yet to be liberated; but the thing didn't work out quite that way. In the first place, I learned that the British were restricting each correspondent to a total output of five hundred words a day, so heavy was military traffic at the wireless head, whereas down in the American sector there was no limitation at all. I had therefore to strip my piece down to the bare bones, by necessity excluding nearly everything but the bald military fact that Caen had now indeed fallen to the Allies.

After filing a truncated dispatch that greatly disappointed me, I went to Greene's billet to see if he had any of his NAFFI (a kind of British USO) whiskey issue left. He did; and as I was taking a drink, in lurched a correspondent for Reuters named Monty Something, crying out in a most un-British fashion that he had just been into Caen, Roger, and it was hell, old man, sheer hell.

I had strong reservations about this tale but certainly no proof that Monty had not been in that hell, sheer hell; and so I said nothing about it. The next day the British Ministry of Information flew over the London papers. My Caen dispatch was in all of them, but on page one in none of them. Old Monty's piece, however, was out front—and so was Roger Greene, with a sad dispatch about the death by German dive bombing of a little French boy named Michele with whom Correspondent Greene—"carrying my bloody knapsack"— had been walking down a country road. Correspondent Greene had ended this little confection (which did not appear in the *London Times* but was writ large in the *Mail, Express,* and the like) with this sentence: "I wish I had a picture of Michele."

"Roger," I said to him in a strangled voice, "I, too, wish you had a picture of Michele. I wish you had a picture because I don't believe one goddam word of this piece." Roger flushed a bit and muttered: "Now, Bill . . . now, Bill."

Correspondents generally played it fairly, or reasonably so, in Normandy and beyond; but there *was* a strong temptation for the Americans wherever correspondents for the popular, or mass, British press were thick on the ground. These fellows had almost universally a habit of personalizing the war as lying between them and Hitler, and the use of the perpendicular pronoun was universal. It was quite common to see a dispatch in some paper flown over from London setting off in some such manner as this: "Monty [Field Marshal Montgomery] told me last night. . . ."

Greene's imaginative effort therefore caused no surprise whatever in the British press camp, which to a man knew it to be nonsense, and I myself was able after a couple of drinks and a couple of hours to laugh over rather than curse at it. Bob Cooper of the *London Times* handled all such transgressions with real style. Unlike many of the "specials," he went to the front daily, sometimes with me or another press agency correspondent, but he never intimated that he had ever been anywhere near the scene of real action. Indeed, once when he and I had been up where things were extremely hot and had returned to write in the press camp, I happened to glance at his dispatch as it lay on the censor's table and read in it this line of the ultimate upmanship-through-downplaying: "The action was quite heavy, one was informed at British headquarters."

Not long after the fall of Caen I was posted back to the Americans, specifically to the First Division—the justly famous Big Red 1, of whose officers' association I am proud to be still a member, its regulations having been bent a bit to accommodate me and other noncombatant correspondents. This was, in my view, the elite fighting outfit of the entire Allied force in France, with the possible exception of the Guards Armored Division. The Big Red 1 had been in the field since North Africa and it was by now (just after the village of St. Lô had fallen to American arms in a cloud of rubble, and the British were at last breaking into Caen) perhaps the most highly professional outfit fighting in France, apart from one or two of the Nazis' Panzer Lehr divisions still ranged against the British to the north.

I found my friends in the First Division impatient, not to say disgusted, with the slow progress the British were making up above but unaware of the vast shortages of everything—men, guns, medical and other support supplies—that were endemic to the British everywhere, relative to the Americans. I was unable to explain the true position to my fellow countrymen, for the ordinarily genial and tolerant General Bradley had it fixed in his mind that Marshal Montgomery was a mere popinjay—a word the general himself would have found fancifully foreign to his good old Missouri tongue—and in the American sector what Bradley thought was what everybody thought.

In leaving the British and coming back home to the Americans I had left the have-nots to join the haves, and no mistake about it. Up in the north, Montgomery was contending with the pick of Hitler's armor and the most fanatically able of his SS troops. He and his next in command, General Sir Miles Dempsey, were short of everything. A single contrast may perhaps tell the tale: when I left the British sector, ambulances were transporting wounded men back to rear hospital areas, moving at about fifteen miles an hour on hard rubber tires that surely dated from about the First World War. One of the first and most heartening things I saw when I reached the First (U.S.) Division was ambulances streaking back from the line at sixty miles an hour on great, soft balloon tires. Moreover, in British territory a "hole in the line" meant just that: when a single battalion was overrun it was exceedingly hard to provide a replacement and quite impossible to do so without much loss of time. As to food, the British ate bully beef and hard tack and drank vast quantities of so-called tea, a gray sludgelike mess.

In short, the British position, relative to that of the Americans, was simply pitiable; but it did no good to try to point this out to my American colleagues. They thought I had "gone British." The accusing shade of Colonel McCormick seemed to follow me everywhere, as indeed it did even long after the war when the *Chicago Tribune* would occasionally touch me up editorially as a suspect "Easterner" then on the *New York Times*.

This was the one time in all my experience in the war when I

113

believed the field censorship to be at fault; not deliberately, but simply because its canons could not foresee everything. Had I sought to write the plain facts about the weakness of the British situation, it would have been in the literal sense an undeniable breach of security and a gift of considerable value to the Germans. And yet the circumstance that this story remained unwritten helped to keep alive, certainly in the United States, a grossly inaccurate version of the whole Allied operation in Normandy. That Montgomery was to a high degree unlikable I have already observed. But that he simply sat around and left the Americans to carry the burden of Normandy is an utterly and absurdly wrong notion that will be forever etched into the minds of countless thousands of ex-GIs and, for that matter, into much of military history.

I say this as a great admirer of General Bradley, a man as incapable of conscious injustice or mere professional jealousy as a man could be. In my own gallery of the giants and heroes he stands topmost. Along with him are General J. Lawton (Lightning Joe) Collins, the commander of the greatest corps of the First U.S. Army, General Maurice Rose of the Third Armored Division, and General Clarence Huebner of the Big Red 1.

When American forces had neutralized Paris, Bradley called all of us correspondents back to his headquarters in a schoolhouse for one of his rare briefings. Standing at a blackboard with a pointer in his hand and his glasses down on his nose, looking the very prototype of a tired country schoolteacher, he attempted to explain that Paris was a detail, a matter long since discounted in his strategic approach. At last, he threw down his pointer and said to us in quiet exasperation: "All right, all you fellows want to do is to *git* to Paris. Well, to do that you ought to go and find that French fellow, LeClerc; he's up around Rambouillet."

He was, of course, exactly right; we all burst from the schoolhouse, raced to our jeeps and headed for what turned out to be a most chilly reception by LeClerc. He was commanding something called the Second French Armored Division which High Command back at Supreme Headquarters had

114

decided must have the honor and glory of rescuing Paris. General Courtney Hodges of the First U.S. Army had obediently pulled back his own forces, leaving the field clear for LeClerc. I do not remember how many correspondents attached themselves to LeClerc's division; those I recall distinctly were Ernest Hemingway, Kenneth Crawford of *Newsweek,* and a young soldier-correspondent named Andy Rooney of *Stars and Stripes.*

We soon found ourselves in a seriocomic situation. Hemingway had long since equipped himself with what the rest of us called Hemingway's Guerrillas, perhaps a dozen French youths whom he had put into American fatigues and armed with American weapons. Hemingway himself carried a tommygun, a violation of God knows how many rules calling for unarmed correspondents. (Some of the rest of us finessed this by not carrying arms ourselves but letting our jeep driver bring along a carbine.)

As the glorious Second French Armored Division lurched out northward toward Paris, LeClerc, to whom the sight of an American uniform was an affront, arranged it so that the jeeps of his accompanying American correspondents should travel midway between his two columns of tanks and half-tracks. It was muddy as the devil and LeClerc's people were in some cases pretty excited, to put the matter with kindly euphemism, or pretty drunk, to tell the impolite truth. The consequence was that from time to time one of his columns would start firing at what looked to us in the middle to be very much like the other column. On such occasions we got the hell out of our jeeps, of course, and ran for whatever ditch or defile was available. I recall one occasion when Crawford and I burrowed into the mud side by side and called dreadful maledictions down upon each and every Frenchman ever to walk upon this earth.

At one point in this zany but rather sticky affair, Hemingway went up to a French colonel and tried to tell him that the Hemingway Guerrillas, who were operating on the division's right flank, had spotted three German tanks hulking behind an abandoned airdrome just up the road. The colonel grandly and peremptorily waved Hemingway aside. Whereupon Hemingway and his guerrillas broke off to their right, shortly put a bazooka into action and knocked out at least one German tank. I did not see what happened to the other two, and I never later asked Hemingway about them.

When we approached the West Gate of Paris, Rooney and I decided to try our luck at entering the city *before* LeClerc, who had by this time coiled up his division for the night. We did get into Paris, or at least into its suburbs, and then returned to the divisional command post. We entered the city formally the next day with the French, who continued to be most displeased at the sight of our American helmets or forage caps, to participate in the Grand Liberation. The only action I saw was in front of the Majestic Hotel, in which a few SS troops were holed up. After a brief exchange of gunfire, in which to my knowledge there were no casualties, the Nazis hung bedsheets out of the windows in token of surrender. As they walked out one by one under guard of French troops, a mob of civilians, many of them women using their spike-heeled shoes, beat them into the pavement. No French officer intervened. I wanted to do so but was unarmed. But a little Jewish-American correspondent named Bob Ruben, who was with the British agency Reuters, pulled an illicit Colt .45 from beneath his combat jacket and held the mob at bay.

I was madly typing wherever I could find a place to set my typewriter, and I put this episode into a dispatch that was by now about three thousand words long, since I had not failed to incorporate earlier the fact of the unauthorized sortie through the West Gate of the night before. Distrusting the elaborate arrangements that High Command had made for us to file dispatches through a wireless center in the Scribe Hotel, and not having learned my lesson, after all, on D-Day, I wrapped my long piece in a spare combat jacket, gave it to my driver, and told him to drive back out of Paris and find the nearest American field radio. That was the end of the dispatch, so far as I know. I never saw the driver or the jeep again. The redoubtable Whitehead, for his part, had again shown better judgment. By just what means he had got into Paris I never knew. But he

116

himself drove back to the wireless transmitter at First U.S. Army headquarters and got his copy safely out. Again, I had failed to protect my communications adequately; again, Whitehead had acted on the sound principle of first things first.

Paris was, of course, *très gai* and all that. The lights, incredibly to those of us who had operated for an eternity in darkness, were on; the women looked chic, well fed, and well cared for. There was, however, an adequate supply of sour notes to the handful of us unwelcome Americans. Somehow a French partisan, a Communist I supposed, attached himself to me as guide and interpreter, my French being limited to such expressions as "Cognac, s'il vous plait." Through him I got a worse case of Francophobia—I had contracted it earlier in the campaign when I saw some of the sterling patriots of the FFI, or Free French, shaving the heads of pitiable tarts newly liberated by our forces, for "collaborating with the enemy." I need not say that the French underground on the whole performed great and gallant service. It is, however, a plain fact that within its ranks were many outright hoodlums and bullies, and some who used the movement to settle personal scores.

My partisan guide took me on the night of the liberation to an English-speaking hospital where I got a bellyful of loud complaints about the horrors poor Paris had suffered from Allied bombing. Everything of course is relative, in war as elsewhere, but this struck me as sheer nonsense, since I had toured Paris and seen less bomb damage in the entire city than I had often seen in a single small quarter of London. At the hospital I expressed myself with some force about the alleged atrocities of our pilots. Upon being invited to leave forthwith, I went down to the Scribe Hotel and filed a dispatch saying that Paris and Parisians showed little evidence of vast suffering but plenty of whining. It was perfectly plain that a great many Parisians had managed to coexist fairly well and even rather profitably with the occupying Nazis. My French partisan guide claimed that at least 60 percent of the French had willingly collaborated. I strongly suspected he was right.

I had had enough of Paris after a strange episode there. By

117

chance I was in the party of General Charles de Gaulle when he went to Notre Dame Cathedral for the mass of thanksgiving for the liberation of the city. I sat in a pew just behind that of the general. Midway in the mass, at the moment of the consecration, shooting broke out in the cathedral. De Gaulle to his credit kept his head bowed and never moved a muscle. I had no doubt at the time, and an English-speaking canon of the cathedral later confirmed, that what had happened was this: some of the FFI men in the de Gaulle party, full of cognac, had thought they saw some movement in the nave of the cathedral and had let go with their Sten guns. The people in the cathedral took it for granted that an attempt upon de Gaulle's life had been made. A British friend of mine, Bob Reed of BBC, was standing in the door of the cathedral with his recorder and understandably broadcast that such an attempt had in fact been made.

The melodrama in Notre Dame, so typical of much that I, at least, saw in my worm's eye view of the campaign across France, was followed by a theatrical hunt for "snipers" on every rooftop near Notre Dame. It is true that de Gaulle was not responsible for this nonsense; it is equally true, however, that he could hardly have failed to know what had happened in the cathedral. If he did not actually see it, he had only to do what I did and ask the canon.

The next morning I went to an American military briefing on future operations and got a hunch that the outfit to tie to for a while was the Third Armored Division of First Army, commanded by Maurice Rose. These fellows would become the spearhead of the American advance across the rest of France, across all of Belgium, and finally would be the first troops to break into Germany itself. For a time I was the only correspondent with the Third Armored, and I became a close friend of Rose, an extraordinary man later killed when a German patrol trapped his jeep inside Germany and shot him, on the dubious grounds that in surrendering he had tried to draw a weapon. This was one of the unsung American heroes of the war. I did what singing I could, but our advance across France and Belgium was so rapid, wireless communication was so iffy, and opportunities to write anything at all were so scarce that I never knew just how much of the story I managed to get back home to the States.

Rose, who had come up all the way from the ranks, was an American Jew with what, to me anyway, was a good, sound, cool-headed hatred of the Nazis and all they symbolized. Once his divisional "point," and a few halftracks and tanks, had cleared eastern France, he all but ran the wheels off his outfit, and we liberated Mons, Liège, Verviers, and Eupen in a stride. The Big Red 1 infantry division was coming up behind us but there was an awful lot of space between us; for many days we were a small, mobile island in a sea of Germans.

The poignant hour of our strike through Liège, Belgium, created in me what has remained a lifelong admiration of the Belgian people. Whereas French communities had celebrated their liberation by demanding things—chocolate and cigarettes, mostly—the Belgians in Liège asked nothing but gave what they had. As our tanks ground through the center of the city, gaunt men, women, and children, many of them with faces sooted with industrial grime, stood silent on both sides of our advance, tears running down their cheeks. Hundreds of them held small, pancake-like cakes, and these they gravely thrust into our jeeps. I, a noncombatant, had from D-Day on felt guiltily embarrassed by being hailed as anybody's liberator, and I felt enormously warm toward the Belgiques for their very reticence. And I must admit that at times I hid tears in my own eyes.

As soon as we left a liberated town, so Rose learned, the Germans came back in and dealt very harshly with a few Belgian civilians in order to issue a lesson in Mastership. Rose then picked up a Belgian civilian somewhere, put him in the uniform of an American major, installed him in a lead vehicle, and had him perform a single duty—to get out at every liberated point and warn the Belgian civilians not, for God's sake, to suppose that all was over and that they were safe.

Again and again the division was halted for lack of gasoline or ammunition, usually, for some reason, at the very banks of the Meuse River, whose meandering course we crossed several times. Finally, at Verviers, where we were down to a minimum supply of both gasoline and ammunition, Rose showed me a signal he had sent back to General Joe Collins at corps headquarters asking permission to halt forty-eight hours to perform maintenance of his vehicles. Within an hour back came this signal: "No. Go on. Collins." Rose cursed mutinously, his imprecations beginning on the name of Joe Collins and ending up on that of Eisenhower, and swore that he'd be damned if he would. But of course we went on, and just as the tanks were beginning to cough, up came a supply from our rear. Rose now thought of Collins as a genius, as in his way he was.

My friendship with Rose, meantime, put me in peril of violating every one of the canons governing the conduct of noncombatant correspondents. The general, for instance, asked me on many an occasion to take a German POW into my jeep for transfer to our mobile stockade. This I did. Once my guest was an English-speaking colonel of the regular German army who remarked to me conversationally, and I believe sincerely, that the Nazis were only pigs. Then he sighed and said it had become a most irregular war. I asked him why and he said: "Because you [our division, he meant] are here too soon. Nobody can run armor this fast." With that he went into a gloomy silence. And as I drove him up to the POW compound, to the captured officers' entrance (Rose was meticulous about military courtesy), he averted his face so as not to see the long lines of captured German enlisted men entering the compound through another gate.

The climactic hour of my association with Third Armored came when, with a small forward task force, it became the first invader to enter German soil in modern times. We broke in, over light resistance from the retreating Nazis, to a village called Rötgen—and I found I had correspondent company. Henry Gorrell of the UP had somehow sneaked up on me and joined the division. As we approached the German frontier, Gorrell had the driver of his jeep plunge past mine so that he could be "first."

I took the matter philosophically, or reasonably so, for he and I had a common problem. Very well, we had accomplished

120

the first Allied entry into Germany; now what were we going to do with our copy? We agreed we could hardly trust the division's own shaky communications and decided instead to drive all the way back to Liège in Belgium where, so far as we knew, the excellent press wireless facilities of First Army were still in place. It was a nasty business going back. We were on what the army called the Red Ball highway—that is, the main supply route to the combat troops—and American ammunition trucks were rushing up to the front, almost tailgating each other, at sixty miles an hour, in a total blackout. Gorrell and I were so thankful to arrive in Liège that between us all the passions of rivalry were long since spent.

When we got to First Army we got a shock. Men were in the process of dismantling the wireless transmitter to move it forward. We cursed and wept, and they delayed the process long enough to let us file our copy. As I passed the censor's desk on the way out of the wireless tent, my eye fell on a dispatch by a man I had never heard of, a new war correspondent fresh from the States, thus datelined: "In Germany with American troops." The mendacious fellow had been no farther forward than First Army HQ. But then, the censor had no right or duty to alter any dispatch except for security violations.

Once inside Germany, the focus of action shifted back to the First Division, which I rejoined gladly if only because it was famous for the quality of its chow. Like Rose, General Huebner had come up from the ranks and he maintained morale—in what was perhaps the most shot-at division in the American army, considering that it had landed on D-Day after North Africa and all that—by seeing to it that the men ate well, even in the line. He had a mess officer who, with plenty of money in his pocket, scoured the German countryside for meat and wine, the very best there was. The enlisted men ate the same food as the officers—and always ate first. Once, in a village that was nameless to me even then, I was with a company commander at the corner of a stone farmhouse, round which both of us were peeping while riflemen advanced up the village street by only one burst of fire at a time. The captain, an old-timer who was as calm as an insurance agent sitting at his desk, suggested that before we left the shelter of the farmhouse corner we would do well to eat. We sat down with our mess kits and suddenly found the slightly corpulent figure of Huebner at our shoulders. "Have your men eaten yet?" he demanded. "No, Sir," said the captain, pointing around the corner where a lively fire fight was all too plainly in progress. "As you see, Sir, they are pretty busy just now." Huebner scowled and then said softly and reflectively: "Captain, put your mess kit down on the ground and step in the goddam thing." He did, and I did, too.

As it had been the British who invested the first major city in upper Normandy, Caen, so it was the Americans, specifically the Big Red 1, who took the first big city in Germany, Aachen. The division was down to 26 percent of its effective strength and Huebner was furious at being ordered to attack in that condition. But attack he did. Whitehead and I agreed that I should go in with the first wave on this occasion, and so I did, along with my British friend Peter Lawless, after a fairly heavy artillery bombardment from our side and after General Elwood (Pete) Quesada had put some of his fighter bombers over the city. It was not so nasty inside Aachen as it well might have been, one reason being that the German troops had just had an issue of schnapps and some of them had drunk it all up at once, perhaps because by this time it was pretty apparent even at foxhole level that their whole cause was going very badly.

Lawless and I got the required eyewitness stuff and returned to the wireless head at Spa in Belgium. Lawless's colleague, Stanley LeBaron of the *London News Chronicle,* was still in his bunk overtaken by *mal de cognac,* and pleaded for a fill-in from us so that he could file a dispatch. We obliged with full accounts of what we had seen. The next day, Lawless came up to me in a red rage waving a cable from his home office. This most unflatteringly contrasted his Aachen piece with the tremendously moving dispatch—this was how Lawless's editor had described it—that had been carried by the *London News Chronicle.* Lawless strode off to confront LeBaron, who was found to be still reclining in his bunk. Shown the cable and told of his infamy, LeBaron pleaded: "But what could I *do,* Peter; I was drunk!" Lawless sighed—and put out his hand.

122

Lucia Alberta Smith White and John VanDyck White,
the author's parents.

The author, at right,
with brothers Goen
VanDyck White (left)
and John Archibald
White.

Above: With fellow correspondents in Normandy; left to right: the author; Roger Greene, another AP correspondent; Robert Bunnelle, AP chief correspondent in London; Lloyd Stratton, AP vice-president; and Bill Downs of CBS.

Below: The author with Canadian tank troopers in Normandy, 1944.

With Roger Greene in Normandy, 1944.

With Lyndon B. Johnson at the LBJ Ranch in 1957.

Mrs. White sits with Lady Bird Johnson and Lynda and Luci Johnson in the Senate Press Gallery to hear President Johnson's first address to Congress after the assassination of President Kennedy.

Above: With Mrs. White in a White House receiving line greeting President and Mrs. Nixon, Chief Justice Warren Burger (left), and others, about 1970. Below: With General George C. Marshall at Marshall's home in Leesburg, Virginia, early 1950s.

Left: Leaving for a three-month assignment in Africa for the *New York Times,* 1952.

Below: With an aide to vice-presidential nominee Hubert Humphrey at the Democratic Convention in Atlantic City, 1964.

Right: With Speaker Sam Rayburn of Texas, about 1947.

Below: In the Senate Press Gallery as *New York Times* chief congressional correspondent, 1955.

With daughters Cia and Victoria in 1957.

With Dean Acheson in the Maryland countryside, about 1960.

It was about this time that some of us, including Lawless, decided to forgo the spartan comforts of the army press billet and install ourselves in Spa's leading hotel, the Portugal. Here, in a place where Madame-the-proprietor was still counting up the marks left to her by her former guests, a group of German officers who had only recently retired eastward, there gathered nightly a collection of convivial friends. We went up to the front each morning; we returned each afternoon to the wireless head, filed our dispatches, and then settled down in the bar of the Portugal.

We were largely a company of First Division correspondents, though we had frequent visitors from other outfits. Among these was Ernest Hemingway, who had attached himself in the deepest of senses to the Fourth Division and was a strong partisan of it. He was one of the bibulous members of our little club, and certainly one of the best liked. He was then writing for *Colliers* magazine at some fantastic sum per word, and in his cups he would declare that he was only the rich man's Ernie Pyle. But this period was not all fun and games for that singularly tormented man. One night in the fall of 1944 he stood openly weeping at the bar. I asked him what ailed him and he told me. Nearly all the assets he had, it appeared, had gone into a place in Cuba and he had just heard from his agent in New York that a hurricane had wiped it out—after the storm insurance had expired. And it had expired because a substitute army censor had stopped a service message from Hemingway to New York directing its renewal. In violation of standing instructions to all censors to notify a correspondent if any message had been killed outright, this dolt had never told Hemingway. I have often thought since that this shattering financial blow, to a writer who had always been improvident anyway, may have lain at the root of Hemingway's lowering of his writing standards after the war. I think he desperately needed money, or at any rate was himself convinced that this was the case.

The winter campaign in the Huertgen Forest and along the Ardennes settled into a slow tempo and one began to look upon the war as a more or less permanent condition of life. By

November 1944 our unit of correspondents had lost casualties in about the same ratio as the combat forces, and in nearly every instance they were needless casualties, suffered by "new" men among us in search of stories that had already been written. The old-timers among us—it *had* been a long time since June 6—increasingly drew together and developed an unspoken code as to what in our professional rivalry was permissible and what was not.

Those of us who had taken up residence in the Portugal became a Spa café society of sorts, as distinguished from those who remained in the official press billet. Lawless (to whom no harm can be done in this recollection since he is long dead and his wife and son had died before he came to Normandy, his wife in a London air raid and his son in a Guards regiment) had established a certain relationship with Madame. He thus became unofficial host in the Portugal. All sorts of people turned up there from time to time. Among them, for instance, was Erika Mann, daughter of the novelist Thomas Mann. She came in one night under escort of an American OSS officer and lectured us at length on the evils of the Nazi system. This rubbed some of us the wrong way, perhaps because somehow we had already heard that the Nazis were evil. At any rate, Hemingway and I took offense. Miss Mann and the OSS officer took offense at us, averred that we were all barbarians, and went out angrily into the night.

As Christmas approached, I was overdue for home leave. I decided to take it, since Supreme Headquarters, we were informed, was looking for a pretty well stalemated war through the winter. Our own Intelligence people at divisional and First Army level were crying warnings in vain that a good many German divisions were ominously inert in the vicinity of Bastogne. These caveats, however, we nearly all cast aside, so strong had become the habit of supposing that "they" back at Eisenhower's HQ surely knew more than anybody else.

I got my orders cut (in fact I cut them myself, as I had often done, using the army style and typing the line "Lt. Col. AUS" at the bottom) for jeep transport back to Paris, as a stop on the way home. In Paris I found that press headquarters in the

Scribe Hotel were teeming with "war correspondents" for trade publications dealing with women's lingerie and the like, and a second lieutenant of the Military Police braced me for being "out of uniform" because I was wearing an unbuttoned field jacket and, at the moment, no forage cap. In a word, I enjoyed Paris even less than I had on the day of its liberation. Nearly every American I met seemed to be far more involved in a business deal of some sort than in journalism of any kind. The hucksters were moving in; that was clear. I could and should have written about this; but I didn't. I was tired, I was on leave, and I was going home. Then, too, that subject was scarcely military in nature, and I knew the cable desk back in New York would be distressed by some quasi-essay on how the buzzards were gathering around the carcass.

I got out of Paris within a day or two on a military air transport aircraft, a DC something-or-other (I never could keep those designations straight). We landed at breakfast time in Gander. It is a fact that one's essential balance, both chemical and psychic, can be thrown off, even painfully so, by abruptly encountering something healing and unbelievably pleasant after a long habituation to harshness. This may seem a precious and implausible observation at this point, but it is not. I still vividly remember that breakfast in Gander, after the long flight home from years overseas and seven unbroken months at the front. We ran into an officers' mess that was brightly lit, warm, unrestrainedly hospitable, and stocked to the roof with food of all kinds. I had bacon and eggs, eggs for the first time in years, and thought of the K field rations that I had been eating in Germany less than forty-eight hours before and to which I had been so long inured. Suddenly I ran to the door of the mess, stepped outside, and vomited. It was a case of too much amenity, too much pleasure, too much North American welcome too soon. I could not immediately accept all this because I was not conditioned to *believe* all this so quickly.

I was in an indescribably nervous state as we flew over Boston. In some crazy way, nostalgia was now working in reverse and I missed my friends back at the front. When we landed in New York I felt foolish and ostentatious to be in battle dress, the only kind I had then, and to be carrying as a souvenir the ghastly gas mask that we all had to take with us on D-Day. I was relieved that in passing through the formalities of customs one of my group was Van Johnson, the actor, in the uniform of a captain. Johnson was the focus for all eyes, of course, and I got through my business at the airport quietly. I do not know why, but it felt immensely good not to be exposed to people asking questions about the war. Because my civilian clothes had been left back in London before D-Day I had to go around New York in a uniform—of sorts—for several days until I could buy a new suit.

Nothing worked out as I had long supposed it would in my homecoming. I felt half drowned in a great sea of gross materialism; I felt that a beloved city had itself become almost monstrous. I detested the leering question put to me by a head waiter at an East Side hotel—the Barclay, I believe: "How do you like the dames, eh?"

When I dropped around to the AP offices in Rockefeller Center it was to meet strangers for the most part. It seemed to be a giant factory; and I came then and there to a conclusion that I had already begun to ponder before leaving Europe. I decided that I would move from the AP to an individual newspaper before I went back overseas. Bob Casey of the *Chicago Daily News* had suggested to me at some point early in the campaign that I might join that paper's foreign service. I also had friends in London from the *New York Times* who thought that I might catch on with that paper.

For the first time in my life, too, I had some surplus money in the bank, apart from six weeks' leave pay in my pocket. A former colleague on the Cable Desk, Fred Vanderschmidt, had now become managing editor of *Newsweek* and he offered me a job there as associate foreign editor. The money was attractive but the position was not otherwise tenable, since I fully determined to return overseas, to the European Theater or possibly to the Pacific, toward which some of my old ETO comrades were turning.

I woke one morning to learn that something called the Battle of the Bulge was in progress and I knew then that given an Allied victory there, the war in Europe would be over, for all practical purposes, before my leave was up. This changed everything for me. For I realized suddenly that I was in pretty bad shape emotionally, the letdown having been much harder than the buildup, and that I had to do something to settle my life a bit.

CHAPTER EIGHT

I CALLED the *New York Times* and made an appointment to see its legendary managing editor, Edwin L. (Jimmy) James. Surely no job interview has ever begun more curiously. As I approached James's office at the agreed hour I saw him standing in its doorway, a short, compact man in his shirtsleeves, bellowing out this extraordinary malediction: "The goddam Catholics! The goddam Protestants! The goddam Jews!"

"Mr. James," I said, "you have left one out." "Which one?" he growled. "Why, the goddam Arabs!" I assumed that what had so disturbed him must have been some sort of flap involving the *Times* in a disputation between rival religious groups, the sort of flap of which every newspaper editor lives in dread. James, however, did not explain. Come to think of it, he never explained much of anything.

It was a happy meeting. James, who had been a distinguished foreign correspondent before being called home by Adolph Ochs, was pro-correspondent and extremely pro-war-correspondent. We settled down into a long conversation having to do with our experiences abroad and nothing whatever to do with my purpose in calling on him. Growing nervous at last, I insisted on saying that I had come to apply for a job as a correspondent for the *Times* and that I thought I would like to go back to Washington, where I had been long ago. James grunted without comment; and there the matter was left for the time being.

A couple of weeks later he telephoned me and said: "How

soon could you report to Arthur Krock in Washington?" Any time, I told him. "Well," he said, "go when you get ready, but before you do, come by and see me again." We had still discussed nothing whatever about the small matters of salary and rank and so on. When I was ready to go down to Washington I went again to see James. Again, the conversation meandered everywhere until at length he threw a salary figure out of the corner of his mouth and I agreed to it. As I got up to go, he said sharply: "Wait a minute. I want to tell you something." Now, I thought, would come the lecture about working hard and doing a good job and all that. But what James said was this: "Go on down there and have a damn good time."

I had not been in Washington for any substantial length of time since the distant days of the first Roosevelt New Deal and I was a bit apprehensive about picking up the threads I had dropped back in 1935. I need not have worried, however. Krock, whom I had always supposed, from reading him, to be a stuffy type, turned out instead to be a brilliantly witty man in person and a very generous and fair-minded boss. He ran the Washington bureau of the *Times* like a sovereign state, paying little heed to "New York" and none at all to any lesser creatures there, such as news editors. He assigned me to "the Capitol," which I translated, as soon as I had got my bearings, as the Senate. The place had always fascinated me, though my earlier work in Washington for AP had only occasionally taken me there. Because Krock ran a laissez faire shop, leaving men pretty well on their own, I chose to concentrate on foreign affairs in the Senate whenever I could.

This was by no means all the time, for I usually got stuck with stories that were long in the telling. I covered the triumphant return home of General Eisenhower; President Truman's proclamation of the Japanese surrender, or V-J Day; the Navy's release of the dramatic details of radar, a weapon I had known about during the war but had not been able to write about then. I was also the resident expert on the story, centered mostly in Senate investigations, of the vast ideological clash that resumed immediately after the war as the old isolationists and America Firsters began again to raise their heads.

"McCarthyism" was only one aspect of this complex of matters. On one issue or another relating to the possible, probable, or indubitable mistakes made before and during the war by a Democratic administration, I wrote for the *Times* on many a night as many as five thousand words. A man in the promotion department in New York once told me, during the late Forties and early Fifties, that I had had more front-page bylines than any other of its correspondents. I replied, fliply: "Maybe I don't write good; but by God I write fast." In a way it was like being back on the AP cable desk in New York in the days before our entry into the war. For much of the time I was a sort of typing machine—and I loved it all.

There were breaks away from Washington, too. In 1945 James sent me to cover a revolution in Venezuela. In Caracas I found great excitement in the American embassy because a few random rifle bullets had hit its stone facade. It was a fairly routine South American upheaval and within a few days I cabled James that I should be returning to the Washington bureau, which had already assigned me to cover the forthcoming Senate investigation of the Pearl Harbor disaster. "Go on down to Rio," James cabled back.

I had not known that anything was happening in Rio, since communications in Caracas were in disarray. But when I got there I discovered that a far more important revolution had taken place. Getulio Vargas, the supposedly indestructible strongman of Brazil, had been most politely removed from power—by the Brazilian army, no less—for attitudes held to be insufficiently democratic. This was a facer, since I had always associated the military in South America with the right wing, so I went to the American Ambassador, A.A. Berle, for such enlightenment as I could get. There was no shooting to look into; everything had gone off with perfect quiet and decorum.

Sitting on the veranda of the embassy residence (with Mrs. Berle, oddly, off at its farthest possible end), Berle told me what had happened. During the war, it appeared, the United States government had given to Vargas a great deal of lend-lease material, and Vargas had sent to Europe a token military force (which, to be unpleasantly honest, was only a bloody nuisance). The understanding struck in this transaction, said Berle, was that after the war Vargas would give Brazil the first free and open election in its history.

As to this revolution, Berle recalled that at a dinner party a few days beforehand, Vargas had come up to him and observed: "You know, Berle, I really doubt this country could be run with a Congress." Berle took this to mean that the dictator was going to renege on his promise to hold free elections. Berle, whom I found to be a very intense man, had then gone off to Sao Paulo to make a speech in which he observed that "the people" of the United States would be most disappointed if the elections did not come off. The Brazilian army had taken note of this and had, without further ado, gone to Vargas and told him he had to go. Vargas, according to Berle's account, had offered no resistance, not even of the debating sort, and had simply packed up his things and quit his official residence to go off into the mountains.

Berle, for his part, was plainly more than a bit disturbed at the instantaneous Brazilian repercussions to his little speech. Sitting in a stiff-backed way on his veranda, he treated me as a welcome guest—pleased, I thought, to have someone to talk to. He was deeply sensitive to what Washington might be thinking of his actions and of course he knew that Washington certainly read the *New York Times*. In those days American diplomats were just beginning to get jumpy about any accusation of American intervention in Latin American affairs, and I soon discovered that there lay the critical point of Berle's disquiet.

For quite a time his monologue ran along in a somewhat disjointed way, I remaining silent because I had nothing to offer, until finally he visibly braced himself and asked: "Would you regard what I did as American intervention?" Though my private view was that Berle was making too much of the episode, not myself seeing any reason why he should not have spoken about the elections, I was not eager to enter his soliloquy. So I hedged, and finally said hesitantly: "Well . . . ." "Well, anyway," Berle broke in eagerly, "if it was intervention, it was only *intellectual* intervention, wasn't it?" Yes, I said.

Within a few days I was on the way back to Washington,

where the lady I was courting, columnist June McConnell of the *Boston Herald*—now my wife—had promised to try to find me an apartment so that I could escape at last from the series of second-rate Washington hotels in which I had been living.

From Rio to Washington in those pre-jet days was about as far as one could go on this earth, or so it seemed. While we were flying over the vast jungles of the Brazilian interior, I went up to sit for a while with the pilot. (Commercial aviation was a good deal less formal and hedged about with restrictions then.) He pointed downward at an oceanic sweep of aggressively green growth and said cheerily: "Hell of a place to crack up, that. It happens now and then; and nobody has ever yet spotted the wreckage from the air. Seems the natives come and haul the stuff away and hide it."

We put down for the night in Belém and I discovered that my luggage was missing. I had only what I stood up in, flannel slacks and a tweed jacket, along with an infected jaw, the recurrence of a problem I had had during the war, when (and where) the medics wasted no time on such trivia. Not until we got to Miami, a world and a half away then, was I able to buy clean underwear and shirts. The stopover there was not long enough to make an appointment with a dentist. Thus, I arrived back in Washington in pain and fatigue and confronting the prospect of beginning the next morning to cover the longest, most vexatious, and most unnecessary investigation that I was ever to know. This was the majestically solemn inquiry into who did what to whom to bring about the Japanese attack on Pearl Harbor. It was one of those "joint" jobs, meaning that the House, too, was involved on the investigating committee, the strongest member of which was Senator Alben Barkley, later Harry Truman's "Veep."

The Republicans, notably Senators Homer Ferguson of Michigan and Owen Brewster of Maine, were determined to find that President Roosevelt had somehow conspired to get the Japanese to put in the attack so that he could then "get us into the war." The testimony was interminable and the interparty squabbling on the committee bench was indescribably tiresome. The broken Pearl Harbor commanders, Admiral

Husband Kimmel and General Walter Short, sat day after day gazing into the far distances, like men for whom the past was the only reality left, and that a painful one.

Because I had seen so often the operation of the iron law of warfare—expressed, though hardly enshrined, in the old army expression "Situation normal, all fucked up"—and because the most sustained congressional second-guessing since the Civil War was going on before me, my private sympathy was all with the beleaguered commanders. Moreover, I had seen the haunted deathmask prematurely worn by Franklin Roosevelt on one of my first assignments for the *Times*—his appearance before a joint session of Congress to report on the Yalta conference—and I could not subdue my pity for that tragic figure. Nor had I forgotten the ease with which the highly political General Eisenhower had escaped censure for the massive high-command misjudgments that could have lost us the war in the snows of Bastogne. Finally, I suppose I was not yet readjusted, or rehabilitated, or whatever the term was, to civilian life.

Still, I had to cover this Pearl Harbor thing "straight," without expressing my bias, and I think I did so for the daily *Times*. But the Sunday Review section was a quite different matter. In pieces for Lester Markel, editor of the Sunday edition, I undoubtedly exhibited from time to time a certain personal point of view. Arthur Krock, for his part, was sympathetic to the Republicans; he had long since fallen out with Roosevelt, both personally and on matters of principle. At times I would see him scanning my Sunday copy with no marked pleasure. But from first to last, on this and on every other sort of story, he never sought to influence me in any way, and he never took up the subtle forms of punishment of a wrong-headed journalist that any boss is able to.

Long after, at a luncheon meeting honoring the retired Arthur Krock, given by fellow Kentuckians Paul Porter and John Sherman Cooper, I said as much of Krock to his face. A proud and basically very private man, he nevertheless had tears in his eyes as he said: "For many years I have waited to hear something of that sort from any colleague."

I tell this story for purposes beyond the anecdotal. The

personal qualities of men in journalism, or at least of those in highly exposed positions, are often judged—and unduly condemned or unduly praised—by the public and even by the journalistic profession totally on the basis of what they *write.* This is fallacious and unjust.

Arthur Krock was a steadfastly conservative writer on a liberal newspaper—and a most courageous one, too, if it comes to that—and it was widely assumed within the liberal community that he was therefore arrogantly and heartlessly reactionary. The exact opposite was the truth of it. Like his friend Henry Mencken, as a *person* he was deeply humane—so much so, for instance, that he could never bear to discharge an employee, no matter how outrageous his behavior. While one of my associates in my early days on the *Times* was supposed to be helping me out in Senate coverage, he spent months simply resting on a couch in the Senate press gallery. I certainly did not complain, for it was all one with me. Somehow, though, Luther Huston, the day-by-day bureau manager under Krock, learned of this fellow's sins of omission and told Krock that the man must be discharged. Krock agreed—in principle, as he put it—but then nothing happened. The bureau manager finally had to let the axe fall; Krock was absent from the office that day "with a cold."

We had an old-time Morse telegraph operator who for unfathomable reasons, perhaps just that he could follow the interminable hen tracks of Krock's copy and get it up to New York in good shape, was a great favorite of A.K. This operator, however, had his troubles with the bottle, and his frequent absences without leave got to be too much for Huston, who fired him. Krock emerged from his ivory tower to learn of this and was deeply troubled. He did not wish to countermand the orders issued by his second in command, but his compassion for the operator was stirred. Thereupon he took up an elaborate course, going to Huston and saying: "I understand you are *thinking* of discharging that man over there. Perhaps it would be as well if we gave him one more chance."

"Jimmy" James, too, who had the reputation of being both too conservative and too tough, was in some ways like Krock.

Like Krock he had the liveliest skepticism about mankind but the readiest sympathy for one man at a time. A single small incident will illustrate James. On a national election night (in 1952, as I recall it), when Krock and I were in New York to write the "leads," he for the presidency and I for the Senate and House, we had baffling difficulty in obtaining the services of copy boys, the runners who carry a piece from a writer to the copy desk. No matter how we banged our bells, nobody came. Finally, I asked a member of the New York staff what was going on. "Simple," he said. "We have no more copy boys. They're all 'junior clerks' now and don't have to run copy. Mister James did it." A few months before, it emerged, a copy boy had gone to James with a story of family troubles and a request to be promoted to junior clerk, a higher paying job under the Newspaper Guild scale. All the other copy boys, including one who used to place James's bets on the horses, then went to him and asked to be made junior clerks, too. With much cursing and grumbling he complied.

Again, Edwin James the Fierce, who had been known in his days as a foreign correspondent as a wizard at padding expense accounts to cover highly unauthorized expenditures, was perfectly capable of rebuking a subordinate not for putting in too big an account but for not having put in one big enough. "Got to cover the essentials," he would say, "and also got not to set any bad examples by letting the auditors have their way."

All his quirks were engaging, even endearing, ones; and if he sometimes behaved like a character out of *The Front Page*, the Hecht-MacArthur novel, that book could also be said to have been a case of the authors' art imitating James's nature. As managing editor he was a member of the *Times* editorial board; but he held all editorials, especially those of the *Times*, in such poor regard that he would not read them and indeed would loudly and in any company advise his correspondents to ignore them, too. "Forget 'em," he would say. "They might influence your work."

His attendance at the editorial board's meetings was therefore notably lacking in the earnestness with which all other

135

members approached them. If I am permitted to call an earthy and bellicose elderly gentleman an *enfant terrible*, such a one certainly was Jimmy James. A favorite of Adolph Ochs, James nevertheless kept his distance from the publisher, on principle, as he did later with the next publisher, Arthur Hays Sulzberger. Though of course he was on contract, James nevertheless insisted on being paid by the week rather than on the proper executive's monthly schedule. Each Friday afternoon (this I was told by Arthur Krock) James would go in person to the auditors' office, collect his pay, and then walk to Mr. Ochs's office, put his head in the door, and announce: "You don't owe me nothin' and I don't owe you nothin'."

Anyone who supposes that by such conduct James was simply making a legend of himself, playing "a character," would gravely underestimate the man. He was profoundly devoted to the *Times* as an institution, although he would never in the world have used the words "devoted" or "institution," and in his quixotic conduct he knew exactly what he was doing. As I have indicated less directly, he had the most passionate respect for stringent truth, accuracy, and comprehensiveness in the news, and for grace in its telling. He knew that these qualities must be sought for in men, not in rules or gimmicky systems. He therefore treated his correspondents generously because he had the wit to see that a great newspaper lives on the talents and the integrity of its staff, and on nothing else.

Working for the *Times* in James's day was truly rewarding because he on his side was so worthy of the best that his people could give him in performance. Much the same could be said of Arthur Krock. Both were natural enemies of the bureaucratic blight that constantly threatens all great media organizations. Both were also natural enemies of the Rudolph Flesch School, which sought to fit writing into formulas not unlike the jargon of advertising slogans. As James's vast influence over the *Times* weakened with his death, the paper waxed mightily but nevertheless lost something irreplaceable in quality. A news editor named Theodore Bernstein, a born desk-man, set up a staff organ called, with repellent cuteness, "Winners and Sinners." In this publication Bernstein regularly awarded accolades to instances of what he deemed splendid writing. One ghastly example I recall was an article beginning, "The Democrats are having woman trouble"—referring to the growing attractiveness of the Republican party to the country's female voters. And he tut-tutted instances of what he believed to be poor or non-"impact" writing style. Krock and I took pride in appearing from time to time in the "Sinners" list, and when one of us wound up amongst the "Winners" he bought the other a drink in apology.

All this is not to say, of course, that the *Times* went to hell with the departure of James and Krock; on the contrary, it has since improved in some ways and in my view is demonstrably the world's best newspaper, taking all in all. Nevertheless, the old times were the best times, if not the best *Times*, before the operation became so huge as to crowd much of the human factor out of staff relationships. I would bet that the present publisher, Arthur Ochs (Punch) Sulzberger, himself feels nostalgia for and would like to return to the old ways—but he could no more do this than I could turn back my own decades.

I certainly owe the paper a great deal, if only for permitting me to be its chief Senate correspondent for some of the best years of my life. In a peculiar way the Senate became my home away from home, and whenever my work there was interrupted by other assignments I soon longed to get back home. Moreover, these extra-Senate assignments had a way of fitting somehow into the concerns of the Senate itself.

One such was a prolonged mission to sub-Sahara Africa, to which I was dispatched in 1952, principally to cover the endemic racial crisis in the Union (now Republic) of South Africa. The Nationalist party that had been founded by Field Marshal Smuts, Churchill's great friend, had by this time grown progressively more nationalist and progressively more rigid toward the blacks. Prime Minister Malan, when I first met him in Capetown, strongly reminded me of an Old Testament prophet or patriarch, harshly and utterly honest by his lights and, in my perhaps somewhat impertinent view, wholly unable to understand the true nature of that parliamentary system under which his nation operated as a member of the British Commonwealth.

Dr. Malan (the use of the title "Doctor" was sharply urged

upon me by a palace functionary who Teutonically preferred it even to the "Prime Minister" I was using) was a Boer, an old South African of pioneer Dutch descent and a man who sincerely believed that God had ordained the Boers to rule the blacks for the good of their souls and lives. His party was made up almost wholly of Boers, who spoke the Dutch dialect called Afrikaans. His opposition, the United party, was largely made up of British-descended or British-oriented white South Africans. Though it was by no means liberal on the race issue, it had the typical British political instinct to avoid confrontation, especially any confrontation put in emotional terms, and it somewhat vaguely hoped the whites could maintain their dominant position by loosening the screw on the blacks one turn at a time for year after indeterminate year. They stood about where the Boer leader John Vorster stood in 1977.

The immediate issue at Capetown was Malan's declared intention to deny the right of the ballot to the Cape coloreds, that is, to the persons of mixed blood who lived in Cape Province. The Nationalists had just won an election, a victory in terms of numbers of parliamentary seats though not in the popular vote, and were determined to push through this typically harsh repressive measure. Malan wanted to know why the American press, and the American government, too, if much more cautiously, were so critical of his program. He had won the election, hadn't he? He had the votes in parliament, didn't he? It was no good saying to him that under the American Constitution and under the unwritten British Constitution alike a parliament was forbidden to strike down inherent personal rights no matter how large its majority.

All the same, the situation was far less clear, far less subject to the right-and-wrong treatment, than it had appeared from Washington. For while the Nationalists were full of unjust convictions (most of them springing from the doctrines of their church in South Africa) they nevertheless *had* convictions. The United party fellows, on the contrary, themselves had no intention whatever of really freeing the blacks; they only wanted to finesse the problem with that well-known British technique called muddling through. One *liked* them the better, but one

138

had to respect Malan's people more. For the Nationalists had a bitter candor, concealing only that some of them had been openly sympathetic to the Nazis during the war and that they were secretly maneuvering to force an issue with London so they could secede from the Commonwealth while pretending to have been kicked out. And in their harsh way they were actually more concerned for the blacks than were the British South Africans generally. These latter, in fact, were all but unconscious of the black man, since, however incredibly, they almost never saw him at first hand. The difference was this: the mine owner, the top boss almost anywhere, was British; the foremen actually dealing with the blacks were Afrikaaners. (The parallel with the Quebec of the Fifties was not lost on me—the owner a British Canadian, the manager a French Canadian.) At a gold-mine pithead near Johannesburg I asked a black which kind of white man he preferred—the Englishman or the Boer? Why, he said, the Englishman; the Boer straw boss was his recognized enemy.

South Africa was, below the surface, a place of measureless melancholy in these years of the great liquidation of the white man's power in nearly the whole continent. Colonialism was dying all across the landscape, giving way to new independent governments that two decades later would all too often be brutal dictatorships and/or absurdly incompetent regimes. The Union of South Africa was free of this traumatic revolutionary movement; it was not a colonial power but rather a member of the British Commonwealth with a long established two-party system. The country did, however, have a sad sickness that was unique on the continent, the almost total cultural alienation between its two white groups, the Boers and the British South Africans.

I was appalled to see this bitter and senseless dichotomy: the whole white population of the nation in total disunity confronted an ultimately insoluble crisis with the black man. For practical purposes there was not one white race but two; there was not one white language but two; not one life-view but two. This schismatic apartness, this voluntary system of white apartheid, was carried to quite unbelievable lengths. In a saloon in Capetown or Johannesburg it was commonplace to see the Boer drinkers ranged on one side of the bar and the British drinkers carefully ranged on the other side talking of some cricket match eight thousand miles away.

In the parliamentary press gallery in Capetown, I found that while Boer- and English-oriented journalists would join in sending a messenger out for beer, they would not *talk* together as professionals. Toward the end of each working day, one set would retire to one end of the gallery, shut the door, and communally work out how all would interpret the day's proceedings of Parliament in their papers the next day. The other set would caucus behind a closed door at the *other* end of the press gallery and proceed in exactly the same way. In our country I have at times seen (what journalist has not?) a fair amount of mutual back-scratching, not to mention blacksheet swapping (which means one man trading a carbon copy of his story with another man for *his* carbon). But never have I seen the blatant abandonment of ordinary professional standards that I saw in South Africa. One would have thought that elementary personal pride, if nothing else, would have exercised some restraining influence on the practice.

In the Civil Service Club in Capetown, which is at least as "British" as White's London, I dined one night with an old gentleman who had come to South Africa as a British subaltern in the Boer War and now, half a century later, was still there. I mentioned to him that I found it difficult to understand why the white South Africans did not come together, if only for mutual defense of their position *vis-à-vis* the blacks. He agreed that it was too bad. "Take the matter of Afrikaans, for instance," I observed. "It is the native and preferred language of your own government. But do you yourself speak it?" He stared at me in astonishment: "Good God, no!" And yet he was in business in Capetown and had to deal day by day with Boer businessmen—who were never so foolish as not to be reasonably accomplished in both languages.

Here were two instances of a kind of deliberate deafness, a slow death of reason, because white men were sunk in puerile self-petting and self-esteem while a great tidal wave of black

140

resentment and black demands approached, all but unregarded and as inexorably as the juncture of the mighty waters of the Indian and South Atlantic Oceans at the foot of Capetown. One of the great upheavals of history was in the making, an upheaval sure to alter everything and everybody below the Sahara. And what did white South African journalists do? Why, they met in solemn daily conference to figure out small ways of doing the Boers (or the English) in the eye.

I did not, regrettably, send such portentous reflections as this home to the *Times*; journalism lived (as a good deal of it yet does to this day) on the principle of see-no-evil, hear-no-evil, speak-no-evil of other members of the tribe. As for the old businessman in the Civil Service Club, he was not very important in himself, since the business of businessmen is simply business, and no commitment is made by them to the spreading of information and intelligence. But even he was important in the sense that he pretty well typified the complacency and smugness of the Englishman who used to "go out there to the Colonies." I thought there was no evil in this archetypical old boy—and I saw a lot of his kind before my African tour had finished. But there was an emptiness in him and his sort that helped to explain how it was that not merely hostile world opinion but also a weakness in the British head was losing England the last of its vital influence in the world.

Sometimes, the gathering of such an immense tragedy may be discerned in seemingly trifling events and circumstances and attitudes which in themselves are as tiny, relative to what they foreshadow, as was the city of Capetown to the great oceans beyond its harbor.

I do not claim that at the time my discernment of what was happening in Africa was nearly so clear as it was in hindsight. I do claim, however, that before the African assignment was over I got a piece of the reality. Indeed, when I got back to Washington I went to half a dozen friends in the Senate to tell them what I had observed. I also went to a meeting of men who I am very much afraid were connected—dare I say it, given the prevailing climate?—with the State Department and even with a thing called the CIA. I hasten to add that nobody "recruited" me or paid me anything and that there was nothing "covert" about my actions. They were only the actions of an American journalist concerned that his own government should get all the information it could upon a developing international crisis with which, plainly, one day it must deal.

And from only a few countries in Africa, by my observation, was the United States government getting that information from its diplomats. Some of these were just serving out their time before retirement, all dreams of the glamour posts of Europe at last unfulfilled, and they wished only to be left alone. Our ambassador to South Africa, for instance, had me to dinner but immediately made two points quite plain. The first was that *he* talked only to the South African officials currently in power, and to them as infrequently as possible. The opposition party . . . the blacks . . . these simply did not exist. The second point was that the ambassador was far from happy at my presence in the country and had no intention of helping me in any way whatever, whether as an American journalist or simply as a wandering American citizen. I gave up on him and made friends with the British and Canadian high commissioners, both of whom were actually sensitive to what was going on.

I sent back to New York a series of long dispatches attempting to give an overview of the position in South Africa that was less simplistic than the sort of thing Americans were reading elsewhere. The press agencies were offering a kind of staccato Uncle Tom's Cabin as their contribution to American understanding—perhaps understandably so, since the facts were so complicated and the nuances so numerous that an untruncated report on it all would have been impossible to fit into the eternally crowded news tickers.

Copies of my series of pieces ultimately reached me—and the South African government—with the arrival of copies of the *Times* itself. The copy desk had not messed up my work, as during this post-Edwin James era it quite often did, with Rudolph Fleschisms. I was amused, however, to note that where I had used the term "blacks" New York had substituted the word "Negroes." I learned later that some copy reader held

142

me in active suspicion because I was a southerner. Within less than two decades American blacks were themselves to adopt "blacks" in preference to "Negroes."

Once the general pieces about the situation in the Union of South Africa were out of the way, I stayed on in Capetown only long enough to see Dr. Malan have his way with his bill to disenfranchise the Cape coloreds. By the time I was ready to leave the country I was in bad odor with the minister of information, a straightout Nazi type whose name I do not recall, but this circumstance caused me no pain. More senior members of the government, including Dr. Malan, were not happy with me but were not hostile, either. A Boer journalist acquaintance even went with me to the airport and said, with the stiff pomposity that unhappily is a fairly common characteristic among Afrikaaners, that anyhow I had "*tried* to be fair." I can recall no country from which I was more glad to make my exit, not only because the whole country was positively a breeding ground for melancholia, notwithstanding its immense material riches, but also because never, it seemed to me, had I as a journalist encountered any national problem that was so damned insoluble—using "damned" in its most literal sense.

I flew up to Southern Rhodesia with spirits lifting from the very moment of takeoff. For up there the British whites were, so I had learned in South Africa, making earnest and honest efforts to set up a Central African Federation with Northern Rhodesia and were determined to make genuine concessions to black rights—not enough to satisfy the black leaders, to be sure, but enough all the same to justify the term "genuine." The capital, Salisbury, could have been set down in some giant movie "location" as the very model of an Edwardian British colonial city. My hotel was large, rambling, wooden, turreted—and achingly *correct* and uncomfortable. The old British belief that a little bit of plumbing should go a long way was emphatically expressed. My request for a room with a bath attached was treated with cool incredulity. To reach such facilities I had to walk a long, inevitably dark corridor with coconut matting on the floor.

143

As we sat with pre-dinner drinks in the vast and gloomy hotel lounge, where three pale and very thin, very English ladies were sighing away at piano, violin, and cello, gladdening the air with "Ah, Sweet Mystery of Life" or something equally spirited, two British colonial service officers earnestly congratulated me on having found such a superb billet. The hotel, it seemed, was quite choosy about its guests. It was, so I learned later, the local Claridge's.

The general atmosphere of Salisbury almost made one think that time had slipped backward fifty years. But what was going on in the government was anything but fusty. Sir Roy Wilensky was energetically trying to find a middle way across the race problem and, incredible as this may seem now, it appeared that he had every chance of making a real breakthrough by which white influence could be retained while black interests were progressively satisfied.

Liberal men in Salisbury truly thought Wilensky was onto something, as did Wilensky himself. They pointed to the fact that the *only* barriers to intra-African immigration that the Rhodesian government had set up were against Boers from South Africa, whose racial extremism was feared and condemned in Salisbury. I have often wondered how Wilensky felt when, later on, he heard himself denounced in the United Nations as a kind of racist stooge. The rejection of his moderate course by so much of world opinion, by the way, led eventually to the Ian Smith government in Rhodesia.

What was going on in Salisbury seemed to me to be full of cheer and hope, and so I wrote to the *Times*, perhaps in unconscious reaction to the contrast between the energy in Rhodesia and the drawling lethargy among British types I had so lately observed in South Africa. I was highly premature in my optimism, as it turned out. In the easy labeling process that is an unfortunate habit of my profession, Wilensky had somehow been put down in most of the press as something close to a racist. The absurdity of the categorization did not diminish its impact.

Unaware, of course, that the brave try in Salisbury was to be only that—a try—I set off for the Belgian Congo to the last teetotally colonial outpost on my African tour. Leopoldville was, physically and atmospherically, a European oasis in what by this time had been a pretty long arid spell for me. Getting there, however, took a bit of doing. Twice the aircraft had to turn back over the jungle, once because a generator failed and again because lightning knocked out most of the radio gear. The touchdown at Leopoldville was at about three o'clock in the morning and the Belgian colonial office man who met me was understandably not in the chirpiest of humors.

In the Congo, the Belgians—my favorite Europeans of wartime days because of the magnificent work done so quietly by their White Army partisans, work so consistently underplayed by them—were frankly bucking the whole anticolonialist tide that was sweeping the world. *Their* reform efforts had nothing to do with politics; instead they were giving the blacks material advantages I had found nowhere else in Africa. Black wages were higher, black housing and medical care were, relatively speaking, superb. The colony was rich in uranium, much more in demand then than now, and the Congo was to a large extent carrying metropolitan Belgium on its back.

Indeed, a Belgian official told me that the Congo was rapidly clearing up Belgium's war deficits and was in fact at the base of the high early postwar stability of the Belgian franc. I am no financial expert, by any standard, but the assertion seemed to me plausible. For the Belgium I had seen in the days of the liberation was economically on its knees far more visibly than was France—but the word *economically* should be stressed. In spirit, Belgium never bent the knee to the Germans, so far as I could learn, and, on the necessarily fragmentary personal observation available to me in the campaign, was damn short of collaborators of any stripe. Perhaps I carried too many fond memories of Belgium of 1944 into Leopoldville. At any rate, I reached the journalistic conclusion that the colonial administration was going to last indefinitely simply because the whites themselves had no suffrage, either. Of course, it all came bloodily apart within a decade. Remember the names: Lumumba . . . Katanga . . . and all that?

Whatever else might be said of the long African assignment,

one thing was beyond debate: variety it most certainly had. I arrived in Accra, in what had been the Gold Coast, on the day after the British, under spur of the United States and the United Nations, agreed to grant independence to what had become Ghana. There had been some shooting and some bloodshed. The British had dared not risk any more and so they were virtually thrusting independence upon the rebels. The day I got there they led Kwame Nkrumah out of jail, dusted him off, and announced to him that he was now prime minister of the nation of Ghana. I had an hour's conversation with him—his English was good, for he had been to college in Pennsylvania—and thought him more nearly a dazedly happy man than a formidable one. He seemed, too, to have a good deal of humility—a bad misreading if ever I made one, since he turned out to be a self-worshipping megalomaniac.

Having put in a parliamentary system, a British Colonial Office official explained to Nkrumah in my presence, they would now like his recommendations for the appointment of an opposition leader. Nkrumah said he would think it over. Whether the leader eventually chosen was nominated by him I never learned. About the whole affair there was an air of unreality so great that I dared not express it explicitly in my dispatches lest I seem to be making irresponsible sport of a most serious matter.

At length, Nkrumah asked eight or ten British colonial officers to remain indefinitely in Ghana as members of his cabinet. While I was there, it was divided about fifty-fifty between black and white, the British fellows usually working on one side of the wooden, Somerset-Maughamish cabinet building and the new black ministers on the other. Among themselves, the British went in their shirtsleeves and used first names; in going to speak to their black colleagues they put on their jackets, if only to cross the hallway, and in conversation they used the salutation "sir."

The British public relations officer in Accra (actually he was an ex-major of the Irish Guards and I suspected him to be the head in Ghana of MI6) was cheerfully outgoing about all that had happened but was oblique upon one point. Remarking

146

that I had just come from an area, Rhodesia, where the British were desperately trying just to hold on, I observed that here in Accra they seemed to be trying not only to let go but to let go in the greatest possible hurry. What, I asked, was the explanation for all this. "Ah," he said, "you know that Biblical line . . . *In my father's house are many mansions.*"

My notion was that these Colonial Office types, though utterly correct in their deportment and though refusing ever to say a word in criticism of their superiors in the London government, were disgusted with London and reckoned to give the erstwhile Gold Coast a true bellyful of independence. Their excessively punctilious conduct rather supported such a speculation, at any rate, and that line of conduct came directly down from the governor general, a man named Arden-Clarke.

Accra was my last port of call on the Africa assignment, for at home the 1952 presidential election year was approaching its first climactic phase—the national party conventions—and I had already been ticketed to work on these.

147

CHAPTER NINE

As A SORT of appetizer that turned out to be for both parties more of a robust entree, the national governors' conference met in Houston, a city scarcely recognizable to me. Gone was the old bayou drowsiness, replaced by frantic expansion and the seemingly limitless sprawl of an industrialization that made this one of the great cities of the country and seemed to promise that it would rival in economic power the cities of New York and Chicago.

The governors' conference in effect settled the Republican National Convention before it began, and settled the hash of the party's leading aspirant for the presidential nomination at the forthcoming national convention in Chicago. The Eastern Establishment cadre that eventually broke Senator Robert A. Taft of Ohio—a cadre headed by Thomas E. Dewey of New York and Henry Cabot Lodge of Massachusetts—actually dealt the fatal blow in Houston. Already, the Dewey and Lodge people had managed to make a great scandal of a so-called "steal" by the Taft forces of prospective convention delegates in Texas. Now, at Houston, they adroitly got even pro-Taft governors to sign what was billed as a generalized manifesto in support of "morality" in politics but was in fact a death warrant for Taft's candidacy. What this paper actually did was to show the Taft forces *conceding* that there had been a "Texas steal."

The Taft people at Houston, far less sophisticated and smoothly articulate than the Dewey-Lodge operatives working for General Eisenhower, never knew what hit them, never really knew what had happened. And neither, to my rage and frustration, did the subeditor on the *New York Times* news desk who handled my dispatch that night. Though I put the story as plainly and simply as I knew how, this clear intimation of mortality for the Taft candidacy wound up far inside *my* paper—and on the front page, where it belonged, of the *New York Herald Tribune*, under a streamer headline.

Since I flew from Houston direct to Chicago, where the convention was being assembled, I did not know until my arrival of the outrage that had been worked upon my piece. Inquiry to the home office brought word that the deed had been done by a copy editor named Sam Sharkey. He was a subordinate of Bernstein, he of "Winners and Sinners," and, like his boss, he had had no experience worth mentioning either in gathering or writing news, but was ripe with expertise on nit-picking and comma-chasing in the copy of correspondents in the field. My Washington-based colleagues in Chicago naturally gave me no quarter, since Sharkey had not only buried my story but had so slashed at it with his pencil as to leave it looking like a model piece of Rudolph Fleschism.

Still, nothing could be done about it all; the damage had been done and could not be undone. My own first instinct was to go out and get drunk, but my *Times* associates in Chicago pointed out to me that I had been assigned to write the nightly lead-all story of the convention and this job would be demanding enough without approaching it under the cloud of a hangover. I did at least manage to get a message through to the home office asking somebody to tell me what in God's name had moved Sharkey to act as he had done. The reply was a tiny classic in journalistic idiocy: "Sam doesn't believe that *state* politicians like governors have anything much to do with national conventions."

But Houston and the governors' conference had been critical not only for the Republicans. There, too, Adlai Stevenson made the first in the series of monumental errors (or perhaps they really should be called fearful acts of indecisiveness) that so doggedly pursued him through two unsuccessful presidential campaigns. Though Stevenson finished his career as the perfect symbol of advanced liberalism to the East and West coast "reform" Democrats, he was at the onset of the 1952 battles actually the most conservative among the Democratic presidential possibilities. He had at least the tentative good will of the powerful southern wing of the Senate, even of crusty old Squire Harry Flood Byrd of Virginia, no less. And no one seriously doubted that in order to win in November the party *had* to hold the South, whether the Republican adversary should be Taft or Eisenhower.

The litmus-paper test to the southerners—not only the senators but each and every one of the southern governors—dealt with the Senate rule governing, or really *not* governing, the filibuster. Richard Brevard Russell of Georgia, perhaps the most influential member of the Senate in either party, was some sort of cousin or second-cousin of Stevenson's and was also the field marshal of the southern determination to maintain a substantially unfettered right of filibuster. Russell had told me that early on, when his kinsman's name had first been noised about for the presidency, Stevenson had given him a commitment that he would do nothing to alter the filibuster rule, Rule XXII. Therefore, when Stevenson held his first press conference in Houston I asked him for his views on Rule XXII. Unless I misheard him, and unless my colleagues also misheard him, he replied that he favored its retention. After the Democratic convention had nominated him in Chicago, however, he seemed to waffle on Rule XXII, for the liberals were determined upon its destruction or severe modification.

I myself never thought this was a case of intellectual dishonesty or cowardice but rather an instance of the brooding, Hamlet-like quality, the to-be-or-not-to-be syndrome that was lodged deeply in this gentle, appealing, and tormented man. Nevertheless it was (to use a popular cliché) a no-win position for Stevenson. His absolute necessity had been to come down upon one side of the filibuster or the other and there grimly to remain. He wound up, of course, by infuriating the southerners, including Cousin Dick Russell, and not quite convincing the liberals. I think he never could have won in November anyhow, but his handling of the filibuster thing put a stain upon him in what might be called the Officers' Mess of the Democratic Party. It was one of those things that are Not Done in a trade that is on the whole remarkably relaxed about codes of ethics, no matter how endlessly such codes are cried up by that trade. It put a black mark against Stevenson not simply among the southerners but with a great many northern pros as well. One of these was John F. Kennedy, then very young but already thinking wistfully of reaching the top some day.

Nor did Kennedy ever forget his distaste. When he was fighting for the Democratic nomination in 1960 he remarked to me early in April: "A lot of people are saying and writing that if I make it [the presidency], Adlai will be secretary of state. I'll let you in on something, pal, and if you want to you can make yourself some money betting on it so long as you don't even mention you ever saw me. Like hell will Adlai ever be *my* secretary of state—though of course I'll have to give him *something*. He's a goddam weeper." To Kennedy, parenthetically, "weeper" was a multipurpose term: sometimes it meant a self-pitier; sometimes it meant a moralizer; sometimes it simply meant somebody with whom John Kennedy was acutely uncomfortable. (Stevenson's "something" was of course the ambassadorship to the United Nations.)

Harry Truman, though an early supporter of Stevenson for the nomination in 1952, soon reached much the same conclusion as Kennedy. "Damn fella can't make up his *mind*," said HST to friends of mine in Chicago. For myself, I liked Adlai Stevenson, and though I was never anything like a close friend, I always thought I understood him. The powerful overprotectiveness shown him by his mother, coupled with the way in which she pushed him to ever higher high-minded endeavor, was as bleakly familiar to me as my own early life.

Then, too, though I do not wish to nominate myself for the popular office of celebrity, we did undeniably have a few things in common, faded-genteel relatives in the South among them. During one of Stevenson's two presidential campaigns (possibly 1952), Kenneth Harris of the *London Observer* and I were down in North Carolina, where the candidate was working the kissin'-cousin bit for all it was worth, albeit in his usual elegant way. Harris, necessarily something of a novice to American politics, said to me after we had heard the candidate hit this theme for the umpteenth time: "Bill, is he becoming a demagogue? He *can't* have all that many cousins in North Carolina." "The hell he can't, Ken," I said. "Believe me, he can and does; I *know*."

Stevenson was in some ways the most exasperating politician I ever covered. Because of a kind of elusiveness about his personality or character or whatever, one never knew quite how to categorize him, even to oneself. I started out, in 1952, strongly attached privately to his candidacy—though maintaining the well-known canon of Objectivity in my dispatches—in the belief that he was the last, best hope of a *civilized* conservatism agreeably mint-flavored, to my mind, by his southern connections. I thought it shameful that a barrier as gossamer as a prejudice and yet as strong as steel had for a century automatically forbidden the highest office to any southerner. I thought that in a President Stevenson, notwithstanding that his own home was Illinois, the South would spiritually rise again. I never dreamed then of a risen South typified by a politician who called himself "Jimmy" and even allowed himself to be sworn in as president under that boyish nickname.

By 1956 it was impossible to see Adlai Stevenson in such idealistic, and perhaps romantic, terms. Progressively, he had allowed himself to adopt, or had been pressured by stronger men into adopting, some quaking positions, notably on national defense, that were unworthy of what he really was, or at least of what he had been.

My last sight of him was at the United Nations, at the luncheon table of Secretary-General U Thant. It was not a happy occasion and it is not now a happy memory. A distinguished American who had twice campaigned for the presidency, an elevated guest among what was otherwise only a journalistic group, sat silent while U Thant repeatedly insulted both this country and Stevenson himself. U Thant tonguelashed the United States and the West in general for at least

152

twenty minutes. I was sickened. What had brought such a man as Adlai Stevenson to the point where he felt he had to accept such treatment? Had it been a diplomatic occasion of delicacy, one in which our ambassador *had* to take a beating in the country's interest, one could have understood it. But this was nothing more than a press briefing, if of a most grandiloquent and unpleasant kind. Stevenson had no need to remain for a moment.

When I got back to Washington I went to President Kennedy with the story of the episode, believing that he ought to know what sort of secretary-general was being supported by the United States. Kennedy, sighed, showing, I thought, some atypical affection and even some pity for Stevenson, and then quickly reverted to the Kennedy I knew better. "That son of a bitch," he said of U Thant. "Sometimes I think we'd be better off with some outright Commie [as secretary-general] rather than that pious Third World fraud." In point of fact, the White House did later begin some inconclusive consideration of the possibility of putting American support behind, say, a Yugoslav, once U Thant's term at the UN was ended.

But while I see Stevenson to this day as essentially a tragic figure, it is not so much the business of journalists to weep over the weaknesses of public men as it is to try to penetrate the reason for those weaknesses. All of us professional politician-watchers should have been perceptive enough as early as the 1952 convention to see that Adlai Stevenson had a fatal flaw as presidential material, for the first requisite of a president is possession of an iron gut, an adamantine courage such as Harry Truman, say, had. And Stevenson's acceptance speech at the convention, a speech insufficiently interpreted to the country by me and by all of us correspondents, was enough to set the alarm bells ringing in even the most amateur analyst of public men. He said that he had prayed to have that "cup," meaning the nomination, pass from his lips. Instead of being moved by this actually gross and pathetic reference to the Garden of Gethsemane, we should have roundly reported that Stevenson was what Kennedy was later to call him—"a weeper," in the end.

153

In that same crucial political year a cherished, cantankerous, and nobly wrong-headed friend of mine, Robert A. Taft the Elder, met and mastered a true political Gethesemane and took his beating without tears. He went to the Republican convention as "Mister Republican," clearly the front-runner, only to see Eisenhower's managers take the prize away from him by the great moralizing public-relations campaign about Taft's "stealing" delegates in Texas. The accusation was absolute nonsense; if any "stealing" had gone on it had been done by the hordes of Texas "Eisenhower Democrats" who had overrun the ham-handed regular Taft organization and announced themselves now to be good Republicans entitled to control a Republican delegation at Chicago. Taft, the one politician I ever knew who was in any possible circumstance incapable of even a trace of hypocrisy, watched in numbed amazement and disgust as Eisenhower demonstrators paraded about with signs proclaiming: "Thou Shalt Not Steal."

As a correspondent and friend, I saw much of Taft during those hot hours. And as the nomination he had so indisputably won under the old rules of the game slipped steadily away from him, he showed only a fastidious and total noncomprehension of how it had all happened. He had been far more direly prophetic than he knew when he told me just off the Senate floor before the convention opened that he expected trouble "from the East." "The East" considered him an isolationist, which at times he was and at times was not. Indeed, the eastern foreign policy establishment, which a generation later still largely controls the State Department (and on the whole probably rightly so) was mortally resolved that he should never be president.

Of this group Thomas E. Dewey was the current political leader and Dewey put more of his back into beating Taft at the Chicago convention than he had ever put into his own two unsuccessful runs for the presidency. He told me about as much when, in 1954, I was working on a posthumous biography of Taft, called *The Taft Story*. When we had finished reminiscing about Taft (whom Dewey hated, as Taft despised him), I asked: "Governor, since you had so much to do with the

Eisenhower victory, it has puzzled me that you did not come down to Washington for a Cabinet job." "I didn't want any job," said Dewey. "I tried twice for the big one and never made it. But by God"—and here he looked icily at me and all but willed me to write his words down then and there—"*I* elected Eisenhower president." Though, as I have already confessed, I never liked the man, I could not seriously dispute, even inside my mind, that what he had said was true, or as nearly true as to make no difference.

Dewey told me, too, of a most affecting reconciliation which, so he said, he had made with Taft while the senator lay dying of cancer in a New York hospital. "I was always *fond* of Bob Taft," he said to me, with as forked a tongue as ever I had heard wagged in politics. A Taft family friend who was present gave me the true account of this meeting. Dewey, said this friend, had twice called at the hospital, and Taft, refusing to the end to be two-faced, had twice refused to see him. On Dewey's third attempt, Taft snapped in his twangy Ohio voice something to this effect: "All right, damn it, tell him to come on up."

This was not long after the senator, old "Mister Republican," finished his last days in the Senate with only an unspoken farewell to his colleagues. On their side, goodbyes were implicit, since everyone there knew that his illness was terminal. On Taft's side goodbyes would have been impossible; he was far too reticent for that sort of thing. He did, however, have a final meeting with an old adversary, Harry Truman. Truman, now an ex-president but forever a senator under the customs of that place, came marching one day into the chamber. He walked to Taft's desk. Taft rose on his crutches, imperfectly masking the pain from the horrible cancer that was eating at his hip bone. They shook hands warmly, Truman in barely restrained tears and Taft smiling a white smile.

This is one of a hundred memories I carry of the Senate of the United States; it formed the core of much of my adult professional career and in the personal sense it long served me as a second home. I made fast friendships there without trying (the only way I ever could really make friendships) and I was

155

peculiarly empathetic with the place. By historical inevitability it became, after the interregnum of the Eisenhower years, the seedbed for presidents, where earlier the statehouses had more or less been their source.

The Second World War and its aftermath brought about a sea change in the official Washington I had known as a young reporter in the Thirties. Then, Roosevelt had been urgently seeking to save the country from economic peril from within; his earlier presidency was essentially inward-looking and domestic in its concerns. Washington reporters heard very little in those days of either foreign or military policy but a great deal about public works programs, "money-changers," anti-drought measures, soil reclamation, public power, and so on. These were essentially home—and homely—issues, and national political eminence could be reached without expertise in world affairs.

Postwar disenchantments—the "loss" of China, the recognition by the Truman Administration that Roosevelt's view of Russia had been far too sunny, the descent in Europe of the Iron Curtain—helped turn toward the outer world a focus of national concern heretofore turned inward. The staggering magnitude of the necessity simultaneously to contain Soviet incursions in the basin of the Mediterranean and to restore Europe's war-ravaged economic base created a revolution in American politics and political thinking of a scope never before seen. The presidency became a worldwide office, only secondarily a home office.

Athwart the Soviet Union's expansionist drive in Southern Europe, Harry Truman cast the Truman Doctrine's program of assistance to Greece and Turkey—and dragged Congress, crucially the Senate, along with him in the enterprise. When Western Europe itself became endangered he put forward the North Atlantic Treaty Organization, directly demanding of the Senate its constitutional Advice and Consent. This, more than any other of the extraordinary acts of leadership of a president whose roots went back to a parochial political machine in Kansas City, deeply and enduringly involved the Senate in a series of first-priority international issues of which to this day

156

it remains "seized," to use a favored term of the United Nations. For Truman was for the first time in peacetime committing this nation to a permanent and many-sided military alliance, was in advance committing it to go to war in an all-for-one and one-for-all pledge of blood and treasure.

NATO brought one of the Senate's truly Great Debates (the phrase has always been used too loosely) of the twentieth century. I shall always be glad that I was there to cover it. By carefully courting the recanted isolationist Arthur H. Vandenberg of Michigan through Dean Acheson, Truman managed to cast the NATO treaty into a bipartisan framework. Vandenberg had become the foreign policy leader of the Republican side of the Senate, whereas Taft was the party's overall senior spokesman. Though I was on the treaty's side and thus on Vandenberg's side as correspondent, I found the senator to be a shallower and more prolix man than the public perception of him. The Democratic administration needed him so badly that they deliberately built him up as a public hero, the perfect Internationalist, while dealing rather brusquely with Democratic senators such as Tom Connally of Texas who had *always* fought isolationism. Truman and Acheson knew they could count on the Connallys anyhow; "Van" had to be stroked carefully and given the best of care and feeding.

I was strongly reminded of one of my earlier assignments for the *Times*, that of helping cover the postwar meeting of the Allies in the discussions leading to a treaty with Italy. Secretary of State James F. Byrnes for the United States, a former South Carolina senator who in the glib labeling of the time was put down as highly conservative, was so solicitous of V.M. Molotov, the Soviet delegate, that he made me a trifle sick. In the briefings given daily to correspondents at the Waldorf in New York, it repeatedly emerged that Molotov was crudely snubbing and even insulting the Labourite British cousin's defense. Even then, the White House was only doing what had to be done, that is, placating real or potential troublemakers and putting its real friends on a very thin diet. I got the impression that Bevin, a politician's politician, entirely understood the American necessity, treating it as part of the game.

Nevertheless, Ernie Bevin, tough cockney Labour leader that he was, had resources enough to take care of himself. At length, on an occasion when Molotov appeared in the Waldorf three quarters of an hour late and offered no apology to him as the Allied chairman of that day, Bevin took official note of the slight and told Molotov: "*I* have the honor to represent a country that *always* fought Hitler." Molotov, so a briefing officer told me that evening, was for the first time in the conference cut down to size. The Russians, of course, were immensely sensitive to any reference to the years in which Hitler and Stalin had been in tandem.

One morning, off the Senate floor, when Connally was in a low mood because of the extreme nature of the Vandenberg buildup and the painful shortage of *any* Connally buildup, I told him of the Bevin-Molotov incident, to say to him that he was not alone. "Hell, I know that," he responded. "But I just get damn tired of hearing Vandenberg this and Vandenberg that." One might make here the unoriginal observation that politics, especially high politics, is a rough business. The NATO treaty debate was a rough business; but then nobody had ever supposed Harry Truman or Dean Acheson to be made of sugar candy, to borrow a Churchillian term.

Endlessly cosseted, "Van" kept the faith and held steady for the treaty, which almost to the end was in a precarious position because Taft, the intellectually dominant force among the Senate Republicans and also a possible future Republican president, was against it. Vandenberg, as I recall, did not relish encounters with Taft on this issue, perhaps not so much from feelings of positive inadequacy as from a general Republican disinclination to challenge the painfully blunt Taft on anything. It fell, therefore, to a Republican newcomer in the Senate, John Foster Dulles, to try to handle "the Taft Problem" in behalf of the party's internationalist wing in the Senate.

Dulles, later to be Eisenhower's secretary of state, was too new in his Senate seat to realize fully that Taft's mind was formidable indeed, even though for the time he was getting a generally bad press and to the media was, in fact, a kind of anti-hero to "Van's" hero. Therefore when these two—Dulles, late of an international law firm in New York, and Taft, a long inactive partner in a typically provincial law office out there in Cincinnati—met in combat, the galleries were full and even the Senate itself was attentive. Dulles set out more to explain away than to explain the treaty, arguing from a clever corporate lawyer's brief that it really didn't commit us to so much as some people thought.

Taft was incredulous at this line and coldly angry. He intensely disliked evasiveness and, for his part, celebrated candor in his every act. He proceeded to tear Dulles apart, forcing reluctant admission after admission from his adversary. At the end, I sent a page in to ask Taft to come out to see me. He did and I said to him: "I'd like to compliment you on the finest speech made *for* NATO today." He looked appalled, and I quickly added: "I mean that Dulles diluted it into nothingness and you gave it dignity and brought it back to what it really means."

How I ever became Taft's warm friend among Senate correspondents I shall never know and can only guess, for underneath my turtleback shell of Objectivity I was, indeed, a hereditary Democrat, and God knows *he* was a hereditary Republican. But warm friend I did become, to the amazement of my colleagues in the Senate press gallery. To a man they regarded Taft as a forbidding and glacial figure and as innately anti-press to boot. My supposition was and is that my more or less unique relationship with him developed through a personality weakness we shared: we were both introspective in what was generally a highly extroverted milieu. What was seen as "coldness" in Taft was more nearly another thing altogether—shyness. Having a pre-dinner drink with him one night in a Pennsylvania Avenue restaurant after a long day in the Senate salt mines—Taft making news down on the Senate floor and I writing about it up in the press gallery—I lightly commented to him upon certain drinking feats I had witnessed involving Churchill. To my astonishment he took these purely idle remarks as a criticism of himself and said to me: "Do you think I would be a better politician if *I* drank more?"

The episode was oddly touching, and it illustrated one of the great and enduring shortcomings of national political journalism in general. This lies in our seeming inability to present public men for what they really are; the whole profession tends instead to offer thin caricatures. John Kennedy is forever seen as "gay" (of course I use the term in its original and not its modish meaning) whereas John Kennedy's real life was one of great physical pain, of much bleak disillusion, and of a constant search for almost exactly the reverse of the kind of regard he actually received. Where he longed for the approval of solid—even conservative—types, he was idolized mostly by the equivalent of fan clubs. He never liked uncritical admiration and never respected those who extended it. At times he would call them, with wry distaste, "the jumpers and squealers."

Dwight Eisenhower did not really care for all that "I Like Ike" business, though as a natural public-relations-expert-without-portfolio he encouraged it, for obvious political reasons. Nor was he at all the gentle "father figure" he was so often made out to be. He could be ruthless with a wide smile, though ruthless, to be sure, only in pursuit of what he perceived to be high public interest. He was a kind of closet power-seeker. His posture as only an honest, bluff soldier set amongst the wicked "politicians" was just that—a pose. He was, in fact, extremely adept politically; he simply had an untypical way of politicking, both in his army career and as president.

Richard Nixon, however manifold his sins, was never an "Imperial President." He had almost no self-confidence, inside, and he had literally to sweat to untense himself in the many private conversations I had over the years with him. Even such a man as Taft was, by comparison with Nixon, almost gregarious. I knew Nixon in the House, in the Senate, and in the White House, seeing him off and on for nearly thirty years, and I never once saw him truly at ease.

It is a habit in my trade to speak of the "loneliness" of the presidency. But I think that Nixon's loneliest moments of all were spent in the Senate. He never really fitted in there because the cliché is correct: it *is* a club and it was made for men at home in clubs, as Nixon never was and never was to be. It is

160

not that one must be a hand-shaker or back-slapper there; on the whole it is better not to be. Rather, to be at home there one must be naturally or deliberately individualistic, a "character," whether aggressively and easily so or simply shyly so makes no difference.

Nixon was never hated in the Senate but neither was he ever much liked, partly because he was overly constrained and almost robot-like in his manner, partly because he had been badly scarred by enmities arising from his role in the Alger Hiss affair in the House and was walking very softly indeed. Then, too, his senior colleague from California, Senator William F. Knowland, was surely no friend. Precisely to the contrary, Knowland, highly conservative though he was, was a protegé of the liberal Earl Warren, who even from the pinnacle of his career as chief justice could, and did, unsparingly curse Richard Nixon to most anybody at any private party.

Then, too, Nixon impressed me, and I think many senators, too, from the beginning of his service in the Senate as more nearly a transient visitor than a settled member, a man for whom fate had other, if enigmatic, designs. He had hardly warmed his chair before he found himself ("found himself" is precisely the right term, for he had never supposed the thing would come about) on the 1952 ticket as Eisenhower's running mate for the vice presidency. At any rate, he left no mark in the place where he had been, nor did he really mix in once he returned as the Senate's constitutional presiding officer. As vice president he still went about the Senate with a tentative air, careful not to intrude, careful not to push himself forward, very respectful of the Senate's patriarchs, and obviously longing to be "Downtown," meaning active in the Executive Branch, far more frequently than he was welcomed by Eisenhower's hostile White House staff people. Whether he was around or not was a matter of indifference to the Senate types, who in the Eisenhower years were largely running this country, a not inconsiderable circumstance which I, for one, tried many times to report to the country. I believe I had some luck as a bearer of this message; at least, many of my colleagues followed suit.

Eisenhower himself, who was far more concerned with what he called his "national security arrangements" than with any domestic issue, and who was fortunately more nearly expert in the former than in the latter, was serenely unaware of any home problem unless it rose and struck him smartly in the face. In his years as a serving army officer he had allowed the Democrats of the Senate and House to believe that if only propriety permitted, he would identify himself with their party. I suspect, parenthetically, that he really meant this, just as I am quite certain that had he chosen to play the game differently he could have been nominated and elected as a Democratic president.

I believe Eisenhower had second thoughts about his proper party affiliation because of his late-coming awe of rich men—meaning mostly Republicans—and because he was horrified at the undeniably squalid, if minor, money scandals that the excessively humane Harry Truman allowed to occur within his retinue. In one sense, at least, to be brief about it, Eisenhower was possessed of the authentic Puritan ethic: pecuniary crime was to him the most unspeakable of sins.

He came to office on the most cordial of terms with the Democrats in both houses, and uniquely so with their leaders, Lyndon Johnson in the Senate and Sam Rayburn in the House. Though he had long since cast off the early years of his life as a Texan, preferring a global personal image if tolerating occasional mention of Abilene, Kansas, as his real home town, the president from the moment of taking office began to perform just as he had performed as the supreme Allied commander in the Second World War. That is, he accepted the fact that he was in a war, Cold this time instead of Hot, and that he needed troops wherever he could get them and must above all keep them from fratricidal infighting.

Nobody on either side ever said as much, to be sure, but Eisenhower had not been six months in office before every adult observer in Washington knew that a tacit understanding had been struck between Eisenhower and Congress, especially its upper house. The unuttered understanding was that Eisenhower would do little to try to undo what Roosevelt and

Truman had done in domestic matters and that the Democrats for their part would protect him from the unwelcome pressures of the right-wing Republicans, who had never liked him, never wanted him, and never trusted him.

This was to Johnson and Rayburn, both internationalists (as have been so many southern politicians), a splendid arrangement. Apart from the fact that they wanted the domestic structures of Roosevelt and Truman left alone, they recognized that the country's vital problems lay in foreign policy, a field in which Eisenhower differed in no important respect from the philosophy of the long era of Roosevelt and Truman.

The inevitable consequence of this state of affairs was that the Senate of the United States was elevated to its highest plateau of power in history. Not only was its role in foreign policy mandated by the Constitution, but it had in this case the special (if ad hoc) power given to it in the Johnson-Rayburn-Eisenhower entente. Things would have been somewhat different had Taft lived, for *he*, much the stronger man, might have been directing Eisenhower, most of the time anyway.

Since it surely required no journalistic genius to see what was going on and why, I dug myself in and pivoted my work upon a forum which had both great puissance and a pleasing corporate personality, the Senate. I would have in any case found the place congenial because it was the very core of all that was *human*, whether good-human or bad-human, in all of Washington. "Downtown," including the White House itself (if I dare utter the heresy), was then and is now an appalling bureaucratic bore for a journalist, and certainly no place for a free spirit.

It was only in the Senate that one could mingle with gentlemen, with gentlemen-rogues, and, occasionally, to leaven the mixture, with a few outright, outsized, and unqualified bastards of politics. It was a highly tolerant place, too tolerant compared to the Executive Branch to suit some of my colleagues on "Downtown" news beats. But their standards of comparison were unwittingly beclouded. For while practically everything that went on in and about the Senate was open to the view of any enterprising journalist, so long as he was not

163

looking for tittle-tattle about senatorial sexual mores and the like, a vast lot of what went on in the bureaucracy was—and to this day is—off-limits.

To be sure, the Senate of the Eighties is a far different place from the Senate of the Fifties, of which I wrote in a book called *Citadel*. My old Senate had a full complement of big egos; but on the whole those who thought extremely well of themselves had good reason so to think. Too, it had an entirely adequate quota of headline hunters, but the Senate of the Fifties did it all with a certain grace and a good healthy dash of self-humor. The old Senate was quite unimpressed by television and could take it or leave it. The new Senate has a groveling addiction to the Tube that is painful to behold.

Above all, the Senate in its great days had a sense of national responsibility, notably in foreign and military policy, that has all but disappeared from current life in the Capitol. It was, in short, a forum largely of *big* men; increasingly it has become a forum of littler men. The members of what in *Citadel* I called the Inner Club had certain self-imposed limitations upon demagoguery that rarely exist anymore, and on the whole they believed in Lord Chesterfield's maxim that manners come just below morals in the scale of values. Peculations there were, of course, as there always are in politics; pettiness was extremely rare.

When, for instance, Foster Dulles at the State Department "leaked" to the *New York Times* a set of papers dealing with the Yalta conference between Roosevelt, Churchill, and Stalin, he dealt a series of metaphorical slaps across the face to many Senators who had been yearning to get into those documents. Such an incident in the contemporary climate would lead to loud, self-pitying ululations from Capitol Hill about "Executive arrogance." In the old Senate, which never heard of self-pity, the episode caused heart-burning only among some of the lesser figures. These insistently pressed Senator Walter George of Georgia, as chairman of the Foreign Relations Committee, to order an "investigation" of Dulles's crime against the dignity et cetera of "the Senate of the United States." George was monumentally indifferent, but at length, in order to have some peace, he directed an "inquiry" by the committee. This lasted about fifteen minutes, in closed session, and George emerged to announce that the book was now closed and that he had nothing to add to that observation.

Carl McArdle, a former newspaperman himself, was then Dulles's press officer, and a Senate correspondent demanded of George: "Aren't you going to call Carl McArdle to testify?" "Who?" replied George in astonished incredulity, ending his press conference then and there. To those who understood the Senate, his monosyllable told a long tale indeed. He was saying that his committee (and he regarded it as *his*) had better things to do than to harrass a junior officer for what Foster Dulles had done. He was saying that, come right down to it, Dulles, not the Senate, was responsible for running the State Department. (Currently that is very far from the view in the Senate's New Dispensation.) And he was saying that he was bored with the whole damn thing and didn't care who knew it. There are men in today's Senate who would be capable of calling a second lieutenant to testify of Pentagon villainies.

George's attitude, his automatic rejection of the small and the small-minded, fairly typified the Senate of those distant days. Once, when Harry Truman came to town from his retirement in Independence, Missouri, I went to see him at his hotel and he unloaded upon me his testiness about the way the Democratic leaders were cooperating with Eisenhower. Among other things, Truman, who had been shabbily and small-mindedly treated by Eisenhower during the transition of White House power in 1952, told me: "I am damn sick of seeing these fellows [the Democratic leaders] kissing Eisenhower on both cheeks." It being understood that Truman was speaking for publication, I reported what he had said in the next day's *New York Times*. Lyndon Johnson was deeply distressed, and of course far from happy with me, when I ran onto him that morning in "the President's Room" off the Senate floor. Johnson began to cry out rather piteously at the unfriendly act committed against him by Truman and by me until George interrupted: "Ah now, Lyndon," he said in his great, pipe organ voice, "don't distress yourself so. You're

165

lucky. Knowing Harry, I'm surprised that he didn't say that you are kissing both cheeks of Eisenhower's *ahss*."

A greatly underrated pillar of the Senate, Eugene Millikin of Colorado, was another embodiment of imperturbability and candor. Whenever the president sent up a major message to Congress it was my job and that of my assistants to go about the Senate seeking the "reaction" of members. I made it my policy to refuse to go pencil in hand to senators, knowing that when they knew they were to be quoted directly they would say pompous and utterly predictable things. The message would be "historic" if it was a Republican speaking of Eisenhower, "disappointing" or worse if a Democrat. To try to find out what senators really thought using the direct quotation system was patently ludicrous, producing only pap. One of my colleagues, Charles Trussell, looked upon this, my deviation from procedure, as dangerously outside the proper form.

Upon the occasion of one of Eisenhower's messages, Trussell and I happened simultaneously to approach Millikin. Trussell had his pencil and pad earnestly at the ready and asked Millikin for his comment. "Will you promise, Trussell, to quote me exactly?" boomed Millikin. "Oh, yes," said Trussell. "Very well, then," replied Millikin. "Here is my comment: I didn't listen to the Goddam message; I haven't read the Goddam message, and I don't intend to. And I couldn't care less." Trussell did not file this story, though I begged him to; but even if he had, Millikin would have been wholly untroubled, notwithstanding that he was a member of the Republican leadership group of the Senate.

A great deal of the real work in the Senate of the Fifties was done in places even more remote than committee rooms and subcommittee rooms. Much of it of course was accomplished, most informally, in the carefully segregated Democratic and Republican cloakrooms off the chamber proper. These I could not enter, nor could any other journalist, but among those who could I developed a network of amiable informers who kept me abreast, day by day, of what was going to happen on the Senate floor itself. What was currently going forward on the floor at any given time was easy to keep track of; the *Times* supplied all its Washington correspondents with a United Press teletype service that covered all the routine news extremely well and one could always fall back on it for the obvious stuff.

What I tried to do, in my dispatches for the *Times* and in the book *Citadel*, was to report and comment upon the inner and institutional life of the Senate, and on the subtle evolutions of its consensus on large issues. It goes without saying, I suppose, that my writing was sympathetic, for I *liked* the place. It would have been impossible not to. To some, its enormous respect and affection for Tradition were fusty; the very fustiness, if that was what it was, appealed to me in the way, for one, that the Inns of Court in London had during the war. Nowhere else, as it seemed to me, could I have met and known so diverse a group of men of a likably flawed brilliance in one direction or another. There were among them none of the Mister Cleans of a later political era, and if they were not so loud about their own "ethics" as senators are today, they also were quietly and effectively merciless toward the rare moralizer or sermonizer within their ranks.

When Tom Connally of Texas once observed to me with cheerful tartness that Estes Kefauver was "out running for president with his cock in one hand and the Bible in the other," his was the sort of rough idiom that would no doubt provoke all manner of shrilly righteous protest from the blandly blended and professionally "good" younger members of today's Senate. Nevertheless, in the mores of the old Senate, in which no judgment that was real, adult, and perceptive could be put down merely by flinging at it the word "vulgar," Connally was far more than an acerbic critic. He was putting out a signal, in the most casual and offhand way possible, that the essential Democratic power center of the Senate, a Concurrent Majority that never met except in spirit, had tacitly and by common consent reached the conclusion that one of their colleagues wouldn't do for the presidency.

Though the contrary might reasonably be supposed, this was in no way meant as an indictment of Kefauver's well-known fondness for nubile ladies; nobody objected to *that*, in itself. What Connally was saying was that sustained and jejune hypocrisy was regarded by the Senate leaders as a disability fatal for a contender for the highest office. When he tossed out this highly colloquial line to me he was illustrating precisely the sort of in-house evolution of a Senate consensus to which I have referred, and which a correspondent with a sympathetic eye and ear could apprehend. I stress the word *sympathetic* simply because that quality was a necessary antecedent to grasping the nuances of the place.

Now, I was not able, of course, then and there to inform the readers of the *Times* that Kefauver was not going to make it. For Connally was speaking in confidence and, had I violated his trust, my work and my contributions to my paper would shortly have become as pedestrian and obvious as my UP news ticker. All the same, the incident was highly useful to me and to my career. For, putting Connally's comment together with what Rayburn had told me, I now knew that no matter how many primaries he might win, Estes Kefauver had been so devalued within the Capitol Hill hierarchy that his nomination was profoundly unlikely and his election substantially impossible. I filed it all away for future reference and was thus able, early on, to write with a sense of realism that otherwise I would never have had.

In those old days much of what was truly significant in the Senate (one is tempted to say almost *all* of it) came to light in seemingly haphazard ways; it was available if one knew how to break the code. Nor did it matter whether a journalist's writings were pleasing or displeasing to the hierarchs, so long as he was not an intellectual fraud and so long as he gave no evidence of using his position with malicious intent. For my part, I made unabashed use of my "connections," though being extremely careful never to ask anything for myself as a person as distinguished from a journalist. I was able to serve, for one illustration, as a human bridge between the then very young and raw Hubert Humphrey and the bottled-in-bond southerners who, at every critical juncture, ultimately controlled the operations of the Senate. I had seen Humphrey at the 1948 Democratic convention where, fresh from the office of mayor of Minneapolis, he had forced the adoption of a strong civil-rights plank in the party platform. I should not have been impressed at all but for the fact that this young man really meant what he was saying—as a good handful of "civil-rights leaders" already in the Senate did not, because they preferred a standing issue (endlessly useful among the minority groups) to a legislative solution.

I had never been comfortable with racial injustice in the South, no matter how much I loved my native region. But I had also always been repelled by southern journalists who upon coming North found it useful to sound like Harriet Beecher Stowe and by politicians from whatever region who did nothing but blather earnestly about the problem.

All in all, in a word, I wished Humphrey well from the day he arrived in the Senate. There for a time he managed to get himself thoroughly disliked and locked into a position of ineffectuality because his deeply humanitarian impulses had a way of springing from his voice box with a strongly pietistic tone. So far as I can recall, I never *directly* suggested to him that Manner was a big part of the Message in the Senate, but I did try to nudge his awareness in that direction. More importantly, I carried good words about him to the Senate powerhouses—Lyndon Johnson, Walter George, Richard Russell, Harry Flood Byrd the Elder, and others. Typically, Johnson at once moved in on "ol' Hubert," knowing a promising talent when he saw one, and very soon struck up with him a private friendship as well. George, Russell, and Byrd, who had felt a melancholy sense of outrage at Humphrey's civil-rights activity at the Democratic conventions, at first looked at me, as a self-nominated sponsor of Hubert Horatio Humphrey, rather as three fond uncles might look at a nephew who had committed some unmentionable social solecism at a dinner party in Charleston honoring the memory of Robert E. Lee. They knew, however, that five of my forebears had died in the armies of the Confederacy. And so, as they say in the South, they *understood* me, meaning that they tolerated me as one tolerates an old friend who is a perfect mess in his cups.

Still, time did its work. Russell, the youngest of my three old southern friends, was the first to melt, this because he too concluded that Humphrey really *meant* it. George signaled his conversion only by occasionally halting at Humphrey's desk on the Senate floor and absently peering at its occupant with a vaguely benign look. Byrd was the last holdout, perhaps understandably so since one of Humphrey's first acts in his brash early days in the Senate had been to attempt (and calamitously fail) to have abolished a small watchdog committee over federal spending of which Byrd was creator and chairman. Byrd finally came around not because he ever agreed with anything Humphrey said but because, as he eliptically put it to me, "You know, old fellow, you may be right that Humphrey isn't such a bad sort, after all."

Back of it all, however, back of Humphrey's rise from near-pariah to liked and even beloved Senate colleague, was his success in schooling himself to be serious without being solemn, and committed to a cause without being pompous about it. The trouble with the present Senate is that it is too moralistic, too multisyllabic, too "meaningful", and too ridden with "press secretaries" and canned speeches. Alben Barkley and his peers needed no prepared speech. Barkley could do a better job with the English language strictly impromptu, after flying in at three o'clock in the morning red-eyed from some dreary lecture in Wheeling, West Virginia (to which he had gone to earn fees to support an invalid wife) than can any contemporary senator's ghostwriter.

As it happened, my period of active service at the Senate encompassed the incubation of three successive presidents from within its membership: John Kennedy, Lyndon Johnson, and Richard Nixon.

CHAPTER TEN

JOHN KENNEDY actually began the long climb upward in 1956 with a determined (and with what seemed then an improbable) attempt to get the vice presidential nomination. Adlai Stevenson, blowing a characteristically uncertain trumpet once he had been given the top nomination, announced that he would "leave it to the convention" to choose his running mate. This threw the Stevenson rank and file into turmoil, and Sam Rayburn, the convention's chairman, into a kind of resigned rage. Rayburn ever since 1952 had planted his squat bulk resolutely against the attempts of Estes Kefauver of Tennessee to become president.

Before the political and journalistic contingent had left Washington for the Chicago convention I had gone to Rayburn's hideaway office at what he called "drinkin' time" and asked him whether Kefauver, who had done extremely well in the primaries, was not going to beat Stevenson at Chicago. "No," he had replied. Why not? "Because, by God, I won't let him," Rayburn had growled. As presiding officer he would be in position to interpret the rules at the convention. He meant to use, and in due course he did use, those rules to make certain that Kefauver never came close to the presidential nomination.

Now, at Chicago, here was Estes Kefauver hammering again at the gate, this time seeking the vice presidency, since Stevenson already had the main prize in hand. The scene was reminiscent of one of the oldest of all newspaper jokes, wherein a young reporter, dispatched to cover a great flood on the Mississippi, telegraphs his home office: "All is confusion; can send nothing."

Stevenson's abdication of the traditional leader's obligation to choose the vice presidential running mate instantly transformed into a real possibility what had been only a somewhat wistful dream by Kennedy of receiving a nomination for national office. His people went to work with the ruthless energy that would always characterize his organization. They also quite unintentionally did a good deal to diminish in advance the shibboleth that he was to destroy in 1960—that a Roman Catholic could not be elected president or, by extension, vice president.

This bonus was brought about because Kefauver, though he was from the border state of Tennessee, was not welcome in the southern caucus in the Senate. At Chicago, then, the southern delegations were put up against it: support Kennedy, Catholic and all, or see the despised Kefauver ascend to within "a heartbeat of the presidency." Most of the Dixie people did not long hesitate. Deeply influenced by the Senate, southern delegations on the first roll call began casting their votes for "John F. Kennedy from the *greeatt* State of Massachusetts." The convention had an electric device to keep the tally; at the *New York Times* press bench I kept our own. By my count, Kennedy actually won the nomination; the electronic counter gave it to Kefauver, and that was that.

I saw Kennedy briefly after it was all over and found him, as always, wryly philosophic and outwardly determinedly smiling. He told my wife in private candor that he was "heartbroken." Even then, however, he was thinking long thoughts about "the Catholic issue," as was his father, Old Joe Kennedy. He retired in good order from the field, making no enemies in the process, and went back to the Senate bearing that curious stamp of not-quite-a-loser.

We had been friends since his days as a freshman member of the House, which he had entered along with Richard Nixon. I had admired his work on the House Labor Committee while his seniors were putting together the Taft-Hartley labor act. As a young member of the House Labor Committee sitting far down the table, he was refreshing in that, though he came from a labor state and district, he accepted no ordering about from the labor leaders, turning to them instead a soft voice and smile in which there was always a touch of irony.

I saw a fair amount of Kennedy socially, too, particularly after he came to the Senate. In fact, my wife and I, along with others, had dinner with him just before he married Jacqueline Bouvier. Though he was in many ways the very model of the rich and privileged young sophisticate, he was, that night, as nervous as any prospective bridegroom in a Victorian novel.

As a senator he established a model to be followed later by his youngest brother, Teddy, of smiling deference to his elders and a quietly persistent campaign to win the friendship if not necessarily the actual political approval of the southern Democrats, even at the cost of risking a degree of displeasure from the northern liberal Democrats. My unusually close journalistic and personal relationship with the southerners, who formed in fact the unofficial Board of Governors of the Senate Club, was not wholly unconnected, I was aware, with John Kennedy's markedly favorable view of me as a political journalist. I had good southern "connections." Nevertheless, I thought then and think now that our friendship stood in good part on a genuinely personal footing, as would later be the case with Ted Kennedy, if never quite with the middle brother, Robert. John and Edward Kennedy, products of a Boston version of Tammany Hall, had an instinctive empathy, as had Tammany before its effective demise, with the southern wing in politics. Perhaps they knew, as Jim Rowe once remarked, that the Irish and the southerners have historically made common cause in Washington far more often than they have been in contention.

For many years I have reflected from time to time on the reasons for this odd compatibility, beginning long ago when I was a young AP reporter covering Tammany in New York. The nearest thing to an explanation that has occurred to me, as a distinctly amateur psychologist, is that the two sets had one atavistic quality in common: both had similar ancestral memories of communal injustices and hardships on the way up. As for the southern Anglos, their forebears had had to climb up over the harsh hurdle left by Reconstruction. As for the Irish, *their* forebears, only two generations back from, say, John Kennedy, had had to endure the social condescensions and religious prejudices of the Anglo culture of the eastern seaboard. I once tried out this notion on John Kennedy; but he was atypically reticent about it, saying only, "You might have something there," and then quickly turning the conversation elsewhere.

I should never have dreamed of putting my notion to Robert Kennedy, who was a very different man indeed from his brothers John and Edward. John Kennedy brought him into public life by way of the Senate. Robert first served as an eager aide to Senator Joseph McCarthy, whom his elder brother always regarded as an unsatisfactory sort of Irishman, and later as a staff assistant to a committee headed by Senator John McClellan of Arkansas which was investigating labor racketeering. Because I had first known Robert Kennedy as a very junior participant, and in such roles as these, I always tended to underrate him, though not, I think, ever to misunderstand him. He had a fire-in-the-belly attitude that deeply troubled John, who saw all of life with a certain ironic detachment in which, as far as politics was concerned, there was little room for much loving and no room for any hating. Bobby, quite unlike brothers John and Ted and also unlike father Joe, for that matter, was fond of the southerners only long enough to use them on his way up.

McClellan, for illustration, as a powerful figure on the Senate Judiciary Committee, was enormously helpful to Robert Kennedy in early 1961 in bringing about a flatteringly swift Senate confirmation of his appointment by his brother, then president, to be attorney general. Indeed, McClellan, Senator Sam Ervin of North Carolina, and other Dixie types rushed the nomination through on a wave of paternalistic affection for Bobby over which John Kennedy smiled in enormous relief when I chanced to see him in the White House a day or two after the fact. The president had, in fact, been deeply embar-

174

rassed when, as he told me that day, immediately after the election of 1960, Bobby had demanded the Justice Department for his prize. A good many people who knew John Kennedy well had been astonished at the appointment, thinking it far too much a manifestation of the operations of what was just beginning to be called, partly in affection and partly in censure, Kennedy's "Irish Mafia."

I myself was by sheer chance involved to some slight extent in this episode, if "involved" is not too portentous a term. In the hiatus between the election and the inauguration I was down in Mexico along with others, as I mentioned earlier, and eventually my wife, June, and I wound up in Acapulco. Bobby and Ethel Kennedy, among other members of the clan, were down there, too. June and I gave a beach party (at which Bobby introduced me to the dubious delights of touch football on the sand) and he and I fell, naturally, to talking politics. He told me what he wanted from his brother—the attorney generalship—and flattered me by asking for my "advice." "Good God, *no*," was my reply. "They'll eat the president up if you insist on going into the Cabinet." He only smiled.

The thing troubled me for more reasons than one. While as a Senate correspondent I had been neither a Bobby-intimate nor an especially interested Bobby-watcher, I thought that his unfitness for what should be at least the even-handed and judicially-minded job of running the Justice Department was too obvious for words. Actually, as a senator, Jack Kennedy had more than once been privately discomfited and troubled by Bobby's punitive zeal, first in support of Joseph McCarthy and later in aid of John McClellan's shotgun assaults in an investigation which, while undeniably hitting some richly deserving human targets, was also subtly putting black marks on labor in general.

Now, with Robert Kennedy as the new attorney general, the embarrassment for the president was doubly painful. For when the great test had come in the Senate on the motion to condemn McCarthy, John Kennedy had not voted. To be sure, he had had a good excuse—he was in bed and in traction at the time, with the bitterly painful back injury he had suffered as a

175

PT boat commander in the war. As a matter of fact, I called on him while he was in this condition and there was no question in my mind (though I did not go there to "investigate" him) that he was indeed disabled. All the same, he *had* said neither nay nor aye to the censure; nothing could change that fact. And the Stevenson-Eleanor Roosevelt wing of his party circulated a cynical witticism that Kennedy's book *Profiles in Courage* had been written by a man whose profile was higher than his courage.

The fact that Kennedy was not recorded on the McCarthy censure issue was long to pursue him. Indeed, Lyndon Johnson used it against Kennedy in the 1960 Democratic convention in Los Angeles when these two became locked in a struggle for the presidential nomination. This was fair comment. But Johnson's people, if not he himself, also strongly suggested that Kennedy's father, Joseph, had been pro-Nazi, and this was neither permissible nor sensible. The consequence was an irredeemable bitterness not in John Kennedy but rather in his brother Bobby which was to have incalculably damaging effects upon Johnson for all the rest of his political life, not excluding his time in the presidency.

Johnson himself never told me as much but I have always thought that he allowed himself, or perhaps simply panicked himself into, a kind of personal attack on an adversary that was wholly uncharacteristic of his ordinary methods as a national politician. Normally he believed in simply talking up Lyndon Johnson, not in talking down the other fellow. My conclusion that the Los Angeles episode was an aberration, and my suspicion that it might well have arisen from one of those extremely rare instances in which Johnson forwent his own intuitions for those of others, was based in part on a conversation early on in 1960 with John B. Connally. At lunch in the Mayflower Hotel in Washington, Connally, at that time a Johnson intimate, both startled and annoyed me by announcing in hortatory tones that "we" *had* to do something very quickly to stop John Kennedy by "going after" the record of his father.

I had no intention whatever of becoming any part of a Johnson apparatus. Our friendship was, and would to the end remain, purely personal. Professionally, I went my independent way, as of course did he. Connally had misunderstood the nature of the relationship (he was only one of a cast of thousands, so to speak, who ultimately did so) and had mentally put me with himself on the Johnson "team." I therefore straightened out Connally's thinking rather briskly; or at least I thought I did. I remarked that I didn't "have" to do anything, that Joe Kennedy was not running for any office, and that John Kennedy had no form of responsibility for anything Joe Kennedy had done. I said, as I recall it, that the kind of "gut" politics Connally was proposing was not only highly unattractive to me but in all likelihood would in the end do Lyndon Johnson no good at all. I added that no matter the outcome of the Democratic convention, Johnson and Kennedy would still have to live in the same party.

For whatever reason, Johnson at Los Angeles *did* create an implacable enemy in Robert Kennedy. John Kennedy, for his part, wasted no time or emotion on the matter, perhaps simply because he too knew that he and Johnson had to live in the same political party. The "drama" of Kennedy's selection of Johnson to be his running mate has been more than adequately celebrated in dozens of colorful "inside stories." What happened was not only natural but almost inevitable, considering the highly rational and pragmatic nature of both these politicians. Kennedy's nomination for president was brought about by big city and largely Roman Catholic party bosses, Richard Daley of Chicago prominent among them. And, coolly estimating his position afterwards, Kennedy realized that the tableau presented to the country of so much raw urban Catholic power might so alienate non-urban Protestants as to revive the very "Catholic issue" that he had surmounted in the primary campaigns. He therefore called upon Johnson, a member of the fundamentalist Protestant Church of Christ and a man of rural roots, to help redress the balance by going on the ticket.

The real "mystery" was not that Kennedy had offered Johnson the nomination but rather that Johnson had agreed to take it. After all, he was still majority leader of the Senate. His reelection from Texas had been assured through a special act of the legislature permitting him to run for two posts at the same time. He told me that he had accepted because Kennedy had calmly told him that if he refused, the presidential ticket would lose and Johnson would rightly be blamed publicly by the Democratic party—and personally by John F. Kennedy.

Though one or two other journalists played some honest broker's roles in putting Kennedy and Johnson on the same ticket, I myself had nothing to do with it. Two years before, I had left the *Times* to become an internationally syndicated Washington columnist for the United Feature Syndicate, and also a regular essayist for *Harper's Magazine.* My syndicated column was prospering, appearing then in about 175 papers in this country and in perhaps a dozen overseas, these later memorably including the *Japan Times* in Tokyo, the most faithful foreign "outlet" I ever had.

My decision at Los Angeles to stay out of the kingmaking process had, in short, nothing to do with any fear that I would lose "clients" within the press. Of "clients" I had plenty, and month by month was getting more. In fact, one of my reasons for leaving the *Times*—which was a risky business for a fifty-two-year-old journalist, cutting loose from a paper famous for "job security," with no way to project whether the new syndicated column would survive—was simply that I wanted to be wholly my own man. I carried this ambition pretty far, I might add. Much to the distress of my syndicate, I informed its president, Laurence Rutman, and its sales manager, Harry Gilburt, that I would attend *no* conventions of newspaper editors or publishers to point up my availability, though most of my competitors were busy each year in these spring rites. I also asked Rutman and Gilburt to withhold all letters to me from client editors, whether written in praise or in condemnation of my work. "It is my job to write the column and I will accept full responsibility for its quality, good or poor as it may be. But it is your job to sell it and distribute it. I am not going around to the editors and publishers like a traveling salesman carrying a brief case." There is no question that they thought me a rare kind of fool, but they were kind enough to respect my wishes, and the pain they felt they manfully kept pretty well to themselves.

So Los Angeles in 1960 presented to me the first opportunity as a full-fledged, certified editorialist to pitch in vehemently for or against some presidential aspirant or another. I abstained for several reasons. In the first place I had, then as now, a strong native preference for exploring issues rather than men; and any political convention is the very last place for such as that. In the second place, I was genuinely fond of both major contenders at Los Angeles, Johnson and Kennedy. For though my friendship with Johnson was much the older, that with Kennedy was no light or trivial thing. In the third place, I had only a few months before done, strictly out of a sense of duty, a thing I never liked to do—I had attacked a third presidential aspirant, Senator Stuart Symington of Missouri, in personal terms. This I had done not in my syndicated column but rather in my regular space in *Harper's*, in a piece called "Symington: The Last Choice." It was not typical work for me, and I didn't enjoy a line of it. The circumstances, however, were compelling.

At the onset of 1960 it seemed to me that Kennedy and Johnson might well so wound each other at the convention as to open the way for Symington, a man nobody hated, to slip into the nomination. This I thought would be utterly disastrous. I had closely observed Symington for years in the Senate and while he was an amiable, decent, and highly personable man, he wholly lacked the guts to be president of the United States. He was the sort of fellow who could speak to the CIO in the morning, to great applause, and the Chamber of Commerce in the afternoon, to great applause.

So I had already involved myself in the presidential context to a degree and in a way that I did not relish, having done it simply because I thought *some* writer had to. Moreover, I had done a service, though this was not my intention, to both Kennedy and Johnson in helping to cripple the third man in the race. Johnson never orally referred to the *Harper's* piece; he only rolled his eyes. Running into me shortly after it came out, Kennedy was quite forthright. "God," he said to me, "I'm glad you did that piece, though if you ever quote me I'll put you on my shit list for the rest of your life. Yeah, sure, I know I am a party in interest. But beyond all that, that guy [Symington]

179

simply has got to be stopped. I honestly don't see how I could vote for him *myself* if he should ever get the nomination. He just isn't up to it. And, Christ, even us politicians have to have *some* regard for the interests of the country."

Symington himself never mentioned my hostile essay to me. But when I ran into him after its publication and for years afterward, he turned upon me, every time we met, a sad, reproachfully *forgiving* face that was harder to bear than a good, cursing attack would have been. I somehow felt guilty even though common sense told me that I had done a job that, while harsh, was both just and in the public interest. Far better had Symington roundly attacked me, as Estes Kefauver had done when, in the book *Citadel*, I denounced his abuse of the Senate's function of inquiry in putting on a television spectacular in a klieg-lit "crime investigation" that served to give him what is called national "name recognition" when he first set out to try to become president.

My first meeting with Kefauver after the appearance of *Citadel* came at a dinner party at the home of Senator Lister Hill of Alabama. Soon after I arrived at Hill's house, along with my wife, June, Kefauver turned up with his wife, Nancy. Pausing only long enough to gulp down his first drink, Kefauver glowered across the sitting room at me and said very loudly that my book was lousy. I had quickly conferred with myself when I saw who my fellow guest was to be and had concluded that no matter what he said I would make no rejoinder. After all, I had already had my say—in *Citadel*—and Kefauver was surely entitled to his. I therefore stood mute, as the lawyers say, all through the evening, insofar as both the book and Kefauver were concerned. I never replied in any way to his several attacks upon my opus. At length, he tired of the exercise and before the party broke up we had a drink together at the insistence of Lister Hill. My younger daughter, Victoria, and Kefauver's daughter, Diane, were later close school friends.

My observation of politics had taught me that there are times when silence is far more effective than speech—even in the Senate, for a paradox. This maxim was surely part of John Kennedy's technique. As a senator he spoke only rarely, and almost never, to my recollection on any trivial or parochial subject. He thus was able to campaign against Richard Nixon in 1960 unencumbered by any excessive burden of past rhetoric and, even more importantly, unbloodied by any unnecessary past feuding with Senate colleagues.

In the campaign I took a line as a columnist of only quiet support for the Kennedy-Johnson ticket. This comparative reticence sprang partly from an aversion to shouting in print, partly from some anxiety as to whether Kennedy had enough mature experience for the presidency, and partly from distaste at the theatrics of some of the more extreme Kennedy partisans, a distaste felt by Kennedy himself and expressed by him in private. If Kennedy ever felt any resentment at the limited nature of my backing, he never once indicated it. To the contrary, he always welcomed me to the White House in his time. I made sparing use of my entree, however, to avoid intrusiveness and because I assumed that the method of osmosis, of largely waiting for information to come to me, would continue to work as it had done in the past. In point of fact, it *did* work. And because I had not been constantly knocking at the door, I was always able to see the president when I really and urgently needed to do so.

Kennedy bore the mantle of the office with less discernible self-consciousness than any other president I ever knew, with the possible exception of Harry Truman. It was a special treat, almost a joy, to lunch with him (something I did only occasionally) because he could let down easily and naturally, without ever letting down the dignity of the place that he held. He had an extraordinary memory of even the trivial preferences of a guest (he remembered, perhaps from his own visits as a senator to my house, my preference for Jack Daniels whiskey) and a good capacity for a deprecating self-mockery. Once he dismisssed as "all that jazz" the strenuous and continuous efforts of some of his White House staff to present him to the country as a high-domed intellectual. Again, when we were idly talking of Barry Goldwater and of Kennedy's own days in the Senate, he observed with a quizzical smile: "Old Barry was in here the other day and was shown into the oval office while I was outside—in the john, as a matter of fact. When I walked in, he was sitting in my chair, in a kind of pensive way. I walked up behind him, put my hands on his shoulders and said: 'Barry, you can have this fucking job any time you want it, as far as I am concerned.' " The incident occurred during one of those "Berlin crises" that were more or less endemic in his time.

And when he was in trouble with business for having denounced a steel price rise and for having allowed Robert Kennedy to send out FBI agents in the middle of the night to inquire into what steel executives were saying to correspondents, he was widely reported to have said: "My father always told me that businessmen were sons of bitches." I had an appointment with John Kennedy some days afterward and he greeted me thus when I walked into his office: "Can you believe that I, John F. Kennedy, could *possibly* have said that those sons of bitches *are* sons of bitches?" Though Kennedy never said so, I believed then and believe now that he had not in fact authorized Bobby Kennedy to go as far as he did, and that he actually was deeply chagrined about such a use of the FBI. My impression, from this and other episodes, was that President Kennedy became only Jack Kennedy when Robert Kennedy was involved and was either unable or unwilling to put the rein on his younger brother.

Certainly, he was visibly uncomfortable when he told me, some days ahead of the announcement, that Ted Kennedy was going to run for the Senate from Massachusetts. Still, the president was very much a president and was quite unamused when McGeorge Bundy, referring to Ted's ambitions, later made some jocular reference to the possibility that there might be a surfeit of Kennedys in Washington.

With Kennedy—as with the two other presidents whom I knew very well, that is, Johnson and Nixon—I maintained a relationship of total confidentiality in this sense: I kept no diary, no notes, no aides-mémoire of any kind. I sustained this policy because two of them, Kennedy and Johnson, dealt with me in great trust, so much so that I often deliberately tried to put out of my consciousness things that had been told to me in the highest of secrecy. I did so because I feared that I might some time and somewhere unwittingly break a presidential confidence. That used to be the gravest sin a national journalist could commit.

I suppose that in the present mores of journalism this attitude would be regarded as at best quaint and at worst a betrayal of "the people's right to know." For my part, I believed then and believe now that, quite apart from any consideration of ethics or taste, mine was the right professional course to follow. I *could*, for example, have written, with complete accuracy, that all was not well between John and Jacqueline Kennedy, just as I could have written more than a year ahead of time that Johnson was not going to seek reelection in 1968. But suppose for the moment that I had written either of these two stories. The first consequence—again, ethics and taste aside—would have been not only to destroy my personal code as a journalist but also to close forever an enormously useful journalistic pipeline, to use a cliché term, into the White House. Other unacceptable consequences would have been involved, too. As to Kennedy, I would have broken a confidence and injured a sorely pressed world leader had I written of his shocked anger when Jacqueline Kennedy took herself off to cruise, along with others, on the yacht of the Croesus who ultimately became her second husband, Aristotle Onassis. What price such a "beat"? That kind of journalism was not my kind and never could have been. And had I disclosed prematurely Johnson's private determination not to run again, I should have broken a poignantly given trust, befouled a friendship of half a lifetime, and left this country with a lamed leader at a time of immense national trial.

It may be that "hard-nosed" Investigative Reporting is the wave of both the present and the future. Certainly it is the way to best-selling books, Hollywood movie contracts, and the esteem of the "celebrities" of this world. Any journalist who plays the game the old-fashioned way will surely never get rich. But then, look at it this way: while a Jack Anderson or certainly a Barbara Walters makes more money in one year than a Walter Lippmann could ever earn in ten, there was only *one* Walter Lippmann. There are, or will be, many Barbara Walterses, many Jack Andersons and Bob Woodwards.

There is a journalism of theater or of soap opera—bad guys

pursued and pursued again in print, huge audiences charmed and lulled five nights a week in their sitting rooms by the capsules and captions of TV news. There are political journalists and there are journalistic politicians. And then there is a journalism that is strictly—well, *journalistic*. If one assumes as I do that its purpose is to serve neither as a punitive force nor as entertainment, but rather as a source of information and opinion, then this Old Journalism had much to recommend it. At any rate, it is the kind of journalism I have always practiced. And, say whatever one may choose about it, it is the only kind of journalism that can put a correspondent into genuine communication, beyond the superficial level, with those who ultimately run the affairs of this country and, to some extent, of much of the Western world.

The methods of the New Journalism often reflect an oversimplification. Should not the journalist approach the mighty in a spirit of total independence and healthy skepticism? Of course he should. But the New Journalism assumes that the so-called adversary relationship between press and politicians requires not just tough-mindedness on the part of the journalist but a state of outright and automatic enmity. This notion extends the obligations upon journalism that are implicit in the First Amendment into a position of extremism which, to counterparaphrase something the unfortunate Barry Goldwater said in 1964, is a vice and never a virtue. It is a vice because it presupposes that the media (I dislike that ad-man's term but confess that at times it is irreplaceable) are by definition constantly in a state of secular grace and are the people's uniquely righteous protector from government. This is simply not so and the profession shames itself whenever it arrogates to itself so much piety. Editors as individuals know this to be the case and some of them have designated staff members to keep watch upon the watchers, that is, to function as critics of the performance of the papers on which they serve. Alas, editors collectively in their annual meetings tend to abandon all self-criticism, to no-bill all complaints against the press, and in short to demand the novel right to try and to acquit their own industry, claiming this unique privilege by virtue of the

First Amendment. In the Great Depression of the Thirties some newspaper publishers even invoked that amendment to justify their claim that newspaper carrier boys were really "Little Merchants" and thus should be exempted from the age-hour provisions of Franklin Roosevelt's National Recovery Administration.

A more serious disability of the New Journalism is that its supposition that public men are guilty until proved innocent alienates it from full human contact with those who make the news. No president or senator, for example, is really going to open his mind and purposes and actions—that is to say, the real news—to any correspondent who is obsessed with the idea that he is in all probability dealing with a crook or a rogue. In the early years of the television show "Meet the Press" I was frequently on its panel of inquiring reporters at the invitation of Lawrence Spivak. I lost interest, however, when Spivak made it increasingly plain that most of all he wanted rhetorical blood on the floor, of either the interviewee or the interviewers. He believed, and said, that a journalist who really knew an interviewee would surely "like" him too much. Under this extraordinary theory, of course, the ideal would be a correspondent psychologically qualified by reason of knowing no important public figure at all. But reporting and commentary beyond the level of paraphrasing handouts are necessarily based upon human contacts, which is not at all to say that a servant-master relationship exists between journalist and politician.

My own relationship with President Kennedy may illustrate the point. In his tragically short tenure I was often critical of his administration on impersonal grounds, but the closest he ever came to resentment was a wry observation he made to Lyndon Johnson, his vice president: "Bill White is kind to you and to me but he is against *us*." By "us" he meant the Kennedy Administration as a whole. He was remarkably perceptive in this judgment. Looking back now over old clippings of my long-forgotten syndicated columns written during Kennedy's first year in office recalls to me that my support for Kennedy was almost totally in the field of foreign affairs. This was perhaps partly because on domestic matters he was not able to accomplish much in Congress anyhow; the great victories on civil rights and social welfare to which the Kennedy name is indelibly attached among American blacks were actually to come later under the administration of Lyndon Johnson. Primarily, I was concerned to do what I could to help this president, a Democrat whom I liked very much, in almost the same way that I had sought to help a Republican president, Dwight Eisenhower, for whom I had respect but no personal affection.

As I read these faded relics of a time long gone (a process that stirs a warm nostalgia), relics mostly cut from the *Washington Star*, refreshed memory informs me that I was in fact seeing the president more frequently than I had thought throughout 1961, the year of his first trials of strength. These meetings were indicated by the code terms then common to journalists who were able to see a president on condition that they not say so outright and that he never be directly quoted. "To talk to the President is to . . ." occurs in a piece from April reporting the chill loneliness he felt toward the end of 1961 after a series of foreign crises. There had been the failure of the Bay of Pigs invasion of Castro's Cuba. There had been Nikita Khrushchev's deliberate test of Kennedy's nerve in that most shuddery ever of our perennial Berlin crises, leading to the August showdown in which Kennedy sent troop reinforcements and Vice President Lyndon Johnson into Berlin to confront the Russians head-on. Kennedy, in a word, had faced up to the imminent possibility of nuclear war over Berlin, as in another year he would do over Cuba. Here, as I wrote, was no longer a "young" president but rather a man suddenly looking much older and a man from whom all real gaiety had forever departed.

It was of this president that I wrote favorably and sympathetically, but not of the President Kennedy who handled domestic matters. As to these latter, I was later berating Kennedy for risking a break in the bipartisan consensus that had supported him on Berlin by his partisan maneuvers designed to bring a big Democratic majority into Congress in 1962. *This* Kennedy so annoyed ex-President Eisenhower, now out of of-

186

fice, that he attacked the Democrats with incomparably more heat than ever he had done in office. (Moreover this same Kennedy-the-party-leader said to me in private that he himself did not relish what he had done.)

Before leaving the White House, Eisenhower had been habitually and majestically nonpartisan, scorning mere "politicians"—among whom he definitely included a young senator named John Kennedy—and giving a minimum of grudging support to his fellow Republicans in Congress in their various struggles for reelection. Once, all but dragged before television cameras to make a speech for Republican congressional campaigners, he angrily observed afterward before a handful of reporters that he was damn glad this partisan clackety-clack was over. On another occasion the general made even more memorably obvious his displeasure with his role as party leader. Leonard Hall, then the Republican national chairman, told me of this. Hall, after a wait of some weeks, had finally been allowed to see Eisenhower in order to make a guarded and deferential complaint that far too many Democrats and far too few Republicans were being given good jobs in the Eisenhower Administration. Old-pro Hall was struck dumb by Eisenhower's angry reply: "Hall, I believe you are trying to get me into *politics!*"

When next I saw Kennedy, after my column denouncing him for endangering his foreign policy by playing some congressional "politics" of his own, I thought to turn away his wry and controlled wrath at me by relating Hall's anecdote. Kennedy, who was sometimes in wonder and awe at Eisenhower's atypical (and to Kennedy incredible) approach to both politics and public office, repaid me in kind. He recalled that some time after his own inauguration as president he had paid a courtesy call on Eisenhower at his Gettysburg estate, where the former president was living in a certain undeniable splendor. "My God," said Kennedy, rolling his eyes, "the gifts that man has accepted you wouldn't believe. If Lyndon or I had ever done that we would have been impeached." I then told Kennedy yet one more true story in what was by that time a large (and still growing) golden treasury of Eisenhowerana. This had been given to me by Senator James Duff of Pennsylvania, a red-headed millionaire politician who had been one of the earliest of Eisenhower's supporters. I had just asked Duff why the president so often had only wealthy men and women to dinner at the White House. It was simple, said Duff. Eisenhower had earned about a quarter of a million dollars from his postwar books. A group of Republicans who already were looking upon him as a presidential candidate for their party called upon him in his office at Columbia University and asked to be allowed to invest his money in Wall Street. They did, and Eisenhower wound up, said Duff, with perhaps two million dollars. Ever since, Duff went on, the president had believed that rich men *had* to be "very smart."

This tale, too, cheered Kennedy up no end; for at this point, as I have said earlier, he was rather fed up with the same rich types of whom Eisenhower was, quite innocently and honorably, such a fond admirer.

Nevertheless, Kennedy always managed to keep a certain comity with Eisenhower (apart from the occasional partisan blows they swapped almost perforce at congressional election time) in order to retain his predecessor's enormously useful backing in foreign affairs. Actually, I saw in Kennedy's time and even more intimately in Johnson's time that there was one supremely elevated "Establishment" in this country of which, so far as I can recall, none of my colleagues ever wrote. This was an informal club that was certainly the most exclusive in the world—the Club of American Presidents, past and present. Beginning with Harry Truman, those who had served before stood with the man currently in the post whenever and wherever this country was in trouble abroad. In every ordeal of Kennedy's involving foreign crisis, Eisenhower came forward to help, as Truman had come forward to help Eisenhower, and as both Truman and Eisenhower came forward to help Lyndon Johnson in his time.

Personal circumstances permitted me to see the operation of this extraordinary sort of old-boys' club close up—very close up in both the Kennedy and Johnson administrations—and I was deeply moved and deeply influenced as a journalist by it. I came to realize that all those who occupied the White House must draw the sharpest possible line between domestic and foreign issues, the former being designated an area of permissible and sometimes even obligatory interparty fighting, and the latter absolutely off limits to it. During the transfer of power in 1952, Eisenhower had snubbed Truman almost brutally and Truman repaid this conduct by backing Eisenhower faithfully "beyond the water's edge." It was remembered by every politician that Truman had been scornfully critical in 1960 of Kennedy's presidential ambitions, as too fervid and much too early, but Truman never failed to answer the alarm bell on foreign policy when Kennedy chose to ring it.

One Sunday night at the White House, where my wife and I were dining with the Johnsons, the president, who as a matter of course kept in the closest touch on foreign relations with both Truman and Eisenhower, told me ecstatically that Eisenhower had been over that afternoon and had been "wonderful" about the impenetrable problem of Vietnam. I asked wryly what the general had said, then, about the "Great Society"? Johnson laughed ruefully and said: "Goddam it, don't bring that up!"

I myself had had an experience with Eisenhower that had sharply illustrated how presidents feel about attacks on them, or support of them, in foreign affairs. In my monthly column in *Harper's* I had done a piece suggesting that Eisenhower had never truly been a soldier, in the way of a Patton, a Bradley, or a Montgomery, though as commander-in-chief in the European Theater he had of course been much more. The instant the thing appeared I was banished from the White House, not literally but effectively so. For months not even James Hagerty, the president's press secretary, would return my telephone calls. At length, however, Eisenhower got into trouble over the disclosure that the United States had been operating a so-called "spy plane," the famous U-2, over the Soviet Union. Khrushchev used the incident, it may be recalled, to cancel a projected summit conference and in general to accuse Eisenhower of high crimes against the peace. Our State Department spokesman got entangled in a net of lies disclaiming this and denying that until President Eisenhower himself was forced to go on television and concede that we had indeed put the Soviet Union under surveillance and that he had ordered it.

While many journalists were hitting the president hard over what they believed to be a reckless sacrifice of coexistence, I took the line that he had done not only what he had a right to do but also what he had an inherent obligation to do, as the man ultimately responsible for the security of the United States. Almost instantly the barriers were lifted at the White House, and on my next birthday the president sent me an autographed photo warmly inscribed: "For William S. White, with admiration and best wishes." The president had not theretofore felt toward me the one, nor expressed to me the other.

Years afterward, while he was president, I told Lyndon Johnson of this incident, and he glumly observed: "Any guy in this office will always have a place in his heart for any other guy who helps him on foreign affairs, no matter how much they may differ about anything and everything else."

Certainly this was true of Kennedy. After the failure of the Bay of Pigs invasion of Cuba, I was weekending in Virginia with Vice President and Mrs. Johnson at a country place not far from Glen Ora, at which President Kennedy himself was spending the weekend. Kennedy got in touch with Johnson (or perhaps it was the other way round) and Johnson, my wife, and I drove over to Glen Ora. Kennedy, in chino pants and a sweat shirt, was mooning about at the edge of the unused swimming pool while Jacqueline Kennedy was entertaining Caroline in a pony cart. The president met Johnson and me with a rather wan smile and then drew me away with him back to the swimming pool, leaving Johnson on his own. This, by the way, was a gracious act, one of many traded between these two men, notwithstanding many reports of "trouble" between them. It was meant to underline the fact that Johnson was not to be involved in the Bay of Pigs disaster since he had been out of Washington during the period of decision.

Kennedy, as I later wrote, was in a state of shock and acute sadness and plainly wanted a friendly ear. He told me in detail about all that had gone wrong in the invasion, tears on his face when he recalled the list of casualties, and said that the armed services chief of staff and the CIA had let him down. He asked me whether I thought he should order a public investigation of who had failed at what and I replied that I thought he could hardly do a more vexatious and harmful thing. The Republicans, I suggested, would see him as attempting to "get out from under" while in point of fact there was no possible way that he could, as commander in chief, fail to accept *all* responsibility. He agreed, and within a day or so publicly took all the blame upon himself. I tell this story not to suggest that I was some high advisor to the president or that he would not have reached the same conclusion on his own. I tell it only to illustrate again the great difference between presidential reactions to criticism on domestic and on foreign affairs. I had never much supported Kennedy on home issues; I had never failed to support him on foreign issues. That was why I was at Glen Ora that day.

Again, when in a later year Kennedy and his advisers in "Ex-Com" (a crisis committee he set up, with Robert Kennedy and Lyndon Johnson among its members) decided to risk nuclear war to force the Russians to remove their missiles from Cuba, I was again a beneficiary of the president's trust. He asked Lyndon Johnson and Senator Richard Russell, then chairman of the Senate Armed Services Committee and a participant at Ex-Com meetings, to tell me everything that had been said in the climactic discussions that brought about what Secretary of State Dean Rusk called the "eyeball-to-eyeball" confrontation with the Soviet Union. Johnson, Russell, Mrs. Johnson, and I lunched that day at the Elms, the grand house occupied by the Johnsons during his vice presidency. Johnson, occasionally reminded of one point or another by Russell, unfolded the whole heart-stopping tale to me, saying in substance at the end of the lunch that the next twenty-four hours would bring a period of "maximum danger" of a third world war. Russell was on the whole moody and withdrawn. Though he offered no word of criticism of the administration's approach, he made it clear that he had recommended an American invasion of Cuba using infantry troops to make absolutely certain that no Soviet missile remained concealed anywhere on the island. Johnson remained silent at this.

Even before the great showdown with Khrushchev, Kennedy was aging before one's eyes at an extremely rapid pace, even by the melancholy standard common to men in the White House in my time, with the single exception of the indestructible and indomitable Harry Truman. All but unconsciously I had already ceased writing of a "young" president. Indeed, in no context whatever did I any longer even think of him in terms of his youth, though at the time of his inauguration, only a little while before, I had thought of him, ten years my junior, as of another generation. The multiple crises that had preceded the transcendent crisis over Cuba—the crisis over Berlin notably, but troubles also in Latin America and, somewhat distantly, in the Far and Middle East—had gathered like sullen and sinister clouds over his administration. One by one these ominous challenges were biting alike into his physique and his psyche, and more and more he retired in spirit, though not in literal fact, from the frenetic and sometimes frivolous gaiety that the world believed to abound in his White House. History in its most pitiless aspect was standing at his shoulder, seeming at times to fling back into his face almost mockingly the brave and challenging words in which, in his inaugural address, he had laid down the foreign policy he intended to pursue. We would bear any burden; we would breast any peril. Would we? Yes, so far as he was concerned we would.

But we would and we did at very great cost to John Kennedy. If privately he still kept his sense of humor, it was not without effort and strain. If publicly he sustained confidence in his political future, he did not, in intimate contacts with personal friends, seek to deny his misgivings and his fears that his reelection in 1964 would be a very near thing, if not in fact an unlikely one. For in meeting what he had to meet abroad he had knowingly, and unhappily, twice attenuated himself at home. Many of the liberal intellectuals—to whom he had a curiously ambivalent attitude, now eagerly seeking a fellowship with them that never quite materialized, now full of angry distaste for them all—were in spirit departing his retinue. They had discovered what others who had known him better and longer (the "Irish Mafia" among them) had known all along—that John Kennedy *was* a Cold Warrior, even though, like many other of that breed, he had never relished the role. The spiritual exodus of so much of academe and of such inter-related politico-academic groups as Americans for Democratic Action (with which he would never deal gladly and which he never joined) hurt him personally as well as politically.

He felt he had given much to academe—"too fucking much," he once told me over a carefully Spartan single glass of whis-key—and that academe had ill repaid him. He had made Ken-neth Galbraith ambassador to India without joy; he had tolerated the Eleanor Roosevelt Democrats with inner bore-dom and pain. Of all the crate of eggheads he had brought in from Cambridge, only one I can recall, Arthur Schlesinger, Jr., could differ with the president without being a self-righteous bore. As I saw at the time, and now reaffirm, Kennedy was, apart from all his other troubles, becoming increasingly sen-sitive to the fear that he himself was not an authentic intellec-tual. He was suffering also some of the strange pangs of guilt of those who are rich and privileged without special effort of their own, and, as they inwardly fear, without special merit of their own. (I have always thought Nelson Rockefeller had this malady right up to the eyes, for all his hi-fella acts of extrover-sion.)

I took my amateur's diagnosis up one night with another nonpolitical well-wisher of Kennedy, Justice Felix Frankfurter, whose tart and sometimes belligerent manner covered a soft and sensitive heart. I told Frankfurter, as I have elsewhere written, that the president was suffering a moderate but nev-ertheless damaging neurosis because he had been no whiz kid at Harvard. All this, I said, was as absurd as it was unnecessary, and why didn't Frankfurter do something about it? "Do what?" asked Frankfurter. I replied in words to this effect: Felix, you are surely the very Pope of Harvard intellectualism. Go see the president and work the conversation around in such a way as to make it clear that you regard his mind as what it really is—a very fine one. Frankfurter, his eyes snapping, was much intrigued. But he had long been bruised by accusations, going back to the days of "Frankfurter's Happy Hot Dogs," that from the high bench he was forever meddling into nonjudicial affairs, so he decided he could properly offer Kennedy no reassurance.

While the president was still sore from the increasing disenchantment of the academics, he was suffering a far more positive kind of wound from another and more important part of the spectrum that lay to his Left—the elected politicians. By the time of the Cuban crisis, the more articulate Democratic Left in the Senate was giving Kennedy far more trouble than ever the Republicans had done or would do. Such men as Senators Joseph Clark of Pennsylvania and Wayne Morse of Oregon were almost constantly at him, sometimes on domestic affairs, which did not greatly distress him, and sometimes on foreign affairs, which distressed him very much. Kennedy longed to reclaim them. But when times were tough there was a great deal of Old Joe Kennedy in him. It was easy to deal with him in the techniques of friendly persuasion, but he got very rough and very "Irish" when somebody was shoving him without apology and, in his view, with insufficient cause. Increasingly, therefore, he turned from a sense of loss to the attitude of Kenny O'Donnell and Larry O'Brien, men who had come down to Washington not from Cambridge but from that very different place called Boston. This attitude, of course, was expressed in the immemorially simple imperative: Go to Hell.

Watching these transmutations as a journalist first but always a friend second, I made it a point to try to see Kennedy pretty often. In this, I had qualified success. For a mare's nest had come into being concerning our relationship—not between the president and me but between me and some of the palace guard with whom it was necessary to cope on one's way into the Oval Office. Kennedy and I had understood each other from his far-back days in the House of Representatives: I asked him no favors and expected none; he asked me for no favors and expected none. I expected information whenever and wherever it could be given without damage to Kennedy's responsibilities, and I always got it. He expected fairness and no exploitation of our meetings by me, and he always got it. The fact of mutual friendship was never in any doubt.

Some of the second-rankers in the administration, however (I name no names here because in the nature of things I had no absolute knowledge of identities and I don't much believe in bellyaching, anyhow), came to regard me as an Enemy. This judgment was based first, upon the undeniable fact that I was an old friend of Lyndon Johnson, whom some of them regarded as the Enemy Incarnate, and secondly upon the fact that I was habitually very far from full of praise for the whole of the administration.

All this is not to say that I was ever shut out of the Kennedy White House; it is only to say that, having never been very good with my elbows, I began sometimes to be hesitant about applying for admission. Whenever I did go in I found Kennedy's old mildly saturnine posture toward life to have hardened into something more mordant, particularly after the congressional elections of November of 1962. These were bad news for the president and, invariably objective in private as he was, he well knew it. He had worried after the 1960 returns that he was in the geographic sense a minority president, having lost nearly the whole of the West beyond Chicago. Now, in 1962, as I wrote at the time (consciously seeking both to tell the truth and to help the president's more sanguine associates begin to grapple with reality), the South, the Southwest, and the mountain states were all in a state of insurgency. (This column was, of course, yet more proof, so far as some of the Kennedy subordinates were concerned, that I was not to be trusted.) This state of affairs was both illogical and unfair. But, as Kennedy remarked (indeed, as he was fond of remarking often), nobody ever said that life was fair. For these were the very sections to which Kennedy's steadfast support of the old doctrine of containment of international communism—in a word, of "the hard line"—should have greatly appealed. Too, he had now begun what would turn out to be his fateful commitment to South Vietnam, and this too was strong medicine—then—for the troops, outside of small liberal enclaves on the East and West coasts.

The farther along he went in his presidency in what was to

195

be the last full year of his life, the more Kennedy's position began to develop striking, if incomplete, parallels with that of Harry Truman in 1948. Foreign crises that had forced the one to let his domestic programs lie largely inert were putting the other, John Kennedy, into essentially the same fix. And the increasing alienation of Truman from the Left and Right wings of his own party was almost precisely replicated in the progressive isolation of Kennedy from *his* Left and Right. Where Truman had had his Henry Wallace, Kennedy now had Mike Mansfield and William Fulbright, who, like Henry Wallace before them, believed their honest but unconscious cryptopacifism to be both intellectually and morally superior to Kennedy's hard-minded view of a hard world. The successor president was in this regard actually more sorely pressed than his predecessor. For while Henry Wallace had, as his 1948 third-party movement proved, no substantial national constituency, Senators Mansfield and Fulbright were both powerful in the Senate and plainly considered themselves as senior to Kennedy as president as they had in fact been to Kennedy as a junior senator. They repeatedly cut the ground from under Kennedy at crisis time, and their voices—Mansfield's as the Senate majority leader and Fulbright's as its senior foreign policy spokesman—echoed abroad a hundred times more loudly than Henry Wallace's ever had.

Plainly, such a state of affairs profoundly touched the public interest; but I am compelled to concede that the facts of the matter were never put before the public by journalism with any force or clarity. I myself tried my hand at it again and again, but I can claim only the smallest bit of success for my exertions. In the first place, though I had then only a vagrant whiff of it, a new reality was in fact at work in the American subconscious. The people were imperceptibly but slowly and surely losing confidence in the foreign policy rubrics—"positions of strength" and "containment of communism"—that had come down in an unbroken descent from the time of Harry Truman and had thus far engaged the loyal support of the elites of Wall Street, the media, and the larger part of the academic community.

196

How much and how deeply Kennedy himself sensed this slippage I could only guess, though I knew that he had some perception of it, if only because he telephoned me at home on one occasion, through no intermediate aide or secretary, to thank me for having written a piece touching inadequately on the subject. Not only was my understanding of it then not at all complete or fully coherent; the truth was that it was difficult to find a real hearing on so amorphous a subject in those days. And, ironically, part of the difficulty lay in an atmosphere that had been created by the "swinging" White House which John Kennedy himself inhabited. People wanted, most newspaper editors wanted, "inside stuff" about the glamorous Kennedys and their cohorts, not dreary depressing stuff about what was happening in an infinitely more real world outside. Never mind that the "glamour" bit annoyed and somewhat repelled Kennedy himself. He was stuck with it, and if he never moved effectively to put a stop to the nonsense, as to his annoyance I sometimes recommended in writing, it may well be that he could not put a stop to it. The Prince Charming legend is most durable, and not in this century, perhaps in no century, had the White House held an incumbent so superficially fitted to that legend. And there *was* charm, at that, in these last few months of Kennedy's life, even though the master of the White House was anxious about the future of the country as well as his own, in the election year of 1964.

CHAPTER ELEVEN

ON THE NIGHT before President Kennedy was to set out upon the trip to Dallas that was to cost his life, my wife and I were among the guests at a typically spirited White House party for the Grand Duchess of Luxembourg, at which the president all but knocked himself out to be the happily untroubled host. The guests, as at any state dinner, were lined up alphabetically to march in the receiving line past the president and his guest of honor, and my wife and I, as W's, wound up in a small and pretty well isolated group including Supreme Court Justice Byron White and Mayor Robert Wagner of New York. I had not seen Wagner face to face in some years (we had, in any case, never been much more than nodding acquaintances) and as it happened I had within the preceding week written a column deploring what I felt to be the absurd cannibalism then besetting the Democratic Party in New York, for which I had heavily blamed Wagner himself. And, by coincidence, I had just a day or so before this dinner discussed the same matter briefly with Kennedy, remarking that it seemed to me that as head of the national Democratic Party he would be better off if the Republicans should win the municipal elections in New York at the first possible opportunity, and give the Democrats there something real to complain about, since in power they were so determinedly bitchy among themselves. Kennedy had grunted noncommittally, meaning that he had far bigger things to worry about.

Nevertheless, as Wagner, Byron White, and I stood together waiting to move by the president, I stood in a good deal of discomfort. Few journalists are tough enough to enjoy small talk with a politician whom they have just skewered. Then I realized that Wagner's amicability proceeded from his mistaken supposition that I was Byron White. Somehow, Kennedy sensed exactly what the situation was. For when Wagner and I reached the president in single file, Wagner being in the lead, Kennedy greeted him somewhat formally and me with a very loud "Hi, *Bill*," and then trumpeted to Wagner: "Bob, I'm sure you know *Bill* White, the *columnist*!" Wagner gave me a chill smile; Kennedy a broad and delighted grin. This was the last time I was ever to see John Kennedy. And in the aftertime, seeking, as no doubt were so many others, some fragment of memory touched with humor rather than sorrow, I consciously nourished the recollection that I had, if unwittingly, given him some comradely amusement in the last night of his life.

Without being mawkish about it, I must say I was to need every shred of happy memory that could be dredged up. On the fatal day in Dallas I was lounging about the Senate press gallery in Washington to no special purpose, simply poking about in my mind for some satisfactory subject for a column. I did three columns a week and never, in sixteen years with the United Feature Syndicate, failed to meet a deadline. Through the desultory hum in the gallery I heard the United Press ticker ringing that series of urgent bells that means that a "flash"—a signal of some momentous news event—is coming. I hurried to peer at the machine and read that the president had been shot in Dallas.

I have never been able to abide the sort of fellow who makes not just a parade of his grief but a majestic procession, suggesting that somehow *his* suffering is incomparably acute and must be seen by others. But the plain fact is that I *was* crushed by grief and shock and all but physically knocked down by my horror that this unspeakable thing had occurred in my home state, where not long before a handful of harpies in Dallas had spat upon Adlai Stevenson. In a rush of precognition I knew that Texas, for which I had never been any booster but which I

199

nevertheless knew was no more hospitable a home for brutality and madness than any other state, would now be in for a long session of harsh condemnation and guilt by association. To this day, the city of Dallas has never fully recovered from its hidden trauma. Nor, I suspect, have some of the most fair-minded and decent and humane friends I have ever had, including the editor of the *Dallas Times Herald* at that time, Felix McKnight, who had steadfastly squelched every nascent lunatic element that ever showed its head in that city.

It would soon emerge in the findings of the Warren Commission that John Kennedy's assassin, Lee Harvey Oswald, had nothing whatever to do with Texas and had had, assuming that ideology had been any motivation in the first place, associations with both Cuba and the Soviet Union. Nevertheless, a trying and sorrowful and hopelessly frustrating time now opened for me, as a journalist and simply as a man, and for my wife. The circumstance that we were widely known to be old and close personal friends of the new president, Lyndon Johnson, and his wife somehow condemned us in the eyes of some of the associates of John Kennedy. The mere fact that I had been born in Texas, irrelevant in any rational context, somehow developed an ugly significance, not only to some of the Kennedy followers but even to some of my colleagues in journalism. One colleague, reviewing a book of mine, referred to me, in no relevant context discernible to me, as a "professional Texan." Walter Lippmann, whom I had known for two decades, was astonished. "*I* never knew you were from Texas," he remarked. "You don't sound like it, either." He meant, I suppose that because I had not assiduously cultivated it, my "Texas accent" had long since vanished by the natural erosion of my many years in the East.

I repeat that I do not wish to apply for a Purple Heart; but telling it like it was remains an obligation. For at least six months, life in Washington, for both my wife and myself, was unshirted hell, both personally and professionally. I think I may justly say that neither of us was in any way paranoid. I know I can say with total accuracy that we met alternately unconcealed and pointless hostility or smarmy courtship from many people we knew. Some of them in journalism, I am sorry to say, wanted something from Johnson and assumed that I was just the man to get it for them. There was not much—there was nothing—that I could do about it all. I could not go around wearing a badge saying that I had been truly fond of John Kennedy. I could not go around with printed slips saying that I did not work for Lyndon Johnson in any way, shape, or form; that our private friendship long antedated his rise to power and status, and that I had no apologies whatever for it; that I would have felt it utterly contemptible to exploit such a private relationship either to feed or to sell my column. The president of my syndicate, Laurence Rutman, told an inquiring reporter the truth—that the sales of my column had only normal growth after Johnson reached the White House.

The Kennedy family, which had its own infinitely graver burdens to bear, remained my friends, collectively and severally. On my side, I retained the posture that I had always maintained with John Kennedy, asking no journalistic favors and offering none. Away back when Kennedy was running for president in 1960 I had written of the plain fact that his great personal fortune, not to mention that of his father, was putting his rival Hubert Humphrey in an essentially unfair position in the primaries. This was poignantly the case in crucial West Virginia, where, to be blunt about it, the real contest was for county organizations, not individual voters, and the Kennedy people were spreading splendid largesse among the court-house men.

Robert Kennedy's wife, Ethel, a warmly human woman fiercely loyal to her in-laws, caused me to be awakened late one night by a special delivery letter protesting that I had been too harsh to her brother-in-law and to the Kennedy family generally. I wrote back to her that in political writing I was not about to make war on the women and children (an expression that would have got me into ghastly trouble had the Women's Movement been active then) and that I admired her for sticking up for her people—as, indeed, I did. But, I added, I *did* have a job to do and in this instance the journalistic obligation had been to point out that West Virginia was something more than

201

a struggle between anti-Catholic bigots and Jack Kennedy, as some of my colleagues, notably Joe Alsop, were loudly implying. I did not add that while her brother-in-law had not liked the piece either, he had felt it was not outside the rules of the game. Nor did I tell her that, before he announced at a press conference that he was taking an enormous gamble (in going into heavily Protestant West Virginia as an urban Catholic against the Protestant and Farm Belt Humphrey), he had cheerfully and impishly acknowledged to me in private that of course it really wasn't going to be all *that* big a gamble.

All the same, Ethel Kennedy forgave me when she had read my note. The anecdote is germane because it so well illustrates the general course of my professional and personal association with the Kennedys after the president's death. We never really broke in any personal sense, but we were rarely in agreement on issues, in part because as a political writer I felt profoundly uneasy about the dynastic cult that arose after John Kennedy's death, believing it to be politically unhealthy. I believed also that John Kennedy alive would have had his own reservations about it. Perhaps I was wrong and even naive in this latter estimate; but I shall never think I was.

To go farther into what I am aware is a highly speculative area of thought, I believe that Ted Kennedy, at least, always had his own doubts about the dynasty concept, though Robert did not. In fact, I was able to write with confidence long before the 1972 Democratic convention that Ted Kennedy was not going to move a muscle for the presidential nomination, this simply because he had told me as much in what we both knew to be totally confidential talk. I use the word "simply" with deliberation; a political writer can easily become *too* skeptical unless he happens really to *know* the politician with whom he is dealing. On the occasion of this conversation I not only knew my politician. I knew, too, that he trusted me as a journalist and would not grossly mislead me even if he could. This was not because of my blue eyes but because Ted Kennedy knew the nature of my relationship with his slain eldest brother, and because I had not leapt upon him personally in connection with the death of his young woman companion along the beach at Chappaquiddick in Massachusetts. I had written that, tragic as the death of the young woman was, the ghastly episode was no fit factor in any public determination as to whether Edward Kennedy was qualified to be president of the United States. My published conclusion to this question was that the answer was no, he was not, on admissibly nonpersonal grounds, so qualified.

Not long afterward, I ran into Ted Kennedy at a small dinner party in the Israeli embassy for Prime Minister Golda Meir. I had not seen him face to face since the episode at the beach or the publication of my column. I thought that piece had given him very cold comfort, but I walked across the room to meet the thing head on. I said to him something to this effect: "Ted, many issues lie between us, as you know, and I am not about to join those who are crying you up for president. But I am also not one of those who are cutting you up about a private matter that I know is a source of grief to you. We are, and probably will remain, apart—but we are apart on *public* issues alone." He said very little. To my recollection he said only, "I know, I know," or some such thing. But he did not forget; and when later I was talking to him about his presidential plans, if any, he made it plain to me that he had not forgotten.

Somewhat similar in spirit, to a point, was an incident involving Robert Kennedy in 1968, when he was preparing to make his run for the presidency. After the death of his brother, Bobby Kennedy had become a vehemently bitter critic of the Vietnam involvement, which that brother had helped to widen perceptibly, if not on any massive scale, because he felt it to be imperative. Bobby's position had seemed to me inescapably to involve a repudiation of John Kennedy himself. At any rate, his choice of close political associates—most of them from the Left wing of the Democratic party and some of them outright and ungenerous adversaries of John Kennedy in his lifetime—was odd indeed. In consequence, my columns were often sharply critical of Robert Kennedy.

In all these circumstances, Robert Kennedy invited me one day to lunch in his office. Having no wish to appear truculent but concerned on the other hand to avoid hypocrisy, I told him, in case he had missed my pieces, roughly what I have written just above. He was throughout absolutely impassive except when I said to him that he was making political associations of the very sort that John Kennedy had scorned—and associations moreover that would never stand the test of adversity should adversity befall him. He seemed to make a mental note of that somewhat astringent observation, where, as it appeared to me, he had been wholly unmoved by my remarks concerning Vietnam. Ted Kennedy came in and joined our luncheon at about this point and I believe he may have heard me say to Robert that people who loved him too much while he was ahead were likely to run away from him, or even turn on him, if he should ever start losing.

I never saw Robert Kennedy again. Within weeks he lay dead in California, victim of yet another assassination. It was with all this in mind—John Kennedy murdered, Robert Kennedy murdered, the young woman dead at the beach—that with some pity I approached Edward Kennedy as I did at the Israeli dinner. He was in a modified state of shock in observing that journalists who had until Chappaquiddick been tirelessly lyrical in his praise were now the very ones most pitilessly attacking him over that episode. I was not graceless enough to point out to him that this perfectly illustrated what I had told Bobby Kennedy. But the extraordinary upshot of this evening was that Ted Kennedy was almost *grateful* to me for having declared in print his disqualification for the presidency because I had not put the case on personal grounds.

The transition from the Kennedy to the Johnson Administration involved one of the gravest crises for this country in this century. And to me as a molder of opinion, in a small way, it presented the most enduringly difficult professional challenges I ever had to face.

The fact was that nobody—not the new president, not the CIA, not the FBI or military Intelligence—knew in the immediate aftermath of the murder in Dallas whether or not something unthinkable in our national history and ethos—some sort of violent coup d'état—might be in preparation. All those in responsible positions *did* know one thing for certain: that

204

the country was in a state of hysterical horror and profound disturbance, and that it was absolutely necessary to take every possible action that would reassuringly underline the existence of continuity, under the Constitution's provisions for orderly transfer of power in whatever circumstances.

When Lyndon Johnson flew back to Washington from Dallas accompanied by the dead body of his predecessor, it was these necessities that preoccupied him. He desperately lacked two things. He had no time to ponder with any real care the proper priorities for his immediate actions, and he had no real information about what had happened in Dallas beyond the bald fact that a president of the United States had been killed, by somebody, for some reason. The authorities in Washington could not be certain, for instance, that the bullets that struck Texas Governor John Connally in the Kennedy car had not been intended for Johnson. The two Texans bore a considerable resemblance in distant profile in that both were tall and well set up and, by simple happenstance or because Connally had always seemed to model himself on Johnson in some ways, were similarly dressed. It also occurred to some, including me, that an assassin might reasonably have assumed that the man riding with the president would be the vice president, not a mere governor.

Private speculations of this kind could not be dismissed out of hand or ignored by the new president himself. On the odd chance that such concerns might be sound, the motivation of the crime would take on a sinister face indeed. Had the intention been to wipe out not simply the president but also his constitutional stand-in and thus cast the burden of leading a shocked and frightened and disarrayed nation upon the frail shoulders of the aged Speaker of the House, John McCormack? So nightmarish a possibility could not for the moment be excluded, however bizarre it might seem, and the Lyndon Johnson who had asked for God's help in his brief comments upon being sworn in as president in the aircraft in Dallas poignantly meant his prayer, though like most of us he had never been a pious or especially devout man.

After his arrival back in Washington as president, Johnson

returned to his old house, the Elms, and asked my wife and me and Abe and Carol Fortas to come over. We found him directing the country's urgent affairs over a single telephone line, with neither presidential assistants nor secretaries at hand. He was telephoning the members of the Kennedy Cabinet one by one to ask them to stay on, speaking very gently in contrast to his usual sharp and crisply businesslike manner. As we were driving to the Elms I made up my mind that my attitude toward Lyndon Johnson as president must be wholly different from what it had been toward Johnson as senator and then as vice president. I would guard my tongue so that I never forgetfully called him "Lyndon" or anything other than "Mr. President." I would under no circumstances offer him any advice on anything unless specifically requested to do so. And I would never ask him, or accept if offered, any kind of political favor, for myself or anybody else.

The fact was that I was in some fear that he would ask me to come into his administration, and I knew that I could not and would not do so. It would never have worked out, as Johnson himself later let me know that he understood. Apart from the fact that I had no appetite whatever for public office, I knew that Johnson, as a triple-distilled perfectionist and a man who never knew what a clock was for, could be extremely difficult to work for, just as I knew that I myself was a bit on the prickly side. Finally, I knew I was a journalist, and only a journalist, and I loved my work and also my independence as a private man. I would not have exchanged my job for the ambassadorship to Great Britain—not, of course, that Johnson would ever have been foolish enough to offer it to me.

Immediately Johnson put down the telephone, he *did* ask my advice and, as I recall, simultaneously that of Abe Fortas, on two matters: how to deal with the Kennedy White House staff, and how to reassure the American public that everything possible would be done, with the most rigid objectivity, to know the whole circumstances of the assassination in Dallas. Fortas successfully favored the appointment of a national board of inquiry—the Warren Commission, as it turned out to be. I suggested leaving the murder in the hands of the state of

Texas, as a gesture of confidence and trust in its judicial processes. With hindsight, that looks to have been a poor idea, but one can hardly say that the Warren Commission was wildly successful in satisfying the public. As to the Kennedy White House staff, I suggested that every member be asked to stay on, at least for a considerable period, and the president quickly nodded assent in such a way as to indicate that he had already reached that conclusion.

I was aware that Johnson was deeply disliked by some of the White House staff, as he most certainly was, but to the best of my knowledge he regarded this as only an awkward and not a significant fact. I never heard him make a cutting remark against any of the Kennedy Palace Guard, though he knew, as did most of sentient Washington, that some of them had amused themselves at parties by using his photograph as a dart board and by calling him "Old Cornpone." This restraint on his part was not, of course, so much an instance of Christian charity as a reflection of the fact that he genuinely admired the talents of some of the Kennedy people—notably McGeorge Bundy, Arthur Schlesinger, Kenny O'Donnell, and Larry O'Brien—and wanted to keep them in service as long as he could.

For my part, I was for the first time unreservedly happy that I had left the *Times* and was now a full-time, wholly uninhibited columnist-commentator, as distinguished from a correspondent for whom the straight reporting function was always primary. Long before, as war editor of the AP, I had chafed at the fairly gentle restraints put upon me, for I was convinced of a moral obligation to contribute something, somewhere, to a national consensus in favor of our intervention in the Second World War. At no point in my work at the *New York Times* had I been entirely free to scatter my opinions about unstintingly; at no time during that association had I felt it proper to use the pages of the *Times* as a forum for W.S. White. So now that I was an independent writer, owing nobody anything, making no pretense about bare Objectivity, and subject only to the sanctions of the newspaper marketplace, I reckoned it to be my duty to take—and without ever looking back I did take—a course candidly designed more to help foster national reunion and what I thought of as national safety than to be simply "out in front" (shades here of Kent Cooper and the old AP!) of the hard news. That it was a self-assigned mission I concede; that it was a needed mission I had, and have, no doubt.

By historical accident I happened to be in an especially advantageous position to serve in a small way as a bridge, a link, between the grief-stricken Kennedy people and the still slightly dazed Johnson people. It seemed to me inconceivably childish and mortally absurd that the country should be deprived of the best leadership Johnson could give it simply because of White House staff infighting, because one side or the other of the Kennedy-Johnson axis did not "like" the other side. I never, of course, discussed this notion in any oracular terms, or indeed in any other terms, with President Johnson, nor did I ever do so with the Kennedy people. I simply tried to interpret one set to the other. For example, I pointed out to the Boston/Cambridge sets that even in Johnson City they did wear shoes and read a few books. And I observed to the Johnson people that it was perfectly human for the Kennedy people to feel some sense of resentful loss that their leader had been killed, by the bitterest of ironies, in the successor's home state. I could have added, but didn't, that for no politician in this nation had the Right-wing fringe characters in Dallas felt so hot an animus for so long as they had for Lyndon Johnson. To them, Kennedy was no worse than an outlander; but Johnson was a "traitor to his class" or region or both, especially because of his sustained advocacy of civil rights, rather as Franklin Roosevelt had been to his fellow members of the stockbroker section of Groton/Harvard alumni.

At any rate, wisely or not, effectively or not, I put a great deal of effort into this missionary work. The temptation is nearly irresistible to say that I got only what the man in the middle usually gets—good solid clouts on *both* ears—but in point of fact the consequence wasn't quite that bad. To be sure, young men avowedly devoted to purity in journalism (none of them having ever held any significant job in it) did push me about a bit on the college lecture circuit; but this I was able to bear up under without lasting pain. What did sometimes make me feel about like the singer-protagonist in "Old Man River" was the fact that a good many grown-up colleagues so wholly misunderstood what I was about and the motivation for it. The ill favor of the pros hurt.

My "in" with Johnson, much more even than with Kennedy, was personal rather than journalistic. True, he did tell me things in confidence that unquestionably involved the highest of national security. So to a lesser extent had John Kennedy done, for that matter. But on such occasions I mentally turned off my switch of recollection, much as old Bernard Baruch would turn off his hearing aid when, giving his advice to congressional committees, he had been asked too awkward a question.

The period of transition was Johnson's finest hour, as even his sternest critics were later prepared to admit. For when he put his mind to it he could be very sensitive to the feelings of others and he was almost uniformly patient and compassionate toward both the Irish Mafia and the intellectuals on the White House staff. Walter Jenkins, who had been Johnson's incomparably faithful man-of-all-work from almost the moment Johnson first entered national politics, performed far beyond the call of duty in tirelessly struggling to keep the Kennedyites and Johnsonites from biting too much at each other. Jenkins was the White House chief of staff. He held enormous power and never once brandished it. He alternately soothed and persuaded Johnson staffers out of becoming jealous of Kennedy holdovers, and vice versa. I never in all my experience as a political writer saw so unselfish, so disinterested, and so brilliant a staff service as was performed by Jenkins. And when during the presidential campaign of 1964 this tragic man's life was smashed to rubble by his arrest on a "morals" charge, I felt, and so wrote, that he was an almost unspeakably pitiable victim of the brutal pressures under which he had worked.

Only the day before this sad business became public, I had Jenkins to lunch at the Cosmos Club in Washington and found

209

him, a man always in danger of exceedingly high blood pressure, all but purple in the face from strain, and suffering from a hypertension patently acute even to a layman such as myself. As we talked I was increasingly alarmed and troubled for him and at last I begged him to go home and lie down and forget about the White House for a while. No, no, he said; there was a mountain of work back at the White House waiting for him. My instinct told me to ignore his demurrers, to leave the table, to telephone President Johnson and recommend that he then and there *order* Jenkins to bed. I did not follow that instinct, as I would have done had I been a truly perceptive friend. But I was not really close to Walter Jenkins; in all my association with Lyndon Johnson I had made it a rule to deal as a journalist only with him and never with his subordinates. This personal policy I had come to early in my days of covering the Senate—talk to a senator himself or talk to nobody. The journalist who sees the staff instead of the boss can very easily receive an incomplete or even erroneous impression of what the top man really thinks, really intends to do, or really has done. There was "nothing personal" in all this; it was simply a working rule that I had found indispensable.

As I later learned, Jenkins was in a state of near collapse that day at the Cosmos Club, not simply because he had been picked up (that very morning, as I recall, or perhaps on the morning just before) in a Washington YMCA on a morals charge. He was in torment also because he had not immediately notified Johnson of his predicament and was thus about to let the whole unhappy affair break over the president's unsuspecting head.

When, on the morning after the luncheon, I picked up the *Washington Post*, I was astounded and saddened to read that Walter Jenkins had resigned and was even then in the George Washington University Hospital. It was a "column day" for me, that is, one of the three days of each week on which I had to do a piece. And so I sat down and wrote a column totally in support of Jenkins, recalling his magnificent work and saying in substance that if he had in fact done what he was accused of, it could only have been an aberration, not unlike the atypical

210

acts of a soldier in a state of combat fatigue. Having sent off my piece by messenger to the syndicate's wirehead in the National Press Building, I went to George Washington University Hospital and brushed past a nurse or two into Jenkins's room. As he caught sight of me, he buried his face in the bed clothes. I jerked them down, as his Roman Catholic priest looked on with what I believed was approval, and shouted: "Walter, to hell with hiding your face. Pull up your socks—and to hell with them all!"

Jenkins within moments was prepared to talk to me with reasonable coherence, and it was clear that, being what he was, he was far more concerned that he had harmed Johnson in the campaign than that the life of Walter Jenkins lay in ruins. I told him there was no possibility that Lyndon Johnson was going to lose the election to Barry Goldwater (who, by the way, was Jenkins's fellow officer and friend in the Air Force Reserves and who with characteristic decency never once in the campaign referred to Jenkins's personal tragedy).

I left the hospital within an hour or so believing that Jenkins had calmed himself, and went back to my house to await what I knew was inevitable—a great many telephone calls, now that my published column had hit the streets in Washington. To my surprise and great satisfaction, most of my callers were civilized people who pitied rather than condemned Jenkins. It goes without saying that this was a source of satisfaction to me; I had been far from certain that the episode would not become the worst of all possible kinds of campaign issues, the sort having no real consequence in the life of the Republic that can nevertheless obscure issues of genuine public importance. In fact, Tommy Corcoran told me later that he believed my piece had "negated" the Jenkins affair; I hoped so, for the sake of Jenkins no less than for the sake of Johnson.

Still, I knew that sooner or later a very different kind of call was going to come in; and it did. A woman whose very voice summoned up a complete picture of venomously outraged virtue, wholly minus that virtue called Christian charity, snapped at me: "Are you William White who wrote that column today about Walter Jenkins?" Yes, I said; I was. "Are *you* a

211

homosexual, too?" she pursued. "No," I observed, "as a matter of fact I am not. But, by God, if *you* were the only alternative I might seriously consider it." I suppose I must have subconsciously prepared myself for some such exchange. A Washington columnist, especially one locally printed, is in all but name a public figure, and is considered by people outside and inside public life to be fair game. Since he is forever dishing it out, it is reckoned that he should be prepared to take it.

Not really enjoying contention in any form, and in truth feeling something approaching automatic revulsion and distress from almost any kind of scene, I never liked this aspect of my life as a columnist. My wife and I went out socially far more often than we really liked, especially to embassy parties where there are usually only two sorts of conversation. There is the parochially social chit-chat of the so-called Cave Dwellers, old Washington residents who over the years have managed, God knows why, to get onto the invitation lists of foreign diplomats and who are handed down from one ambassador to another like the embassy furniture. To sit at dinner with one of the ladies of this set is a cruel experience in boredom and triviality. Scattered amongst these people—who have absolutely no interest in either foreign or domestic affairs, except possibly in the sexual connotation—are usually one or two Proper Sillies (I owe the term to my friend Elizabeth Rowe, wife of Jim Rowe) from the junior ranks of the State Department. Though I do not wish to malign the State Department as a whole, or even largely, it is unhappily true that State *does* manage to collect a good many asses whose sole utility seems to lie in happily attending embassy dinners in positions below the salt. These, too, usually appear to be wholly unconcerned with what is happening in the world except perhaps for gossip.

The second kind of conversation at dinners in embassies, or dinners outside embassies at which foreign ambassadors are present, tends to an ultra-sophistication and a brittleness that get tiresome before nine o'clock in the evening has come around. The honest word "bitchy" is in fact more nearly descriptive. One such evening remains green, or anyhow greenish, in my memory. An old friend, Oscar Cox, then acting as a lawyer for certain French interests in this country, had the French ambassador, Herve Alphand, and Madame Alphand to dinner at his house in Georgetown. As it happened, I was the only male guest who was more or less in public life. This was at a time when General-President Charles de Gaulle of France was being, even for him, insufferable toward his old special devils, the United States and Britain. Alphand was taking up the same cause with great vigor on every possible occasion, and was being rude in that especially feline way of many Frenchmen. Some time before, I had been calling on Lyndon Johnson at the White House and had emerged to find Alphand glaring at me in outrage that the glory and grandeur and so on of France, of which he was the official embodiment, had been cooling its heels while a mere journalist was being lent the ear of the president.

It seems too petty to be credible but I do believe that Alphand was still burning about this incident on the night of Cox's dinner. At any rate, he set out at table to be remarkably offensive about the United States, its government, its habits, and its people. And he was plainly directing his commentaries at me. Had any American official been present I should have kept quiet; but when it became apparent that no one else was going to challenge the ambassador, I undertook that duty myself. I asked Alphand if he had read Churchill's war memoirs, particularly that passage in which the prime minister recalled his final visit to France just before its fall to Hitler. Oh, yes, said Alphand. "Do you recall, Ambassador," I asked, "what Mr. Churchill wrote when upon his asking frantically where the French mass of maneuver was now to be committed, he had been informed that there *was* no mass of maneuver?" Alphand was silent. I went on, "Churchill wrote that thereafter he spoke to his French colleagues in 'indifferent French—indifferent in both senses.' "

To his eternal credit, stout Oscar Cox, French legal account or no French account, remained serene, when he might well have rebuked me for "conduct unbecoming" toward a foreign plenipotentiary who was the honored guest. It goes without saying that I was never again invited to the French embassy, which suited me well enough. My favorites were the British and Israeli embassies, both of which invariably made up with the quality of their ideas—and information—for the absence of *haute cuisine* on their tables.

As for Alphand, his belligerence may perhaps have come down to him right from the top. On the twentieth anniversary of D-Day, June 6, 1964, President Johnson was thoughtful enough to put me on the official American delegation he sent to France for the commemoration. This was headed by General Omar Bradley and it encompassed a dozen other officers whose contributions to the rescue of France from the Nazis had been by any measure historic, if not actually decisive. De Gaulle boycotted the mission from the first day to the last. And at the windup affair, a memorial dinner for Allied officers in the Hall of Battles in Versailles, every one of us "Anglo-Saxons," American and British, was severely informed by a major domo upon entering: "*No* whiskey will be served." Too Anglo-Saxon, no doubt. We were all given medallions showing three heroically struggling warriors with linked arms, the French figure holding the central position. The American ambassador, Chip Bohlen, was after all permitted to speak to the dinner, and gamely he did.

I told President Johnson of this on my return to Washington, mentioning that when the American and British delegations had been invited to go to the Allied cemeteries to commemorate comrades who had fallen on D-Day, we were permitted to stay about five minutes at the British one, about ten minutes at the American one, and about an hour at the French one. The president was not at all upset. He shrugged philosophically and observed that when de Gaulle had come to Washington on the occasion of John Kennedy's funeral he tried to snub the new president, as he had tried to snub the dead president. "How do you mean 'tried' to snub you?" I asked. "I just mean *tried*," said Johnson impatiently. "How the hell *could* he?" He then recalled that upon an earlier occasion, when as vice president he had gone to Paris on a mission for Kennedy, de Gaulle had said to him, "What did you come to learn from me, young man?" and Johnson had replied: "By God, General, just anything you feel like you can teach me."

214

Johnson had by this time become inured to the injustices which in some inexplicable way fall in our generation more heavily upon the Great Powers and their leaders than upon the Small. I recall one Sunday afternoon when, aboard the presidential yacht *Sequoia*, there was a good deal of pained and resigned discussion about one or another of de Gaulle's persistent acts of nastiness toward the United States—I believe it was his theatrical announcement that he was reneging on all French military commitments to the North Atlantic Treaty Organization. The president, Secretary of Defense Robert McNamara, and I were talking of this up in the prow of the boat, while the eternally jealous and suspicious aides who seem to surround all presidents were sitting resentfully at a distance, their ears out like radar scanners, to be sure that no Palace Guardsman got "in the know" ahead of anybody else. The president was quietly and resignedly cursing the turn of events and making a few remarks about the pseudo-power represented by de Gaulle. I made bold to remark that some of my professional military friends in the Pentagon had told me that France in any event had nothing to offer NATO except French territory to defend. If this was the case, I said, then why did the president so persistently turn the other cheek to de Gaulle; why did he not find *some* means to score off this Gallic megalomaniac? Before Johnson had had a chance to reply, McNamara rushed into the breach to say nay, nay; we must do *nothing* to offend the French, for reasons which seemed to me then to be very complicated and which today I cannot remember at all.

This man, Robert McNamara, was to my mind a perfect embodiment of the square peg in the round hole during nearly all the time he served as chief at the Pentagon for Kennedy and then Johnson. I saw a good deal of him, sometimes in fairly unbuttoned circumstances, and about him I reached two conclusions: that he was an able and decent man, if perhaps a bit too sensitive for the job he held; and that as secretary of defense he was wholly misplaced. Curiously enough, though it was Kennedy who had chosen him, whereas Johnson had only kept him on, McNamara was far more influential with the successor than with the predecessor president. This arose from the fact, one that I know hits folklore squarely in the face, that by nature Kennedy was more nearly martially-minded than Johnson, Kennedy was thus far quicker to become impatient with McNamara'a inherent squeamishness about the use of harsh military force, whatever the circumstance. The vision of Johnson as a kind of Davy Crockett of the wild frontier, forever ready to take down the rifle and go hunting for trophies, was absurdly false, though it is true that Johnson himself nourished it by some of his public comments, particularly about Vietnam.

Kennedy as a Roman Catholic held the classical conservative view, in an essentially unpolitical sense, of man's eternal nonperfectibility and, collaterally, of the necessary place of force—even ugly force—in human affairs. Johnson, on the contrary, was heir to an evangelical Protestant liberal view that not man but only the World was vile. Robert McNamara was heir to the same view. I can never recall a conversation with him in which he did not stress most of all what could *not* be done militarily, in Vietnam or elsewhere. I always thought that, given a psychic shove of only an inch or two, he would have been an outright pacifist. Moreover, I always thought something of the same of Johnson, but in his case the psychic shove would have had to be more forceful; indeed, it could never have been effective so long as he had the vast and terrible responsibilities of the presidency.

More than once I saw Johnson weep surreptitiously in the nighttime when the sum of the day's casualties in Vietnam was brought to him in the family quarters of the White House. But this was only in private and only in the sight of intimate friends. I saw Bob McNamara publicly weep toward the end of his tour as secretary of defense, visibly weep at a White House reception. The job at the Pentagon was brutally punishing to him, I suspect, because he had no real heart for his ultimate responsibilities there. And there surely have been few more choice ironies than the irony of the report widely published that Johnson "fired" him as secretary of defense toward the end of the president's final term. Johnson in fact *relieved* him, in every sense of that word, by causing his appointment to head the World Bank.

216

McNamara's tour was, of course, streaked with a hundred aching uncertainties, primarily over Vietnam, and was clangorous with many discordant voices. In the meetings of the National Security Council, which amounted to a War Cabinet, Johnson not only invited but insisted upon advice and dissent rather more than advice and consent. And as the going got harder and harder, in both Vietnam and the United States, the somber chorus of his advisers got louder and more and more dissonant. More than once when Johnson ordered a bombing halt he told me later that in the military sense he had probably been wrong to do so, but that as the elected leader of a free nation turning more and more against the war he could not leave untried even the most unpromising possibility of a bearable solution, *so long as it did not endanger our troops in Vietnam.*

Through most of this long trauma, the Western allies badly let him down: allied prime ministers and foreign ambassadors made popular capital in nearly every country in Europe by criticizing American policy in Indochina—while privately and desperately urging Johnson and Rusk in Washington for God's sake not to give up, lest American commitments to *them* become dubious. I wrote of this double-faced policy on every occasion where the obligations concerning confidentiality of information given to me did not preclude publication, and I was as a result thrown into ever closer personal relationships with European ambassadors in Washington. The Italian embassy, whoever its occupant at a given time, largely scorned to talk out of both sides of its mouth, and so did the British embassy, even under a Labour government in London. Indeed, when at some sticky point (and they were nearly *all* sticky points) Labour Prime Minister Harold Wilson came over from London just as Britain was embarking upon its withdrawal east of Suez, I wrote a column that brought me some embarrassment.

Lyndon Johnson and Harold Wilson, I wrote, had many things in common—a devotion to Liberal welfarism and to reformist programs. But they did differ in one thing: Johnson understood and was ready to use power as an instrument of national policy. At a state dinner for Wilson, as I passed through the receiving line, I saw Johnson pointing to me as he talked to Wilson. When my turn came for the handshake with the two, Johnson, who pulled my leg at every possible opportunity all through our long friendship, remarked to Wilson: "Bill White here is the William S. White who writes a syndicated column. Maybe you saw his piece in this morning's *Washington Post*." Wilson surveyed me for an instant with no noticeable warmth but not with discernible hostility either. "Oh, yes," he said, "we have met before. I *did* read your article this morning. But you really were wrong on one point—I, too, believe in power."

Though I thought he wanted to believe in it, I didn't believe he really did. My judgment was perhaps prejudiced because my own marked preference since the days of Churchill had been for Conservative prime ministers. Harold Macmillan, for one, had in his time been generous to me as a journalist. At the time I was contributing editor of *Harper's Magazine* (the prime minister, like most Britons, didn't really credit the existence of such things as syndicated newspaper columns), Macmillan once gave me a long interview on condition that I not touch anything purely topical. My appointment at 10 Downing Street was for ten o'clock in the morning in the Cabinet room, from one of whose walls Gladstone stared down at a most painfully hungover journalist. I had spent the night and a good part of the early morning in reunion with wartime British friends; when the pubs closed we crawled through a long list of drinking "clubs" and I got back to my room in the Connaught Hotel long after daylight.

The interview was by agreement confined to "politics" in its general sense, with no reference to "living personalities" or that sort of thing. My concern was to find out how Macmillan had managed to bring into the Tory party so many unlikely recruits from the lower middle class and even from among the intellectuals. Macmillan's interest, as I often found to be the case among European politicians, was in the techniques of Lyndon Johnson as a bringer-about of consensus in his various political posts. I soon discovered that most of these techniques—blurring sheerly ideological categories in order to accomplish pragmatic actions—were in operation in the British Isles as well, under Macmillan. He was vastly pleased when I remarked as much, throwing in that his own mother had been "born in Indi*ah*na." As to the fattening of the Tory party, he said, this had been accomplished by building more public housing and by special appeals to "the fellows in the white coats." By this he meant scientists, primarily the practitioners of the physical as distinguished from the social sciences, and the technician class under them.

Macmillan's parliamentary secretary, aide, or whatever was his title, was plainly horrified that I had arrived in so hungover a state (a circumstance that did not make me all that happy either) and that I was staying so long. Again and again, however, as I rose to depart, the prime minister waved me back to my seat and set off on more political anecdotes. The British Foreign Office, however, was put out with me for not having "dropped by for a bit of briefing." I told this to John Kennedy upon my return to Washington and mentioned the matter much later to Lyndon Johnson. Each president in his turn said substantially the same thing: "These damn foreign offices and State Departments *think* they run everything!"

Kennedy and Johnson to my direct knowledge, and Nixon, too, in my estimate, seriously believed that the State Department bureaucracy was essentially ungovernable by *any* president or secretary of state, so inbuilt were its protections and privileges. One of the enduring shortcomings of national journalism, indeed, lies in its unwillingness or its emotional inability to deal with the Foreign Service with the same critical tough-mindedness with which it habitually deals with "politicians." A friend who served in high place in State in both the Kennedy and Johnson administrations, Harlan Cleveland, entered service with stars in at least one eye concerning the splendid barriers thrown up at State against the "Spoils System" of patronage appointments, but he later told me, ruefully, that in practical terms it was simply impossible to discharge an incompetent or disloyal official. To do this, he said, a senior officer such as himself had to spend days before various boards justifying *any* disciplinary action. He had found, he added sourly, that the only effective way to get rid of an undesirable subordinate was to *promote* him to another section. The anomaly, in fact, goes far beyond the State Department. There is the strongest doubt that any president in the lifetime of the current generation will ever be able truly to master the federal bureaucracy in general. The old hands in Washington knew this very well and this is why they smiled so skeptically when Jimmy Carter confidently announced that by "reorganizing" Washington he would bring it to heel.

Many years ago David Lilienthal, then head of the Tennessee Valley Authority, astonished and delighted me by stating roundly, in a conversation at his home, that examination-paper "merit" as the litmus test for employment was all very well in theory but usually worked damned poorly in practice. And while I am about it, I am moved to observe that the supposedly pristine meritocracy of the British Permanent Civil Service is one of the most flatulent myths of political science. The system has some good ones; but it has some bad ones, and that is about it.

All presidents know that our civil service is, taking it all in all, perhaps the largest gathering of dull, humorless, self-important characters extant. This is one of the reasons, perhaps even the principal reason, why presidents, at least from Eisenhower onward, have put such steady accretions of real power into the White House staff, taking power away from the old-line Cabinet departments. An assistant who doesn't carry his weight at the White House is fully as expendable as any executive in private industry. This process of aggrandizing the White House Palace Guard is not really motivated so much by presidential arrogance as by presidential need to have people in sensitive positions who are *directly*, indisputably, and without any nonsense about civil service protections, under constant presidential command. The system is quasi-military in all except nomenclature. (It may be that all this explains why the White House staff dining quarters are called "the White House Mess.")

The Cabinet departments have never in my experience been under White House control in anything like the degree that might be supposed, given the fact that the presidency is constitutionally the fountainhead of all the Executive Branch of government. This is especially true of State, Defense, and what was Health, Education and Welfare—all three such swollen colonies of entrenched bureaucracy as to make it not only impossible for a president but also impossible for the relevant Cabinet officer really to "take charge."

Every president newly arrived in the White House supposes that, whatever his troubles with the co-equal congressional and judicial arms, his authority must prevail at least in the executive departments. Every president soon learns better. I reject, therefore, the mystique of the perilous "Imperial Presidency" of which an old friend, George Reedy, a one-time press secretary to Lyndon Johnson, wrote so vividly, thus providing Jimmy Carter with the centerpiece slogan for his "outsider's" campaign for the presidency in 1976. Far from exercising imperial powers (definable, I take it, as czarlike and uninhibited), the presidents I have known have on many occasions been hard put to obtain mere bureaucratic obedience in matters both great and small. John Kennedy felt constantly uneasy that his foreign policy directives were being short-circuited or at times even emasculated in the State Department, and not by any senior official but rather by faceless people down below. Lyndon Johnson, for all his powerfully demanding personality, very often ate food that he didn't like and that was indifferently prepared—at Camp David and aboard the yacht *Sequoia*, both of them Navy-manned, and even in the White House. So did Kennedy. And so, I believe, did Nixon.

Moreover, Johnson, like all the other presidents I have known, was not always Lord of the Earth even within his own White House Palace Guard. Once, swimming with me in the White House pool and wearing a kind of rubber shower cap, Johnson was thus greeted by McGeorge Bundy, his irrepressible foreign policy adviser: "I see the Emperor is wearing his crown!"

And, on the subject of aggrandizement, the fact is that the number of congressional staff personnel has over the last decade or two swollen far more rapidly than White House personnel. No; the long and the short of it simply is that presi-

221

dents have learned that in order to operate as they *must* operate, each must have a comparatively lean interior structure, apart from and in no way influenced by the sluggishness and unresponsiveness of the Cabinet departments.

The White House Mess is one of the outward symbols of this state of affairs and it is inwardly a citadel of strictly privileged in-house communication. Kennedy in his time was not all that keen to see his assistants invite journalists into the Mess. Johnson frowned strenuously upon such visitors to the Mess except in the most extraordinary circumstances. The place was even more off limits in Nixon's years. Though I had known Richard Nixon, from the day he entered Congress in 1947, no Nixon aide ever asked me into the Mess. I never took umbrage at this. To paraphrase an old expression, the bigger they are the easier they are to reach, so long as the journalist doesn't clamor for the Big Ears of government too loudly, over too little—and, of course, so long as the journalist commands a wide audience. The thing works in a kind of geometric progression. Members of the House of Representatives are necessarily interested in any reporter representing *any* paper in their districts; senators don't unbend much except toward a correspondent of a statewide or national paper. Presidents, not unnaturally, rarely give much time, nor do their White House functionaries, to any journalist or broadcaster who does not have a national constituency of readers.

Like Kennedy, Lyndon Johnson had once been a newspaperman himself—Johnson on a college paper in small-town Texas and Kennedy in metropolitan Boston. LBJ was fascinated by the inner workings of the craft, almost as much as by what was printed about him. He liked to talk the professional jargon of "leads," of "beats" and so on. For his speeches he preferred crisp, very short sentences—too short, I often thought. But for some reason his taste leaned toward the more elaborate in journalistic writing. When a passage in a piece of commentary struck him, he was apt automatically to memorize it (he did this easily, being a very quick study) and then later quote it back approvingly to its author. Sometimes I was the recipient of his kudos; but though many times I wrote articles critical of something he was doing or planning to do, he never once protested during his time as president, though he had occasionally done so earlier in his career.

Our personal relationship during his presidency was much closer than it had been before, simply because I always believed that, like any man in that position, he badly needed detached friends on whose discretion and personal loyalty, if not necessarily political or ideological approval, he could rely. The tacit understanding between us, never once put into words, was simple at bottom. I had my work and my career, and all that was my business; he had an infinitely greater career that was his business. Thus, though we often talked about public issues, of course, we spent more time in casual chatting and in scoring each other off. He often pretended to perceive me as some unreconstructed fellow brandishing a Confederate flag in each hand because, while I had supported his basic civil rights designs from his Senate days onwards, I believed that at times he went too far too fast.

One night after supper at the White House, Johnson announced that we were all going to see a splendid movie. This turned out to be an opus called "Harry Sundown," to my mind a bitter anti-South screed. As it unfolded I was increasingly uncomfortable—a fact of which Johnson was amusedly aware—and I finally reached the limit of my tolerance when a character in the movie, the stereotype of the big-bellied racist, spat into the Communion cup in rancor, as I recall it, at the liberal racial views of the Episcopal priest, who was celebrating a Eucharist that happens to mean much to me. I rose from my seat and departed without ceremony from the White House movie theater, going upstairs to the family quarters and making myself a large drink. I sat there alone until the movie downstairs had ended and the president and his other guests had returned to the family quarters. "Well, well, Bill," he boomed at me, "I always wondered what that S in your name stands for. Stands for *Sundown*, doesn't it?"

Johnson in his time in the White House made it clear to me that he habitually read my column; and there the matter ended. Almost never did he comment upon any piece I had done, either to praise or to protest; it was a degree of self-restraint that must have been very hard on him, though to me it was a welcome thing. This reticence Johnson maintained even when, not long after his accession to the presidency he knew me to be working on a book about Lyndon B. Johnson, later published as *The Professional.* I neither sought nor was offered Johnson's cooperation on that job, which I had undertaken with some reluctance because my intention had always been to do a biography only at leisure, after Johnson was out of office and only after the dust had settled a bit over the career of the most complex man I ever knew.

I wrote *The Professional* when I did, not so much for money (of that I felt wonderfully and wondrously well supplied at that point, from my syndicated column) as out of a sense of national obligation. I was aware that no other writer knew Lyndon Johnson so well as I. More importantly, amidst the enormous aftershocks of the Kennedy assassination then traumatizing not only the American people but to some extent also all our allies, I felt it imperative that the new president be presented as he really was, as soon as possible, to this country and especially to the world. A realistic perception of him, I thought, was acutely needed abroad. Because Johnson's career had until recently been so centered in what is to Europe the somewhat arcane institution known as the Senate, many Europeans, some of them in high position, tended to see him as a sort of cowboy from the outback, not realizing that as majority leader he had directly helped shape American foreign policies throughout the eight Eisenhower years.

In a word, I set out not to defend Johnson but rather hurriedly to explain him, the more so because even his comparatively brief tenure as vice president had, inevitably in that office, tended to cast him into the shadows of national and international public life. (The difference between being vice president and being majority leader of the Senate is roughly equivalent to that between being, say, a personal assistant to the president of a corporation and being the chairman of its board. And yet I had, by the way, several colleagues in journalism who really believed that Johnson had somehow "maneuvered" to get the vice presidential nomination at Los Angeles in 1960. He had sought that designation in about the sense that one of old Alben Barkley's characters, in Senate cloakroom conversation, had accepted distinction. This was a character who, seized by a group of determined men and informed that he was to be ridden out of town on a rail, replied that but for the honor of the thing he had rather walk.)

While I was writing *The Professional* I saw Johnson, and my wife and I dined with him and Mrs. Johnson, very often, and I can recall only a single occasion upon which the subject was mentioned between the president and me. One night he did ask me what my title was going to be and I told him. He was impassive. Bill Moyers, then a Johnson aide and a fellow with whom I always felt uneasy, happened to be present. "I don't like that title!" he said, very sharply, exhibiting the almost universal urge of White House staff people to be seen as "in there fighting for the president." Johnson looked at him and said nothing. I looked at him too, and had it been possible to do so I would have said even less. Though I strongly suspect that Johnson, too, did not "like the title," since it clearly and perhaps even loudly designated him as a professional politician, a term which to political puritans tends to have a certain satanic color, still he exercised adamant self-control in removing himself from the smallest intrusion, even into a book about Lyndon Johnson written by Lyndon Johnson's friend.

At any rate, he never saw the book or any part of it until it was issued, nor ever sought to. It got generally favorable reviews, I was most happy to see. More important to my central purposes, it was published abroad in six or seven languages—including Chinese. In this I was peculiarly interested, since it seemed likely to me that under either Johnson or some early successor president, the American national interest would inevitably require some new understanding with Communist China, if only to serve as a makeweight against the Soviet Union. For this insight I claim no seer's vision. Many conversations with Russian diplomats in that period had made it plain to me that Soviet fear of China was one of the most real and profound (and almost paranoid) forces at work in the

225

world and that this circumstance could certainly be exploited by the United States to promote a *detente* with Moscow resting on something more reliable than exchanges of prolix rhetoric about "coexistence."

By all this I do not mean to suggest that at this or any other time I saw myself as some kind of volunteer secretary of state or backdoor "presidential adviser." I was a journalist and only a journalist. I knew very well that nobody had elected me to anything, or was ever going to. But I thought, and still do, that a journalistic commentator had a professional obligation to apply the best perception he might have to each subtle ground-swell in foreign affairs he might be able to discern. He has no right or writ to *make* foreign policy but every right and writ to suggest, criticize, and propose.

Nor, for reasons I have already indicated, perhaps too laboriously, did I go panting to Johnson with my theories, or seek to engage Dean Rusk or Mac Bundy or Walt Rostow in solemn conversation about them. To imagine that in my casual contacts with Iron Curtain people (of whom one was a Russian "cultural attaché"named Yuri Bobrakov, certainly a Soviet Intelligence officer) I had come upon some unique diplomatic opportunity not already perceived within the White House would have been absurd.

Really, I was more than satisfied that I had, without help from anybody in the government and without intruding upon its official channels, pretty well worked out in my own mind the probable future revolutionary turn in the course of American-Russian-Chinese relationships. When, later, Richard Nixon activated this new policy with his missions to Moscow and Peking, I never joined the general hallelujah chorus in American journalism thanking God for a new and mellow Nixon no longer reflexively anti-Communist. I wrote (while Nixon intermediaries were letting me know that they sure did wish I wouldn't be so tactless) that Richard Nixon was plainly and simply, and very sensibly, taking advantage of an extraordinary opportunity to rub up the already chafed relationship between the Communist superpowers. Period. He was, of course, rearranging the world balance of power, and for the first time, in any fundamental sense, since the onset of the Cold War.

The consensus of the national press was that this tremendous enterprise was essentially the concept of Henry Kissinger. In point of fact it would have been attempted long before, in Johnson's time, except that the burdens of the Vietnam war lay so heavily upon this government that initiatives beyond or apart from Vietnam were hardly possible. This is in no way to depreciate Kissinger's powerful role in our foreign affairs. It is only an effort, of the kind I made repeatedly at the time in my column, to keep in mind the reality, in my experience at least, that it has always been presidents, not secretaries of state, however brilliant, who initiate grand policy designs, and secretaries of state who *implement* those designs. The unexampled elevation of Henry Kissinger into a world figure surpassing the president did no harm to anybody or anything except to the accuracy of history. It may indeed have been a fortunate circumstance considering that the Watergate affair would eventually destroy Nixon; national interest was perhaps better served by the wide oversimplification that our policies toward the end of his tenure were really *Kissinger* policies.

Kissinger himself was not responsible for his dizzying ascent except perhaps in the sense that he was always "good copy." I knew him reasonably well and never saw him devoting himself to self-promotion. On the contrary, he often seemed to me to be privately amused by the superlatives piled upon him by media people—and all too aware that if the Nixon policies should bring stormy weather, the man who had been credited with bringing the sunshine would be the man savagely blamed for the rain, the same Henry Kissinger. In truth, perhaps the best quality he brought to his job was neither his formidable mind nor his undoubted skill and poise as a negotiator. It was, I thought, an inbred awareness, fairly common in Europeans but no so often found in Americans, that *some* problems in this world are not really soluble and so must be approached with a stoic willingness to seek whatever measure of tolerable and partial solution may be found.

Another of Kissinger's contributions, far less significant but

227

by no means inconsiderable, was his resolute refusal to let the enervating and spirit-sapping bureaucratic miasmas of Washington, notably strong in the State Department, trouble him in the least. I often wondered what would have been the consequences had fortune put him into the Johnson rather than the Nixon Administration. *That* would have been a pair to remember, for each had his theatrical side and each was more inclined to see even dreadful obstacles as bracing challenges than as hand-wringing problems. Johnson displayed his streak of melancholy only in the purely private Johnson; Kissinger never had one, so far as I could see. As to the nature of Kissinger's relationship with Nixon, beyond the obvious aspects, I often speculated within myself, but to the end I never attained the smallest notion of what it might really be.

The fact of the matter is that the Nixon years were, for me as a journalist, more nearly years of watching from a certain distance than of the constant, close eye-witness that had been available to me in the Kennedy and Johnson eras. In this sense alone, I was back to Eisenhower's time, with the important difference that in Eisenhower's years I, like many others, unconsciously luxuriated in a distinctly non-urgent national (and therefore professional) atmosphere—an atmosphere neither I nor the country was soon to know again.

I was never invited socially to the White House in the Eisenhower years, a circumstance that suited me well at the time, and which, with hindsight, came to seem positively Edenic. I regard as rubbish the credo of some "hard-nosed" journalists and press critics that a mere social familiarity with the White House and its occupants means that one has been "had" and can never again "write independently." I reject as well the notion that infinite dangers to chaste journalism lie in wait for those who attend off-the-record White House briefings, or "backgrounders." The theory here is that in such meetings the wily politicians are bound to put something over on the honest correspondents and thereby cause them to write too kindly of a president, thus allowing him to "manage the news." The reality is that national journalists are presumed to be grown-up, and it is assumed that if they are unable to discern a ploy to "have" them, then they had better go forthwith into some other line of work.

Still another of the small blessings of the Eisenhower era had been that there were not many—and need not have been many—backgrounders to begin with. I once heard an acquaintance quote Barbara Ward (Lady Jackson) as having said of Norman Vincent Peale that he had rewritten Scripture to read: *Take up thy cross . . . and relax.* No journalist who had observed at close hand the gallant travail of Harry Truman, or would later witness still more closely the Kennedy, Johnson, and Nixon presidencies, could ever forget the blessed peace of the Eisenhower years, a peace achieved though it may have been by White House brooms vigorously brushing things under the rugs.

In the Johnson years, private suppers at the White House were frequent for me and June, and there was not one of them that was not memorable in one way or another. I never wrote of them, not even obliquely, because they were meant to be purely private, and so they must remain. All the same, they were useful to me as a journalist in that they enormously improved my understanding of the presidency.

State dinners under Nixon were particularly stiff because of that president's own lack of social ease. Nixon was, I believe, the most tense man I ever knew, inside or outside of public life. Indeed, a strangely waiflike quality in Nixon persisted all through his public life, and beyond a doubt it influenced me as a journalist to give him the benefit of the doubt on occasions when I would not have given it to a more personally secure man. Richard Nixon was the kind of man, one of his assistants once observed to me, who when strongly moved by feelings of friendship might conclude a letter with "Very truly yours."

Like Eisenhower and Johnson, Nixon came from what most people would consider in one sense or another deprived origins. Economically and socially, his boyhood was lived on the wrong side of the tracks. Johnson, though he came from a money-poor family, also came from an old one with ties to the Texas Republic of Sam Houston. Entrance into such Society as existed in the hills where he grew up he never had to seek; for what it was worth, it was his by birth. Eisenhower, though he too had a hard start in life, had great inner security. Perhaps his rise to the officer class had healed him of any early psychic wounds; at any rate he himself never had the slightest trouble Liking Ike.

Nixon's lack of inner assurance, though often hidden under the mannerisms of the so-called "gut fighter," was appalling, if also unjustified. This was perhaps the quality—or the anti-quality—that destroyed his presidency in the end. As I have said, I do not pretend to be even an amateur psychiatrist; and indeed I dislike and mistrust popularized psychoanalyses, especially those made at a remove from the subject. All the same, one would have to be truly stupid not to discern that here was a man as unsure of his place on earth as most of us are unsure of our place in heaven. Singularly gifted in some ways—in his best days his far-seeing intuitions about what moved masses of people at given moments were almost tactile in their accuracy—he was cursed by what seemed to be a sense of personal insufficiency, a sense of somehow not having measured up. This may have lain behind his wretched confessions in the celebrated interviews with David Frost in 1977. In a certain deep sense he was what is colloquially called a born loser, not just politically so. Among the many tragic aspects of his flawed presidency was the waste of an extraordinarily keen intellect, an intellect that was both wide-ranging and surgically precise when employed in large, impersonal matters—and a shaky tool indeed as Richard Nixon faced the personal problems of life and career.

Nixon's behavior in the Watergate affair, inexplicable to many, if perversely gratifying to others, was grotesquely inexplicable to those who had known him longest and best. The expression "a man beside himself" comes to mind, in its literal aspect. It was as if the brain of Richard Nixon had become dissociated from the persona of Richard Nixon, and moreover had somehow ceased to function. Along with, I gathered, such colleagues as Joseph Alsop and Richard Wilson, I found it at first very difficult to credit the *Washington Post* disclosures of Watergate and the cover-up because the actions imputed to

Nixon (mostly correctly, it turned out) were such affronts to elementary common sense. It was like being asked to believe that a nuclear physicist of internationally proven competence had made an ass of himself when asked what made water boil. Nixon was at no point in the remotest danger from George McGovern in the presidential race of 1972, and Nixon knew it very well from first to last. The Democratic National Committee then housed in the Watergate posed the peril of a popgun.

When Nixon was nominated in 1968 at Miami Beach, I wrote a column in effect reminding him that his had been a divisive course in politics, at least until he went in as vice president under Eisenhower. I suggested that now he had the opportunity to disprove the notion of his most bitter adversaries that he was the embodiment of irredeemable sin. I never heard from him about that piece, not even in the oblique, third-person way that was his method of communication.

Four years later I published a book called *The Responsibles* (dealing with Robert Taft the Elder, Truman, Eisenhower, Kennedy, and Johnson) in which, in passing mention of Nixon, I made many of the same points about him that I had made in the Miami Beach column. I sent a copy of the book to the White House with an explicit request to the president (the only one of that kind I ever made to a public figure) that he try to find time to read it. Whether he did I never knew. All I do know that might possibly bear on the point is that shortly afterward he telephoned me and said, in the guarded and glancing way that was so like him, that he often enjoyed reading my work.

Just what I thought I was up to in this episode I don't know, unless it reflected some atavistic instinct for delivering a homily I'd inherited from the Presbyterian dominies who had been so numerous on one side of my family. I think what had moved me was my hope that Nixon would make as worthy a president as he was capable of being, if he ever conquered his besetting insecurity.

EPILOGUE

FOR BETTER OR WORSE, I am a traditionalist and what I might call an institutionalist. So I have been a traditional journalist with a great respect for our durable institutions, whether the Anglican communion or the presidency. The possibility of real harm sustained by those institutions troubles me deeply and activates a desire in me to *do* something in their defense, however quixotic this may seem. I have not been so responsive to or moved by persons in public life as I have been by the institutional structures they inhabit.

This quirk—and it is a quirk, since I have also always been of the school that believes it is men who make history and not the other way round—has been accompanied by another which has made me an untypical, if not atypical, journalist. As I ascended the shaky ladder in the AP, I began to question the principle in journalism that "hard news" alone has true value. By the time I had become the *Times* chief congressional correspondent I no longer sought "beats" but was moving instead toward what is called in my trade the "think piece." And in the third phase of my career, in my syndicated column, I was more and more drawn to the essay approach to public affairs.

A column, I thought, required a coherent theme, a deliberate treatment, a clear point of view, and a measure of literary grace, to whatever extent one might bring that off. All this, it seemed to me, was quite enough to put on one man's plate. If others wanted to knock themselves out in pursuit of "exclusives," then let them. If others wanted to rummage in Washington's moral trashbins, then let them indeed. I have never enjoyed watching the trembling finger of moral indignation, wherever I have seen it pointed, in public or private life.

I had determined, upon leaving the security of the *Times*, that if I was to risk that rupture, I would write to please myself. It was not that I reckoned there was anything unworthy in searching for the hard news; it was that I grew more and more aware of its evanescent nature, and of the oversimplifications so often codified in it. Not unconnected, of course, was the all too visible influence of television news, which in becoming the prime purveyor of information and instant commentary was beginning to cast the press quite into the shadows. What used to be taken casually and at leisure—the daily summary of news and commentary by press and radio—is now hurled at a public audience that is both captive of and addicted to this product of "communication" (to use another ad-man's term I wish I could easily replace), that is, the evening news on television.

The newspapers, sadly to me, no longer form the cutting edge of the national apparatus of information. They cannot compete as of yore, when gladiatorial Hearsts and Pulitzers and Ochses and Scrippses and Howards fought great battles for the country's attention, for the "scoop." These contests are now of the kingdom of television. More and more the newspaper press interprets, elaborates, analyzes the news. It does not so much direct public thinking as influence the consciousness—and sometimes the conscience—of the Influentials themselves. In that sense, the writing press has become a more elitist institution. In my own time I have seen the national political conventions of both parties progressively push the writing press farther and farther backstage, while the convention's *real* permanent chairman is a troika of the television networks.

The increasing function of the press as a confider of Meaning rather than as a bearer of the Message has brought about nothing less than a crisis in the area of public information. Public distrust of the media has reached an uncomfortably high point. Many nonvoters, when polled, state that their disinclination to vote is attributable largely to their conviction that they cannot depend on the media for unbiased news. The fact is, though, that most people never did really admire the media, even when that plural term meant only the newspapers and magazines and, a little later, the radio. Reporters were almost always seen as snoopy and impertinent, disreputable types—an impeachment not always unjust.

The press commentator or columnist is not all that popular either, except among those who want something from him. By professional necessity, he is an opinionated fellow in an unseemly rush to lay down the law on all sorts of public matters. And sometimes he is pompous, to boot. The truth of the business is that the two kinds of journalists, the editorialist and the hard-nosed reporter, whether of old or new vintage, do stand constantly in peril of overweening pride, and, yes, of occasional rushes-to-the-head of self-righteousness.

Self-righteousness is a particular danger for columnists, and I have no doubt that I have experienced and exhibited that clammily unpleasant trait on more than one occasion. Nevertheless, I am much too human not to prefer to illustrate the occupational fault of self-importance with an anecdote in which others are the lay figures. An AP war-correspondent friend of mine, John Moroso, walked up to Churchill in Cherbourg, not long after the old man had come across to observe the post-D-Day buildup, and said breezily, "Mister Churchill, what have you to say to the Associated Press of America?" Churchill, a world's champion of the putdown long before the term came into the language, looked Johnny up, down, and sideways, then remarked icily, "As it happens, nothing at all."

If this book were a memoir, its content would be overwhelmingly about my wife and daughters. About the time it comes to print, June and I will have been married forty years, so I hope I may be allowed to pay her a tribute. No journalist could have done the work I did, with its odd hours, its traveling, and all its pressures, without a wife behind him. At the time we met I was tired and even somewhat disillusioned. Certainly I was tired of death and of both the nobility and the ignobility of war. I wanted life. And so eventually grew our family—two beauties,

Cia and Victoria. Living with and knowing those three has been the most important thing in my life.

Yet this book is *not* a personal memoir nor any sort of complete accounting of my life, but only the story of how my fifty-year career as a journalist was made. And as I approach my eightieth year, my mind is alive with a sense of gratitude to those who helped me make the journey.

My years with the Associated Press were, by military analogy, my years of Basic Training. Here the hard facts of life taught me the utter necessity for accuracy and the professional obligation to tell things as they were, not as I might have wished them to be. It was a hard but enormously useful school to me.

The years on the *New York Times* were, among other things, full of a feeling of liberation from the slam-bang exigencies of time and event as I had experienced them in the AP. And there was always a sense of pride in being on the *Times*, the feeling of being, as the Marine recruiters say, with a few good men. Having a press card identifying me as a *Times* correspondent was almost as good as a diplomatic passport to a traveler. And I owe a heavy debt to Edwin L. James, the great *Times* managing editor; to Arthur Krock, chief correspondent of the Washington bureau; and to Lester Markel, the *Times* Sunday editor, the best editor I ever knew.

The years of my work in Washington for the *Times* and the early years of my column were uniquely joyous to me. The Fifties, once the political neurasthenia of McCarthyism and "Who Lost China?" had been driven from national life, were far less demanding to a journalist than any decade recently gone before them—or any decade to come after them. There was time for play as well as work, General Eisenhower having set the country a clear example in this regard. There was, in the diplomatic phrase, a relaxation of tensions all around.

In this period, my private life and that of my family got a full measure of my attention, and our pursuits were of a healthy, uncomplicated (for Washington), and joyous sort. With William and Mary Bundy, James and Elizabeth Rowe, and a series of more or less itinerant diplomats from the British embassy, my wife and children and I formed a highly relaxed club of our own which had unspokenly as its core a kind of revolt from official Washington. The Bundys owned a farm in Maryland, and William Bundy's father-in-law, Dean Acheson, our Master of the High Table, had long owned a beloved country place. We all spent a good deal of time at the Bundy farm, less at Acheson's since he moved in and out of our club as the notion moved him. The children (White, Rowe, Bundy, et al.) roamed the fields with such happy enthusiasm as to ruin urban life forever for two of them—my daughters. The adults in the group played charades and various vaguely intellectual games in a curiously innocent way. None of us was in that period caught up very much in Society, of either the official or the cliff-dweller variety.

Rowe was what in Washington is called a "Democratic lawyer," a partner of Roosevelt Brain Truster Tommy Corcoran, and a lawyer of the good and ethical variety. Bundy was a high official of the CIA—high enough to be publicly identified with the agency—and so discreet about any and all public issues as to be an ideal off-work companion. Our British friends, like the rest of us, were more than content to forget all about the Big Picture for the weekends. In the good life we lived when we were off duty, so to speak, there was never much shop talk. Even when the real and working world broke irresistibly into our private lives, as inevitably it did, it was greeted with great reserve.

Donald and Catherine Hiss (he a brother of Alger Hiss) were among our "club" members. Dean Acheson had created a great and bitter controversy when as secretary of state he declared he would not turn his back on Alger Hiss. The whole sad Alger Hiss affair, a crushing weight on the gallant spirit of his younger brother Donald—one of the finest men I have ever known and one of the most honored friends I have ever had—was absolutely off limits for all us, Acheson included.

With Dean Acheson, this splendidly articulate and occasionally splendidly splenetic character, I had a relationship that can only be called abrasively affectionate. In argument, he had a low boiling point; and I had a short fuse when, as his friends put it, Dean "was being Dean," majestically laying down one or another of Acheson's Laws. (I am certain, too, that there were times when friends said that White was "being White.") Alice Acheson, Dean's wife, a charming and beautiful woman who was also a gifted painter, made dinner at their Georgetown house an enormous pleasure.

It was a time that neither I, nor my family, nor our friends in Washington were ever again to know, and a golden twilight sheen hangs over it in my memory.

As to my career as an author, two real pros from Harper's publishing firm whose friendship I look back on gratefully were Evan Thomas, my first book editor and one of a mettle long gone, and John Fischer, the editor-in-chief of *Harper's Magazine*, who occasioned the third ascending step of my career, my decision to strike out on my own as an independent Washington columnist. Jack Fischer came down to Washington from New York in the Spring of 1958 and asked me to take over his column in *Harper's*. I told him I did not like to do that, since I did not want to see him depart as the chief voice of *Harper's*. He proposed that I begin a new column in the magazine; I was delighted, and we settled on "Public and Personal" for a title—his idea. It turned out, however, that the top management of the *Times* would not permit me to write for *Harper's*. As it happened, with Tom Stokes's death, the United Feature Syndicate in New York had a vacancy for a new columnist. Lawrence Rutman, the president of United Feature, came down to Washington and asked me to take the job.

Peering somewhat sadly into the past in these, an old man's reminiscences, I give credit too to my beginnings in Texas and to my father, John VanDyke White, for the making of me as a journalist. The climate I grew up in was utterly unpermissive, and from my teens I knew that no one had promised me so much as tomorrow; I was never very much surprised or thrown by hardships. This was my father's contribution, this and a lifelong awareness of the obligation to "play the game," as my father would have put it. In the rough days of that time in a rough Texas, the children of the Whites were anything but privileged, except perhaps privileged by our family's pride in our ancestry and in our certainty of our parents' love for us.

Accordingly, I have tried, and I hope sometimes with some success, to put some historical perspective into what I have written—and every now and then some humor in the face of the human condition.

INDEX

Brewster, Sen. Owen, 132
Britain: and Mississippi Delta, 20-21; correspondents from, 112; parliamentary system in, 137, 138; Permanent Civil Service in, 220. *See also* D-Day; South Africa; World War II
British Guards, 22-23, 101, 102
Broder, David, 11
Brooks, Henry, 36, 37, 38, 39, 40
Brooks, Victor, 36, 39
Broun, Heywood, 54
Browder, Earl, 76
Bundy, Mary, 235-36
Bundy, McGeorge, 182, 207, 221, 226
Bundy, William, 235-36
Byrd, Harry Flood, Sr., 150, 169, 170
Byrnes, James F., 157

Canadian First Army, 109
Carter, Jimmy, 152, 220, 221
Casey, Bob, 126
Central Intelligence Agency (CIA), 141, 191, 204, 236
Chamberlain, Neville, 70-71, 72, 73
Chappaquiddick incident, 203
Chesterfield, Lord, 164
Chesterton, G.K., 6
Chiang Kai-shek, 16
Chicago Daily News, 79, 126
Chicago Tribune, 75, 113
China, 16, 225; Japanese invasion of, 61; "loss" of, 156, 235
Christian, George, 36
Christian, George, Jr., 36
Churchill, Mrs. Winston, 95
Churchill, Winston, 23, 40, 52, 71, 158, 159, 213, 218; WSW's

opinion of, 26, 77; personality of, 95, 101; as warrior-statesman, 96-99, 234; and Prime Minister Smuts, 97-98, 137; and Unconditional Surrender, 100; and Montgomery, 101-2; and Allied invasion of Europe, 110; and Yalta conference, 164
Citadel (WSW), 164, 167, 180
City News Association (New York), 69
Clark, Sen. Joseph, 194
Cleveland, Harlan, 219
Cohen, Ben, 47, 48
Cold War, 100, 162, 193, 227
Colliers, 123
Collins, Gen. J. Lawton (Lightning Joe), 114, 120
Congress: Eightieth, 3; and journalists, 7, 222; in Great Depression, 46; Texans in, 47-48; and New Deal, 51. *See also* Senate, U.S.
Connally, John B., 176-77, 205
Connally, Sen. Tom, 51, 157, 158, 167-68
Cooper, Bob, 110, 112
Cooper, Sen. John Sherman, 133
Cooper, Kent, 62, 64, 68, 208; and Wirephoto, 57-60; and Flesch system, 67; and World War II, 71, 74-76, 77, 79, 80
Corcoran, Tommy, 47, 48, 211, 236
Cottingham, George, 43
Cox, Oscar, 212-13
Crawford, Kenneth, 115
Cuba, 186, 190-91, 192, 194, 200
Curtis, Lon, 36-38

Daley, Richard, 177
Dallas Times Herald, 200

Davis, Richard Harding, 12
D-Day: WSW as assault
correspondent on, 12-13, 73,
90, 93-94, 100, 102-3, 126;
WSW's description of, 105-10;
twentieth anniversary of, 214
de Gaulle, Gen. Charles, 118,
213, 214, 215
Democratic national
conventions, 3, 150, 168, 171
Dempsey, Gen. Sir Miles, 113
Dewey, Thomas E., 2-3, 4, 35,
148, 154-55
Dickens, Samuel, 36-38
Dinitz, Simcha, 6
Douglas, Justice William O., 40
Duff, Sen. James, 188
Dulles, John Foster, 8, 158-59,
164-65
Dunkirk, 74

Eisenhower, Dwight D.: and
State Department, 8, 9, 158,
220; personality of, 22, 45, 160,
162, 235; and Hoover, 44; and
Truman, 45, 189; and press,
103-4; in World War II, 107,
120, 124, 133; return to U.S.,
129; election of, 149, 150, 154,
155; and Congress, 161, 162,
166; and Nixon, 161, 231; and
Democrats, 162-63; and right-
wing Republicans, 163; and
foreign policy, 163; and
Kennedy, 186-88; and WSW,
186, 190, 228, 229;
nonpartisanship of, 187; and
Wall Street, 188; and U-2
incident, 189-90; journalists
and, 229; origins of, 229-30
Elizabeth, Queen, 70
Ervin, Sen. Sam, 174
Evans, Rowland, 11

Fallon, Wild Bill, 34
Farley, James A., 28
Ferguson, Senator Homer, 132
Fischer, John, 237
Flanders, Sen. Ralph E., 18
Flesch, Rudolph, 67, 136, 142,
149
Ford, Gerald, 8, 9
Fortas, Abe, 40, 206
Fortas, Carol, 206
France, 77, 109-16, 213-14. *See
also* Paris
Frankfurter, Justice Felix, 19,
40, 193-94
Free French (FFI), 117, 118
Front Page, The (Hecht-
MacArthur), 12, 135
Frost, David, 230
Fulbright, Sen. William, 18, 196

Gaitskell, Hugh, 19
Galbraith, John Kenneth, 193
Gallagher, Wes, 103
Garner, Jack, 44-45, 48, 49, 50
Garner, Mrs. Jack, 44
George, Sen. Walter, 164-66,
169, 170
George VI, King, 59, 70, 71, 72
Germany: air raids over, 103;
invasion of, 120-21; taking of
Aachen in, 122
Ghana, 146-47
Gilburt, Harry, 178
Goldwater, Sen. Barry, 6, 181,
184, 211
Goodwin, Mark, 44
Gorrell, Henry, 120-21
Great Depression, 41-43, 46, 185
Greene, Roger, 93, 109-10, 111,
112

Hagerty, James, 189
Hall, Leonard, 187

Harper's Magazine, 178, 179, 189, 218, 237; "Symington: The Last Choice" (WSW) in, 179

Harris, Kenneth, 151-52

Harrison, Gilbert, 6

Hemingway, Ernest, 96, 106, 115, 123, 124

Hemingway Guerrillas, 115-16

Highsmith, Lehlia, 35

Hill, Gladwin, 73

Hill, Sen. Lister, 180

Hines, Jimmy, 2, 35

Hines-Tammany affair, 2

Hiss, Alger, 161, 236

Hiss, Catherine, 236

Hiss, Donald, 236

Hitler, Adolph, 70, 71, 72, 77, 112, 158; invasion of Soviet Union, 81, 101; bombing of England, 109

Hitler-Stalin Pact, 81, 158

Hodges, Gen. Courtney, 115

Hoover, Herbert, 43-44, 45

Hopkins, Harry, 47, 52

Houston, Sam, 20, 25, 26, 229

Houston, Tex., 148-49

Houston Chronicle, 42-43

Howard, Roy, 54

Huebner, Gen. Clarence, 114, 121, 122

Huggins, Roy, 98

Hughes, Howard, 41

Humphrey, Hubert Horatio, 3, 168-70, 201, 202

Huston, Luther, 134

Hyman, Sidney, 6

Ickes, Harold, 52

International News Service (INS), 63, 64, 73, 90

isolationism, 75-77, 81, 129, 154, 157

James, Edwin L. (Jimmy), 128, 130, 134-37, 142, 235

Japan Times, 178

Jenkins, Walter, 209-12

Johnson, Gen. Hugh, 52

Johnson, Lyndon B., 170, 231; 1964 presidential campaign, 6; and Joseph McCarthy, 18; personality of, 26, 47, 221; press secretaries of, 36, 221; and Jack Garner, 45, 50; WSW's first meeting with, 48, 49; and FDR, 50; and Eisenhower, 162, 163, 165, 188, 189, 224; and Humphrey, 169; and John Kennedy, 176, 177-78, 185, 186, 187, 190; and Robert Kennedy, 176, 177; WSW's friendship with, 176-77, 179, 182, 183, 189, 195, 200, 201, 209, 213, 214, 219, 221, 223; and civil rights, 186, 208, 223; and Berlin crisis, 186; and Club of American Presidents, 188; and Truman, 189; on foreign affairs, 190; as vice-president, 190, 224-25; and Cuban crisis, 191-92; as president, 205-9, 214-27; WSW's advice to, 207; and Walter Jenkins, 211; and de Gaulle, 214; and McNamara, 215-16; as Protestant liberal, 216; and Vietnam, 216-17; and National Security Council, 217; and Harold Wilson, 217-18; and consensus, 218; attitude to State Department, 219; and White House Mess, 222; and journalists, 222-23, 229; and WSW's column, 223-24; compared with Kissinger, 228;

244

radar, 129
radio, 18
Ragsdale, W.B., 55
Rayburn, Sen. Sam, 26, 49; and Truman, 5; and Roosevelt, 5, 48; and Eisenhower, 162, 163; and Kefauver, 168; and Stevenson, 171
Reed, Bob, 118
Reedy, George, 221
Republican National Convention (1952), 8, 148, 154
Responsibles, The (WSW), 231
Reuters News Agency, 116
Rhodesia, 143-44, 147
Roberts, J.M. (Buddy), 72, 73, 74, 76, 77-79, 80, 83
Rockefeller, Nelson, 193
Rogers, Otis, 33-34
Rogers, Rebecca Bradley, 33-34
Rooney, Andy, 115, 116
Roosevelt, Eleanor, 50, 176, 193
Roosevelt, Franklin D.: death of, 5; and election of 1936, 28; and Congress, 44, 46, 133; and Jack Garner, 44, 50; Brain Trust of, 47; and World War II, 81; and Churchill, 100, 101; and Stalin, 100-101; and Pearl Harbor investigation, 132, 133; and Russia, 156; and New Deal, 156, 163, 185; and Yalta conference, 164; National Recovery Administration of, 185; as "traitor to his class," 208
Roosevelt, Theodore, 83
Rose, Gen. Maurice, 114, 118-20, 121
Rostow, Walt, 226
Rowe, Elizabeth, 212, 235-36
Rowe, James, 47, 48, 173, 212, 235-36
Ruben, Bob, 116

Rusk, Dean, 191, 217, 226
Russell, Sen. Richard Brevard, 150, 169, 191-92
Rutman, Lawrence, 178, 201, 237

Saturday Evening Post, 27
Schlesinger, Arthur, Jr., 193, 207
Senate, U.S., 46-53, 129-30, 132-33, 155-70; and Joseph McCarthy, 18; friendships made in, 22, 155; foreign affairs in, 129, 156-57, 163, 164; and elections, 135; WSW on, 155-56, 163, 166-68; power of, 163; and television, 164; of Fifties, compared with Eighties, 164-67; attitude of, to WSW, 169
Sequoia (presidential yacht), 215, 221
Sharkey, Sam, 149
Shorr, Daniel, 18
Short, Gen. Walter, 133
Smith, Ian, 144
Smuts, Field Marshal Jan C., 97-98, 137
soldiers: WSW on, 11, 22
South Africa, 137-47; Boers in, 138, 139, 140-41, 144; Nationalists in, 138-39; British in, 139, 140-41, 143; U.S. ambassador to, 142
Soviet Union, 200; invasion of, 81; and Iron Curtain, 156; expansion in Southern Europe, 156; and China, 225-26
Spanish-American War, 83
Spanish Civil War, 62, 65
Spivak, Lawrence, 185
Stalin, 70, 81, 100-101, 164
Stars and Stripes, 115

246

State Department, U.S., 141,
154, 212, 219-21, 228
Stevenson, Adlai, 149-53,
171-72, 176, 199
Stokes, Tom, 237
Stone, Melville, 63
Sulzberger, Arthur Hays, 9, 136
Sulzberger, Arthur Ochs
(Punch), 137
Supreme Court, 40, 46, 66
Symington, Sen. Stuart, 179-80

Taft, Sen. Robert, the Elder:
and Dulles, 8, 158-59; WSW's
friendship with, 26, 154, 159;
WSW's biography of, 43-44, 45,
154; and 1952 elections,
148-49, 150; and Dewey,
148-49, 154-55; as party
spokesman, 157; and NATO,
158-59; shyness of, 159, 160;
and Eisenhower, 163
Taft-Hartley Act, 172
Taft Story, The (WSW), 154. *See
also* Taft, Sen. Robert
Talbot, Gayle, 83
Tammany Hall, 2, 35, 70, 173-74
Tannehill, Judge, 25-26
television, 18, 233
Texas: WSW's origins in, 1,
20-22, 237; WSW as journalist
in, 25-32; murder trials in,
33-41; Great Depression in,
41-44; old-boy network of,
47-49; national governors'
conference in (Houston),
148-49; and Kennedy
assassination, 199-200, 206-7
Thant, U, Secretary-General,
152-53
Thomas, Evan, 237
Thompson, Admiral, 94-95
Time, 17

Timmons, Bascom, 44
trial by jury, 1, 14
Truman, Harry S, 7, 15, 17, 45,
132, 231; presidential
campaign of 1948, 3, 4-5;
character of, 26, 153; and V-J
Day, 129; on Adlai Stevenson,
151; and Taft, 155; and Soviet
Union, 156; and NATO, 156-59;
and money scandals, 162; and
Eisenhower, 163, 165, 188,
189; as president, 181, 192,
229; and John Kennedy, 189,
196
Truman Doctrine, 156
Trussell, Charles, 166
Tugwell, Rexford Guy, 51
Turner, Richard, 55

United Feature Syndicate, 178,
199, 237
United Nations, 144, 146, 151,
152, 157
United Press (UP), 63-64, 73, 79,
80, 120, 167, 168
U.S. News and World Report, 55

Vandenberg, Sen. Arthur H.,
157, 158
Vanderschmidt, Fred, 126
Van Loon, Hendrik Willem, 78
Vargas, Getulio, 130-31
Venezuela, 130
Vietnam, 189, 195, 203, 204,
216, 217, 227
Villa, Pancho, 30
Village Voice, 12
Vinson, Chief Justice Fred, 5
V-1 bomb (doodlebug), 109
Vorster, John, 138

Wagner, Robert, 198, 199
Wallace, Henry, 196

Walter, Emmet, 43
Walters, Barbara, 183
Ward, Barbara (Lady Jackson), 229
Warren, Chief Justice Earl, 41, 161
Warren Commission, 200, 206, 207
Washington, D.C., 48, 49-57; in Great Depression, 46; in New Deal, 49-57, 129, 156; postwar, 128-29, 156; WSW's family life in, 235-36. *See also* Congress; White House
Washington Post, 15, 18, 210, 218, 230
Washington Star, 61, 186
Watergate affair, 14, 227, 230-31
Weller, Frank, 51
Wells, "Cappy," 90
White, Cia (WSW's daughter), 235
White, Dick, 77
White, John Van Dyke (WSW's father), 1, 26, 237
White, June McConnell (WSW's wife), 132, 175, 180, 189, 190, 198, 200, 206, 212, 225, 229, 234
White, Justice Byron, 198, 199
White, Victoria (WSW's daughter), 180, 235

White, William Allen, 76
Whitehead, Don, 106, 108, 109, 116, 122
White House: Kennedy-Johnson infighting in, 208; Palace Guard in, 220, 221; and Cabinet, 220-21; journalists at, 222, 228-29; WSW's private suppers at, 229
Wicker, Tom, 11
Wilensky, Sir Roy, 144
William Allen White Committee to Aid the Allies, 76
Williams, Edward Bennett, 34
Wilson, Prime Minister Harold, 217-18
Wilson, Richard, 230
Wilson, Woodrow, 2, 30
Woodward, Bob, 183
World's Fair of 1939, 71
World War II, 5, 12-13, 16-17, 22-23, 42; WSW as war editor in, 72-82; as journalistic challenge, 74, 78-80; British intelligence in, 93-95; liberation of Caen in, 110-12, 122; and British correspondents, 112; Paris in, 114-18; taking of Aachen in, 122; Bastogne in, 124. *See also* D-Day; Dunkirk; Paris

Yalta conference, 133, 164